Praise for
Conversation Transformation

"A devastatingly insightful look at the ways we unwittingly sabotage our conversations, and as a result, our relationships. So spot on you begin to suspect the authors have been eavesdropping on your own most frustrating interactions. Especially when they then pipe up to provide the practical coaching you need to change old habits and transform your conversations. Hard work? Sure. Worth it? You bet."
> —Sheila Heen and Douglas Stone, bestselling authors of *Difficult Conversations*

"This powerful, practical book shows you how to communicate and influence others in every area of your life."
> —Brian Tracy, bestselling author of *The Psychology of Selling*

"Communication is the cornerstone of success in business. *Conversation Transformation* is filled with invaluable lessons, tips, and techniques to help any professional to avoid communication breakdowns and build loyal relationships."
> —Shep Hyken, bestselling author of *The Amazement Revolution*

"Training in the ideas and skills in this book was great for me personally, as well as for our entire management team—a diverse group of competitive, hard-driving executives. We learned a lot about ourselves and the impact of our communication on others, and we were able to smooth the transition of a difficult merger."
> —Steve Snider, former CEO, Exterran Corporation

"Practical and down-to-earth, this book offers a detailed guide for changing the most common negative patterns of communication. It will be equally useful in business, professional, or private life, wherever people seek to resolve fruitless conflict and promote mutual problem-solving."
> —Judith Herman, M.D., bestselling author of *Trauma and Recovery*

"In my work in healthcare, I've experienced firsthand how conversations that end poorly can lead to suboptimal outcomes, conflict, and moral distress. While I've typically thought of myself as a strong communicator, reading this book showed me just how much I could improve. As I've worked through the clear, practical exercises, I've been able to make positive changes for myself and those around me."
> —Rev. Angelika Zollfrank, Director of Clinical
> Pastoral Education, Massachusetts General Hospital

"To live in a peaceful world each of us has to master the skills of collaboration and the ability to resolve conflict free of aggression either physical or verbal. *Conversation Transformation* contains the keys to begin that journey. I recommend it to anyone who wants to live in a world of love and compassion."
—Lama Surya Das, bestselling author of *Awakening the Buddha Within*

"*Conversation Transformation* is an invaluable work which outlines exactly how to use some basic strategies relevant for people seriously interested in improving their communication skills. This is a 'must-read' book which anyone can profit from reading."
—Susan Friedmann, CSP, bestselling author of *Riches in Niches: How to Make It BIG in a Small Market*

"As I was reading *Conversation Transformation*, I began to think I need to recommend this book to my students . . . and my kids . . . and, well, *everyone I know*. This book is truly transformative. It can help improve not only the way we speak, but also the way we think."
—Dan Millman, author of *Way of the Peaceful Warrior* and *The Four Purposes of Life*

"This is not an ordinary book; it is a tool. If you carry out the suggested exercises, it will help you to solve problems both at work and in your private life. It is easy to read, based on sound theory, and full of illuminating and moving examples."
—Christer Sandahl, Professor of Social and Behavioural Sciences, Karolinska Institutet (Sweden)

"Transforming behaviors is no easy task as the authors of this book so clearly demonstrate. The book provides just what a person needs to be on the path for more successful conversations, dialogues, and ways to deal with disagreements. There are many helpful examples—each scripted for practice. I would like to see every teacher develop these transformative conversations as they work with students. And, I would like to see every student equipped with these habits as they move through school and out into the demanding environment of the 21st century."
—Bena Kallick, Ph.D., Co-Director, Institute for Habits of Mind

"*Conversation Transformation* offers all students of communication, lay and professional, a rich menu from which to satisfy their intellectual appetites. I have an appetite for rigorous practice models linked with sound theories of how change takes place. The authors achieve this with meticulous care."
—David Kantor, Ph.D., Director, Kantor Institute, and author of *Reading the Room: Group Dynamics for Coaches and Leaders*

CONVERSATION TRANSFORMATION

RECOGNIZE AND OVERCOME THE 6 MOST DESTRUCTIVE COMMUNICATION PATTERNS

BEN E. BENJAMIN, PH.D.,
AMY YEAGER, AND ANITA SIMON, ED.D.

New York Chicago San Francisco Lisbon London Madrid Mexico City
Milan New Delhi San Juan Seoul Singapore Sydney Toronto

The *McGraw·Hill* Companies

1 2 3 4 5 6 7 8 9 0   QFR/QFR   1 8 7 6 5 4 3 2

ISBN 978-0-07-176996-9
MHID 0-07-176996-X

e-ISBN 978-0-07-177210-5
e-MHID 0-07-177210-3

McGraw-Hill books are available at special quantity discounts to use as premiums and sales promotions or for use in corporate training programs. To contact a representative, please e-mail us at bulksales@mcgraw-hill.com.

This book is printed on acid-free paper.

To Yvonne Agazarian,
whose groundbreaking theoretical analyses
of interpersonal communication
underlie all the material in this book

———————————

And to Claudia Byram and Fran Carter,
both for their invaluable help and support
during the writing of this book
and for their years of dedicated work and teaching,
which have enlightened and inspired each of us.

Contents

AN INVITATION:

Visit www.ConversationTransformation.com
right now to take our Conversation Skills Pretest
and measure your level of communication savvy.
When you're finished with the book,
go back and take the posttest
to measure how much you've learned.

Note to the Reader

Is This Book for You?

We wrote this book to be accessible to anyone who's interested in improving their communication. As you'll see when you read each chapter, the issues we discuss wreak havoc in conversations everywhere, from the bedroom to the boardroom. Whether you're trying to talk more effectively to your manager, coworker, patient, student, teacher, client, friend, spouse, or child, you'll find a wide range of ideas and skills that are immediately relevant to you.

How to Use the Online Resources

There's much more to *Conversation Transformation* than these printed pages. On the website (www.ConversationTransformation.com, also accessible by the shortcut CTsavvy.com), you can:

- Test your knowledge before and after reading the book with the pretest (CTsavvy.com/pretest) and posttest (CTsavvy.com/posttest).
- Hear a spoken version of any dialogue from the book (CTsavvy.com/dialogues).
- Find additional exercises and quizzes that supplement the training programs in Chapters 3 through 8 (CTsavvy.com/exercises and CTsavvy.com/quizzes).
- Continue your learning with a comprehensive online learning system (CTsavvy.com/LearnIt).

You'll also find links on the site to a variety of other resources, including teleseminars, webinars, and live trainings.

Where Our Stories Come From

This book is filled with stories about communication—mainly focusing on conversations that start out badly and end up with satisfying, often surprising resolutions. All of these come from real-life experiences, either from our own lives or from those of our colleagues, friends, clients, and workshop participants who have generously shared their stories with us. We intentionally included examples from people who do not specialize in communication skills, to illustrate how anyone can use the basic strategies to transform their conversations.

To protect confidentiality, we have changed the names and other identifying details of individuals, except for colleagues who have agreed to be personally identified. In a couple of stories, we have used a composite of two or three similar conversations. However, we've been careful to preserve all the relevant details of the communication, staying as faithful as possible to what happened in the original dialogues.

Where Our Ideas and Strategies Come From

The core ideas we teach in this book have a long history. They're drawn from a comprehensive communication framework called SAVI®, the System for Analyzing Verbal Interaction, developed in 1965 by Anita Simon and Yvonne Agazarian.* SAVI-based strategies have been used for more than 40 years to improve conversations in teams, couples, schools, therapeutic and coaching relationships, religious groups, businesses, and other organizations, but they have never before been the subject of a full-length book. We're excited to be able to share them with you here.

The purpose of this book is to teach some of the practical skills that come out of SAVI, not the theory underlying the system. However, in Chapter 9, we will introduce some basic elements of SAVI theory, to show how it brings together everything you've learned in the previous chapters.

---

*SAVI® is a registered trademark of Anita Simon and Yvonne Agazarian.

1

Can This Conversation Be Saved?

Communication breakdowns are bad news for our lives and work. At best, they're a source of irritation and frustration. At worst, they can threaten our jobs, families, and friendships—and in some cases, even our health. Research suggests that failed communication is one of the leading causes of preventable medical errors.[1]

The Surprising Common Factor in All Communication Breakdowns

How can we go about improving our conversations? First we need to get clear about exactly what's going wrong. We can't solve a problem if we don't know what's causing it. However, when it comes to communication problems, the cause is often tricky to spot. Consider the following conversation between a physician (Dr. M) and his patient's daughter (Sarah).[2] As you read it, see if you can figure out what's causing the trouble between them:

> Sarah began by saying, "It's so upsetting to see my father in this condition. I know this is not how he'd want to spend the last days of his life."
> "I'm very sorry," replied Dr. M, emotionless.
> "I think it's finally time to take him off the respirator."
> "I can see how you'd feel that way now," said Dr. M, "but this new medication may start to improve his quality of life."
> "At this point, that's just not enough. He's never going to get to the point where life is worth living again."

*"Wouldn't it be better to wait and be certain? I'm sure you want to
explore all the options."*

*"We've waited so long already," said Sarah, whining now, "and noth-
ing has helped!"*

*Still very calm, Dr. M replied, "The morphine has helped to make him
more comfortable, and his breathing seems a little easier today."*

*"Look," said Sarah, exasperated, "I just can't talk to you about this
anymore!"*

What's going on here? What made that conversation so difficult? When
we present this dialogue in our training sessions, people usually come up
with two different types of explanations: blaming the people and blaming the issue. In fact, these are the most common reasons people give for
any type of communication failure. Unfortunately, neither explanation is
particularly useful.

Explanation 1: Blaming the People

If you blamed the problem on Dr. M or on Sarah, you're using the people
explanation. From this point of view, communications fail because of psychological factors, such as attitudes, emotions, intentions, motivations, or
personality traits. In the hospital case, we might decide there's something
wrong with Dr. M (he's cold and insensitive, and doesn't care about Sarah's
concerns), with Sarah (she's too emotional or too pessimistic), or with both
of them (they're both too rigid and set in their views).

The psychological perspective has a strong intuitive appeal. It may
seem like common sense—of course people's bad attitudes, hidden agen-
das, and raging emotions ruin conversations; you can probably think of a
few examples off the top of your head. However, this type of thinking also
leaves us in a bind, with no good way to solve our problems.

Suppose you decide that the real trouble with your communication is
someone else's defensiveness or overemotional reaction. That's not something you have the power to control. In fact, if you try to control it and
force the person to change, you're likely to make things worse. If you don't
believe us, ask anybody who's tried to resolve an argument by saying things
like, "Stop being so defensive," "Calm down," or "You need to relax." (Imagine what would have happened if Dr. M told Sarah to be more rational, or

if she told him to show some feeling.) Moreover, even if it were possible to make someone change—perhaps by convincing them[3] to get coaching or go into therapy—that's a long-term process. It's not an efficient strategy for making your conversations work better right now.

Sometimes it may seem as though the only solution is to get the difficult person out of your life—quit your job, fire your employee, seek a divorce, and so on. Even if you haven't gone through this type of thought process yourself, you likely know people who have. You probably know more than one person who's acted on that reasoning, only to end up having the very same conflicts a few months later in their new job or new relationship. And of course, it's often not possible to exclude someone from your life. In our example, so long as Dr. M is caring for Sarah's father, they have no choice but to talk to one another.

The Usual Suspects

When a conversation fails, it's easy to blame:

The people. Difficult personalities, motivations, or emotional states

The topics. Touchy issues and irreconcilable differences

Explanation 2: Blaming the Topics

If you don't blame a communication breakdown on the people, you might be tempted to blame it on the topics being discussed. Perhaps some topics are so contentious or emotionally charged that a certain amount of frustration—or even bitter fighting—is simply inevitable. From this perspective, nobody is to blame because no better result was possible. The conversation was doomed from the outset.

Sarah's conversation with Dr. M, evaluating whether or not her father's life is worth living, certainly falls into the category of highly charged topics. The question of taking a person off life support can stir up a lot of controversy and moral outrage, even when the person involved is a stranger. It's easy to see how this contentious issue could be a big part of the problem.

Unfortunately, that explanation gets us no closer to finding a solution than the people-blaming approach. When you identify the subject matter as the source of your trouble, you're basically admitting defeat. There may be some difficult conversations you can simply avoid. For instance, you could decide not to talk about religion when you're around a particular colleague, or to avoid political debates with your parents. But much of the time, avoidance is not an option. Whenever you have a real problem you need to resolve—your employee is making costly mistakes, your department is facing tough layoff decisions, your spouse is threatening to leave you, one of your kids has started using drugs, or your dying father is suffering in the hospital—sidestepping the issue won't make it go away.

Explanation 3: The Real Reason Why Conversations Fail

Focusing on who's talking or what they're talking about doesn't just leave us without solutions. It also distracts us from the true cause of communication problems: *how* people are talking to one another. We can understand why any conversation succeeds or fails just by listening for the particular combinations of words and voice tones that are being used—the *communication behaviors*.

The Hidden Culprit

All communication breakdowns can be explained in terms of one common factor:

Behavior. The specific combinations of words and voice tones people are using

---

Whatever message you're trying to get across, the communication behaviors you use will have a strong impact on the way your message gets received. You can think of communication behaviors as the packages that carry our ideas out into the world. Often we're so focused on the content of what we're saying that we're completely unaware of the package we're sending it in. We fail to notice that our brilliant idea is wrapped up in the conversational equivalent of a stink bomb or a sign that says "kick me"—making it highly unlikely that our message is going to come across in the way we intend. (See the following sidebar for an example from a business context.)

Failure to understand this sort of effect can also cause trouble when we're on the receiving end of somebody else's message; we may be so distracted by the packaging that we can't see the valuable information it's carrying. For instance, it's extremely difficult to take in feedback that's given in the form of a hostile accusation or sarcastic jab, even when that feedback could potentially be very useful.

Change Your Behavior, Change Your Results

Say you'd like to hire a new administrative support person, but you're not sure whether your manager would support the idea. There are many different behaviors you could use to express your thoughts:

- "Everyone here is working so hard, and day after day we get more overloaded." (Complaint)
- "I know you're going to say we can't afford to hire more staff." (Negative prediction)
- "I realize that finances are tight right now, but hiring more administrative help would free us up to take on more projects and bring in more money." (Yes-but)
- "Don't you think we could use some more help around the office?" (Leading question)
- "The amount of overtime my team is working has doubled during the past three months." (Fact)
- "I suggest we take a look at the budget and see if we can afford to hire an administrative support person." (Proposal)
- "If we could find enough money in the budget to bring a new support person on board, would you support that decision?" (Narrow question)

It makes a big difference which of those statements or questions you use. While some may help get you approval for a new hire, others are more likely to get you into an argument.

Let's return to our hospital scenario. When we look at the behaviors that each person used, we can see exactly why the conversation went downhill. In the course of this book, you'll learn to recognize the six patterns of behaviors that most frequently cause breakdowns in communication. All of them occurred in this one brief dialogue:

1. **Yes-buts.** Token agreement followed by a different idea.
    Dr. M: I can see how you'd feel that way now, but this new medication may start to improve his quality of life.
2. **Mind-reads.** Assumptions about someone else's thoughts or feelings, stated as a fact.
    Dr. M: I'm sure you want to explore all the options.
3. **Negative predictions.** Negative speculations about the future, stated as a fact.
    Sarah: He's never going to get to the point where life is worth living again.
4. **Leading questions.** Questions that make it obvious what the right answer is supposed to be.
    Dr. M: Wouldn't it be better to wait and be certain?
5. **Complaints.** Frustrated, whining, or resentful comments implying that people or circumstances are unfair.
    Sarah (whining): We've waited so long already and nothing has helped!
6. **Attacks.** Venting of strong negative feelings in a hostile or blameful way.
    Sarah: Look, I just can't talk to you about this anymore!

With this perspective, it's easy to understand why Sarah and Dr. M ran into problems. The behaviors they used are enough to cause trouble in any communication. What's more, we can now see a clear path to making some improvements. There's no need to avoid the topic or change anyone's personality. All that's needed is a shift in behavior.

How Bad Conversations Turn Good

This book will give you the tools to turn around all of the most common types of difficult conversations, whether they're driven by mind-reads or yes-buts or verbal attacks. If Sarah or Dr. M had possessed these skills, their conversation probably would have gone in a more positive direction. Here's one possibility:

> **Sarah:** *It's so upsetting to see my father in this condition. I know this is not how he'd want to spend the last days of his life.*

Dr. M *(with feeling): I'm really sorry. I hear how difficult this is for you.*
Sarah: *It is so hard. I'm starting to think it's finally time to take him off the respirator.*
Dr. M: *Many people consider that option when several different treatments have failed, and they start to lose hope. Are you feeling that way?*
Sarah: *Yes, I am. I'm feeling totally hopeless and also feeling guilty. I don't want to prolong his life just to save me from the grief of losing him.*
Dr. M: *I can see how hard it is to face all these decisions, not really knowing what's going to be best for your father.*
Sarah: *I just don't know what to do.*
Dr. M: *We do have a support group here to help family members deal with these types of issues. It sometimes helps people to know they're not going through it alone. Is that something that would interest you?*
Sarah: *I'm not really comfortable in groups, but I could use someone to talk to.*
Dr. M: *Our support services department could set up an individual counseling session for you. Would you like me to connect you with them?*
Sarah: *I'd really appreciate that. Thank you.*
Dr. M: *Great. I'll do that. And as you prepare to make a decision, I want to be sure you have accurate information about your father's new medication and the types of effects it can have. Is now a good time to discuss that?*
Sarah: *Sure. Go ahead.*
Dr. M: *All right, let me tell you what the studies show . . .*

Can you tell what changed? You may have noticed that Dr. M's side of the conversation sounded quite different. Be careful how you think about that difference. It can be tempting to go back to focusing on psychological factors, thinking that Dr. M must have changed his attitude (becoming more open-minded), his emotional state (feeling more compassionate), or his motivation (attempting to help Sarah, rather than just push his own views). He may have done any or all of these things, but that doesn't tell us why the communication went well. Plenty of caring people, with all the best intentions, have conversations that fail miserably. What turned things around was a change in Dr. M's behavior—what he actually did. This is a key point to remember: **Intentions alone do not change conversations. Actions change conversations.**

Dr. M did very specific things that helped show Sarah that he understood her concerns and was receptive to hearing what she had to say. For instance, instead of arguing with yes-buts and leading questions, he mirrored her emotions ("I hear how difficult this is for you") and asked straightforward, nonleading questions ("Would you like me to connect you with them?" "Is now a good time to discuss that?"). Starting out in this way also left Sarah more receptive to hearing his ideas about the new medication.

Now, Dr. M is not the only one with the power to transform this conversation. Remember that when he yes-butted Sarah in the original dialogue, she replied with a negative prediction. A more skillful response might have led to a much better outcome:

> **Dr. M:** *I can see how you'd feel that way now, but this new medication may start to improve his quality of life.*
>
> **Sarah:** *So you're saying you think this new medication may make a difference for him. How big a difference?*
>
> **Dr. M:** *If he responds well to the drug, it could extend his life for several months. It could also allow him to return home, as long as he had 24-hour care available.*
>
> **Sarah:** *Wow, that could make a huge difference to Dad. He's always said he'd rather spend his final days at home. How long will it be before you know if it's working?*
>
> **Dr. M:** *Most people respond within a few days, but it could take up to two weeks to know for sure. I'll check in with you every day to let you know what's happening.*
>
> **Sarah:** *Thank you! This is the first sign of hope we've had in a long time.*

Again, what made the difference here were not just intentions, but actions. The most natural response to being yes-butted is to argue back. It takes skill to resist doing that and try something else instead. What Sarah did was to paraphrase Dr. M ("You think this new medication may make a difference for him") and ask a question ("How big a difference?"). By using this approach, she not only avoided an argument but also gained important information that helped ease her distress and give her new hope.

Part of our aim in this book is to give new hope to you, the reader. Once you understand the factors that cause your conversations to succeed or fail, it is possible to dramatically improve them, even in situations where the people and issues you're facing seem overwhelmingly difficult. We've seen it happen hundreds of times, in families, couples, and all sorts of organizations. Even after a discussion begins to go downhill (for instance, with Dr. M's yes-but), there's almost always a way to turn things around.

In fact, some of the most successful and transformative conversations start out with whining complaints, defensiveness, snide remarks, or personal attacks. What matters is that at some point, someone takes the initiative to do something different. That someone can always be you. At any moment in a conversation, from any position in the conversation, you have the power to intervene and change the course of events. You just have to know how.

Training for Change

One idea we've emphasized throughout this chapter is that how you understand what's going wrong will determine the steps you can take to bring about change. If you blame your communication problems on irreconcilable differences, you may want to go into hiding, or at least into denial. If you blame them on someone else's personality, you may want them to go into therapy. But as soon as you shift your focus to behavior, it's clear that you have a much more effective option: go into training.

When we talk about training, we don't mean the type of training where you sit passively in a seminar while a lecturer explains all the general rules that good communicators ought to follow. The type of training we're talking about is more like sports practice than an academic class. Imagine trying to become skilled at basketball just by being told what to do and watching experienced players do it. You obviously wouldn't get very far. To master the game, you need to get out on the court, get the ball in your hands, and try doing those things for yourself.

In communication, too, what matters most is your level of hands-on skill. You need to be able to respond effectively right at the moment when something sets you off—when your boss yells at you, your colleague shoots down your great new idea, or your spouse starts rehashing the same old complaints you've heard hundreds of times before. This is no easy task. We all have at least one or two fixed habits that we've developed over the years, whether it's a tendency to defend ourselves ("I couldn't help it"), to predict catastrophe ("This will be a disaster!"), to use sarcasm ("Yeah, right, like that's going to help"), or to yes-but everyone else's suggestions ("That's nice, but we can't afford it").

What's the best way to change a habit? Thanks to recent research in neuropsychology, we can now answer that question with greater precision than ever before. Due to the way the human brain functions, it takes particular types of experiences to change the way we communicate. In the next chapter, we'll review that research and show how we can apply it to train our brains in the most effective and efficient way. In the following six chapters, we'll put those ideas into practice. Each time we teach you a new set of strategies, we'll guide you through an intensive training program designed to help you master those skills and transform your own challenging conversations.

Pretest Reminder

If you haven't already taken the Conversation Skills Pretest, we recommend that you do that now, or at least before you get to Chapter 3. You'll get an instant analysis of your general level of communication savvy, plus specific areas of strength and weakness. Then, when you've finished the book, you can go back and take the posttest to measure how much you've learned. Start now by clicking the Pretest link on our website: www.ConversationTransformation.com.

2

Teaching an Old Brain
New Tricks

When we first sat down to write a book on communication, we were troubled by a dirty little secret: people don't actually improve their communication by reading books. Of course, books can teach important, interesting ideas. But we wanted to accomplish more than that. When we imagined what you, as a reader, would take away from this book, we didn't just want you to talk more effectively *about* conversations; we wanted you to talk more effectively *within* conversations. We wanted to give you not just knowledge but skill.

The difference between knowledge and skill is critical, and in some areas of our lives, it's obvious. Take the example we mentioned in the first chapter: basketball. Say you've read a long, detailed book about how to play basketball, so now you can talk very intelligently about offensive and defensive strategies, as well as all the finer points of dribbling, passing, and shooting. Do you then assume you're prepared to get out on the court and play skillfully? Of course not.

And yet, when people talk about communication skills, there's often a sense that if you only understood what you should be doing, you could just go right out and do it, or that if you only understood what not to do, you could just stop. From our experience in training and coaching, we know that's not true. If it were, in a very brief period of time, we could change a person's whole outlook on life, transform a company's culture, or save a failing marriage. We'd simply tell people, "Stop doing this, and do that instead," and call it a day. In reality, it takes a lot more than that to improve the way someone communicates.

The type of teaching that we've seen make a real difference in people's conversations is a series of interactive workshops or coaching sessions. While it's impossible to reproduce the full experience of a live training session in a book, we wanted to come as close as possible. We set out to identify the essential elements of ongoing, interactive trainings that make them effective in conquering bad habits and building new skills. The answers lie in recent research on the brain and on brain-based methods for changing the way people think and act. In the following sections, we'll give you an overview of relevant findings from that research.

Why did we devote a whole chapter to brain-related topics? We realize that you're probably reading this book to improve your communication, not to brush up on neuropsychology. However, even though *what* you'll learn in this book are communication skills, *how* you learn those skills has everything to do with the way your brain functions. Only by learning about the brain can you truly understand why your habitual ways of communicating are so stubbornly persistent, and why it takes more than good ideas and good intentions to change them. This knowledge will also help you to get the most out of the concepts and strategies in the chapters that follow.

We've divided the remainder of this chapter into three sections:

1. **Brain change.** A brief review of what research tells us about the brain's capacity for change (neuroplasticity), and what that means for our ability to change habitual patterns in our lives.
2. **Drivers of brain change.** Descriptions of three essential steps for driving neuroplasticity, and therefore helping to change habits.
3. **How this book helps to drive brain change.** A guide to how we incorporated the three steps of brain change into this book, and how you can use them to help transform your own habitual communication patterns.

Neuroplasticity: New Hope for the Brain and for Understanding Habit Change

As you get older, what do you think happens to your brain? Until quite recently, the picture painted by mainstream science was bleak. According to the prevailing wisdom, by the time we reached adulthood, the potential for positive change was extremely limited. Of course, we could learn and develop new memories, which meant that some of the connections between our neurons (brain cells) could be altered. But the idea that major changes could occur—that regions of the brain could significantly alter their structure or function—was dismissed as preposterous. The concept of lifelong neurogenesis (creation of new brain cells) was relegated to the world of science fiction. With this image of the adult brain, change led in only one direction: toward decline and dysfunction. Neurons could die, but they couldn't be replaced, so brain damage caused by injury or disease could never be reversed.

Fortunately for all of us, the reality is much more encouraging. Around the turn of the twenty-first century, attitudes toward brain plasticity began to shift, in the face of mounting evidence that brains can change—and change dramatically—throughout the human lifespan. It was the start of a new, exciting field of study that would transform the theory and practice of neuropsychology.[1] Far from being an isolated phenomenon largely restricted to our childhood years, plasticity appears to be a defining characteristic of every part of our brain[2] from birth until death.[3]

What's really exciting is not just that our brains keep changing, but that they keep changing *in response to what we do and experience, and even to what we think.*[4] The functions and structures of our brains are continuously adapting to the tasks we perform, whether we're playing a melody on the piano[5] or navigating a taxi through London's complex maze of city streets.[6] Think of this phenomenon as a mechanism for setting priorities. Your patterns of behaving and responding to the world around you tell your brain what it should get good at doing. The way the brain gets better at doing something is through changes in neural connections, or pathways—either creating new pathways or making existing pathways stronger.[7]

In *The Brain That Changes Itself,* Norman Doidge's bestselling book on neuroplasticity, neuroscientist Alvaro Pascual-Leone likens neural pathways to sled tracks down a snowy hill. When you first start sledding, there are many possible paths you could take down to the bottom, but over time, the activity of sledding creates tracks. The more you use a certain pathway, the deeper that track becomes. Certain tracks become "'really speedy' and very efficient at guiding the sled down the hill,"[8] so you're much more likely to take those same pathways in the future.

This is a powerful metaphor for explaining many of the habitual, dysfunctional patterns in our lives. At one time or another, most of us have had the experience of being "stuck in a rut," feeling like we're doing the same thing over and over again—whether it's in our work, in our personal relationships, or just in our own thinking. In neurological terms, that rut is a pathway that has been repeatedly strengthened and reinforced, until it's quite difficult for us to start acting differently. Doidge refers to this phenomenon as the "plastic paradox": "The same neuroplastic properties that allow us to change our brains and produce more flexible behaviors can also allow us to produce more rigid ones."[9] Because our brains can keep changing, our ruts can continue to get deeper. In terms of communication, this means every time we slip into a habitual way of talking, that habit gets more and more deeply ingrained.

A Radically Different Perspective

We want to take a moment to point out how unconventional the plastic pathways explanation is. It's radically different from a much more common explanation for habitual behavior: attributing it to fixed, brain-based characteristics that remain stable over time. We all sometimes talk about people's behavior (including our own) as being the result of personality traits: "She's chronically late because she's flighty and irresponsible." "He keeps arguing because he's highly competitive and has an aggressive streak." "I always expect the worst (or best) because of my deep-seated pessimism (or optimism)."

The plastic pathways approach turns this perspective on its head, showing that it's misleading to think you behave in consistent ways because your personality, or your brain, always remains stable. In a sense, the reverse is true: your brain and personality remain relatively stable because you keep behaving in consistent ways. This type of reasoning transforms the thought "I've kept doing these things because this is the way I am" to "This is the way I am because I've kept doing these things."[10]

From that point of view, it doesn't really matter where your habits come from. Think of the sled track analogy. No matter what drove those pathways to form originally, what's causing them to continue getting used is the nature of the pathways themselves, the deepness of the ruts. The same goes for habits. You may have developed a predictable way of thinking, talking, feeling, or acting for any number of reasons. Maybe you were imitating someone, maybe you were coping with a stressful relationship, or maybe your response served some other purpose. Whatever conscious intention or motivating factor you once had may have disappeared years ago. What keeps you responding in the same way now is the strength of that neural pathway. In Doidge's words, "Neural circuits, once established, tend to become *self-sustaining*."[11] This is why we all sometimes keep doing things that we know are not in our best interest. We're stuck in a self-perpetuating rut.

While neuroplasticity has its downside (turning some unhelpful behaviors into persistent habits), it also brings tremendous potential for positive change, including new, innovative therapeutic techniques. For instance, an understanding of how experience shapes the brain has helped researchers to develop low-tech, noninvasive treatments that restore lost functioning after debilitating strokes;[12] relieve severe symptoms of obsessive-compulsive disorder (OCD);[13] and alleviate the sometimes agonizing "phantom limb pain" experienced by many amputees.[14]

The therapy for OCD is particularly interesting to us, since one of its primary goals is to change people's patterns of thinking (the ways they communicate with themselves). Research psychiatrist Jeffrey Schwartz teaches people with OCD to use plasticity-based techniques to self-treat their condition. By making specific, conscious changes in their thoughts and behaviors, these individuals gain freedom from the deep ruts of obsessive worries and fears (from excessive concerns about germs to irrational fears of having hit someone while driving), as well as their associated compulsions (such as repeatedly washing their hands or circling the block to see if anyone has been run over).[15] Brain scans reveal that individuals who've benefitted from Schwartz's method have altered the functioning of their brains; they show significantly decreased activity in the "OCD circuit," the neural pathways that are overly active in OCD sufferers.[16]

These types of changes provide new hope not just for people with obsessive-compulsive disorder, but for all of us who have developed unconstructive patterns of thinking and acting—in other words, everyone. The same basic steps that help transform the lives of people with OCD—as well as those with chronic pain, stroke damage, learning disabilities, and other brain-based problems—can help transform the conversations we have every day. In the following two sections, we'll walk you through those steps and explain how they can help you get the most out of this book.

Three Steps to Changing Your Brain: Awareness, Action, and Practice

Step 1: Awareness—Seeing the Way Out of Your Rut

Awareness is the basic starting point for any lasting change. When you're trying to change a habit, you need three separate types of awareness: realization, attention, and observation.

Realization

The first type of awareness is simply realizing that there's something particular you'd like to change. Often people are totally unaware of their unconstructive habits, including the unhelpful ways they communicate, even when those habits are obvious to those around them.

We discussed this issue with Ed Josephs, a neuropsychologist who specializes in treating the physical and psychological effects of trauma.[17] Josephs compares people's habitual behaviors to the way they look from the back, or the way their voice sounds to others. Think about it for yourself—everyone around you sees your back all the time, but without outside help (like a mirror), you never do. The same is true of the sound of your voice. Have you ever listened to a recording of yourself and been surprised by what you hear? Even in the most basic sense, says Josephs, "You don't really know what you sound like."[18]

You're probably also unaware of the particular combinations of words and voice tones you tend to use. When we work with clients to start tracking their communication, they're often shocked to learn how often they complain or ask leading questions or say something else they don't consciously intend to say. All of us sometimes need feedback from an outside observer—such as a coach, therapist, teacher, or tactful friend or coworker—to give us insight into what we're doing. Although insight on its own isn't enough to bring about change (see sidebar), it's an important first step.

> ## The Myth of Insight
>
> Notice that realization is only the first part of the first step in changing a habitual behavior. Insight alone won't make you act differently. As Jim Grigsby and David Stevens explain in *Neurodynamics of Personality*, "merely knowing that you habitually do something a certain way is not the same thing as actually starting to do something a different way."[19] When people fail to understand this, they may assume that once they've had an insight, there's nothing more they need to do. Neuropsychologist Ed Josephs warns of that danger: "Having an insight can keep you from changing," he says, "because you feel like you've changed already."[20] In order for insights to be valuable, we need to recognize them as the start, not the end, of the change process.

Attention

The true value of realization is that it motivates you to start paying closer attention. We all know from experience that paying attention to something makes it feel different. For instance, mindlessly eating a meal feels different from savoring the flavor and texture of the food. Gazing absently at a garden feels different from taking in the shape and color of individual plants or flowers. And simply being present while someone else speaks feels different from making eye contact with them and actively listening to what they're saying. As it turns out, in addition to changing what we feel, shifting our attention also changes what happens in our brains.[21]

Earlier, we mentioned that what you do helps your brain to set priorities. In fact, it's not just what you do that matters. It's what you *consciously, attentively* do. Doing something on autopilot doesn't have the same impact as doing that same thing with focused attention. Research shows that attention is essential for lasting neuroplastic changes to occur.[22]

This means that if you want to create a new habit, it's important to perform the new activity with awareness. If you want to change a habit you already have, you face an additional challenge: being aware of your old, habitual behavior at the moment when it happens. Only then do you have a shot at trying a different response. Here again, it's sometimes useful to get help from a coach, friend, or other outside observer. This person can act as training wheels for your brain, providing an external alert when your habit kicks in, until your own awareness develops to the point where you can notice it by yourself.

Observation

Once you're paying attention, you have an opportunity to use the third type of awareness: observation. Observation is a central feature of Jeffrey Schwartz's treatment for OCD. He teaches people not only to attend to their symptoms, but to attend in a particular way, witnessing them with the neutral objectivity of an "Impartial Spectator."[23] When a person experiences an intrusive thought or impulse, they bring to mind two facts about it: what it is and why it's happening. First they label the symptom, naming it as an obsession or compulsion. Then they remind themselves that they're experiencing the symptom because of a medical condition (obsessive-compulsive disorder) that's causing part of their brain to malfunction.[24]

This neutral, impartial observation helps OCD sufferers to resist getting drawn into the content of their obsessions—thinking more and more about dirt, germs, violence, etc.—which would only reinforce and perpetuate their symptoms. Schwartz believes that an observing mindset can help to combat a wide variety of dysfunctional habits. "The key," he says, ". . . is clearly seeing the difference between you and the behavior you want to change."[25]

If you've had experience with the Buddhist practice of mindful awareness or similar forms of meditation, Schwartz's approach may seem familiar to you. That is no coincidence. In developing his treatment for OCD, Schwartz drew upon his long-standing interest in mindfulness.[26] Jon Kabat-Zinn, a leading teacher, researcher, and author on this topic, defines being mindful as "paying attention in a particular way: on purpose, in the present moment, and nonjudgmentally."[27] In other words, you intentionally notice what's happening, while it's happening, without getting caught up in reactions or judgments. That includes noticing the thoughts you're having without automatically accepting them as true (see sidebar).

Thought-Labeling: Not Believing Everything You Think

To help cultivate mindfulness, some meditation teachers recommend "thought-labeling," a technique that closely resembles the first step of Schwartz's OCD treatment. Ezra Bayda, a Buddhist Zen master, describes this process in his book *Being Zen*. As a thought arises, you either identify the category of thinking that it belongs to (perhaps saying to yourself, "planning" or "fantasizing") or label the entire thought (for instance, saying to yourself, "'Having a thought that I have too much to do'").[28] Over time, Bayda says, this helps you to recognize that "even the most stubborn thought is not necessarily the truth about reality, but just a thought."[29] When you observe a thought that's leading you to act in unconstructive ways, you can make a choice to start letting it go.

For most of us, most of the time, mindfulness does not come naturally. It takes mental work to step back and neutrally observe what's going on inside ourselves, whether it's a worry about the future, a feeling of anger, an uncomfortable physical sensation, or an impulse to argue, yell, or reach for a cigarette or a piece of candy. As challenging as this may be, there are many good reasons to put in the effort. Research suggests that over time, mindfulness practice produces a variety of general improvements in the structure and functioning of the brain.[30] We can also use mindfulness to achieve more specific benefits. When we're mindfully aware of a particular bad habit, we have a chance to stop reinforcing the pathways that drive that habit (our old rut). The next step is starting to consciously create a different, better pathway (a new groove).

Using the Three Types of Awareness

1. **Realize** that there's something particular you'd like to change.
2. **Attend** to what you're doing (including what you're thinking), while you're doing it.
3. **Observe** what's happening with the objective mindset of a neutral witness.

Step 2: Action—Getting into Your New Groove

Let's say you've succeeded in cultivating your awareness. You've realized there's a habit you'd like to change, and you've developed the ability to pay attention to it and mindfully observe what happens. At some point, as you're going about your life, you notice the habit start to kick in: a familiar old thought, feeling, or impulse pops up, and you can clearly see where it's about to lead—right into your old rut. What do you do now? The short answer: something different. Resist slipping into your habitual behavior, and try another behavior in its place. For a person with OCD, this might mean resisting the urge to wash their hands and instead starting to garden, play a computer game, or do another activity they enjoy.[31] For someone trying to change their communication, it might mean resisting the urge to criticize a colleague's proposal and instead asking a question or considering what's useful about the idea.

This is a simple technique, just substituting a new behavior for an old one, but it's easier said than done. Because habits are well-worn pathways, they exert a compelling force on us. Even when we know they're destructive—they're hurting our relationships, making us physically ill, interfering with our work, or simply draining time and energy that we'd rather spend on something else—there's a way in which they feel natural and right. As a result, any new, alternative response is likely to feel unnatural and wrong, even though we know in our mind that it's a more constructive thing to do. In fact, at the beginning of changing a habit, feeling uncomfortable is often a good sign that you're on the right track. It tells you that you're doing something different, which is the only way real change can happen.

Of course, responding in a new way once or twice doesn't mean that you've succeeded in kicking your habit. Think back to the sledding analogy. Your first attempts at changing your behavior are like your first few runs on a new path down the hill. At the beginning, the tracks you create won't be very deep; it takes repeated trips to carve out a lasting groove. In the same way, it takes time and persistence to establish a strong neural pathway. You need to perform the new behavior intentionally, with mindful awareness, again and again and again. In other words, you need to practice.

Step 3: Practice—Staying in the Groove

No matter why you're trying to change your brain—to reduce chronic pain, recover from a stroke, overcome an addiction or a learning disability, or change a habitual communication pattern—this change takes practice. The way you practice makes a big difference in how successful you're likely to be. We've already discussed one important factor: you need to be paying focused attention. There are also three additional factors to consider. The most effective types of practice are rewarding, intensive, and incremental:

- **Rewarding.** We learn an action or response much more readily when we get some sort of reward for it.[32] Some activities are naturally rewarding because doing them gives us pleasure. That's why it's best for people with OCD to replace a compulsion with a fun game or hobby rather than a boring household chore.[33] Another powerful type of reward is immediate positive feedback, something that lets you know right away that you've done a good thing. Many computer-based learning games rely on this kind of feedback, rewarding players with satisfying audio or visual effects every time they successfully complete a task.[34]
- **Intensive.** Practice seems to work best when it's concentrated.[35] When stroke patients are rebuilding physical skills, they benefit more from an intensive two-week training than from spreading out the exercises over longer periods of time.[36] In OCD treatment, intensity comes from maintaining a concentrated focus on a new activity for at least 15 minutes.[37]
- **Incremental.** Our brains don't learn by going from 0 to 60, novice to expert, all at one time. Whether the activity we're practicing is physical or mental, it helps to progress gradually. For instance, stroke rehabilitation starts with very simple motions before building up to more challenging movements.[38] Likewise, OCD treatment starts with resisting a single compulsive behavior, often the one that causes the least stress, before tackling other troublesome thoughts and impulses.[39] As you'll see shortly, a gradual approach is also best for improving your communication.

Using This Book to Change Your Brain

We began this chapter by telling you that reading a book isn't enough to change your communication, because reading doesn't do what live training can do. By now, the reasons for this should be clear. In a series of workshops or coaching sessions, there are built-in opportunities to use all three steps for promoting brain change: immediate feedback helps bring your awareness to what you're doing, while you're doing it; exercises and role-plays give you a chance to try out new actions; and, as you repeat those actions over time, you get the practice you need to solidify your skills. Reading to yourself, alone, doesn't have the same effects. You may gain a few insights into your unconstructive habits, but as you've learned, insight alone isn't enough to create lasting behavioral change.

Keeping those limitations in mind, we've written this book in such a way that you can do more than just read it; you can use it as a training manual to actively apply everything you're learning to your own conversations, systematically transforming the way you think and talk. To give you that opportunity, every time we teach you a skill, we incorporate the three essential steps of awareness, action, and practice.

Awareness

In the following six chapters, we'll introduce you to six problematic communication behaviors, from yes-buts to verbal attacks. For each one, we'll suggest specific ways you can build your awareness, so you can start to notice both when you're using that behavior and when other people in your life are using it. We'll often recommend enlisting a friend, colleague, or family member to help you with two forms of awareness: realization (for instance, pointing out that you tend to ask lots of leading questions) and attention (alerting you right at the moment when a leading question comes out of your mouth). In addition, the training programs at the end of each chapter include awareness-building exercises to try either on your own or with a partner.

The third form of awareness, mindful observation, is one of the most valuable of all communication skills. It's easier to develop this ability when you take the approach we recommended in Chapter 1—looking beyond *what* is being said to notice *how* it's being said (the particular communication behaviors being used). When you label a comment as a yes-but, a mind-read, a negative prediction, or any other behavior, you have a much better chance of observing it neutrally, without getting caught up in the content. (This is similar to what happens with the thought-labeling techniques we described earlier, in both OCD treatment and mindfulness meditation.)

For instance, when you notice that you're complaining about your long work hours, you can draw your attention away from what you're talking about (your hours) and toward how you've been talking (in complaints). When you notice that someone has asked you a leading question, you can step back from your habitual reaction (such as automatically agreeing or automatically disagreeing) and think more objectively about what's being communicated and how you'd like to respond.

Shifting into this observing frame of mind is far from easy. It takes patience, practice, and no small amount of mental work. The effort is well worth it, however. Observation gives you the gifts of freedom and choice: freedom from slipping unthinkingly into an old, unhelpful habit, and choice about what to do instead—a new action.

Action

In addition to helping you stay neutral and objective, labeling communication behaviors can also help you plan effective strategies. Throughout this book, every time we teach you about a troublesome behavior, we teach three different skills for dealing with it: a transformation skill, a response skill, and an intervention skill. For instance, in the chapter on complaints, we show you how to transform your own complaining, how to respond when another person complains to you, and how to intervene when you hear other people complaining together. That way, whenever you notice complaining in a conversation—coming either from you or from someone else—you'll have specific actions to take that are likely to be more productive than what you might habitually do. By performing these actions, you start to train your brain in more effective patterns of behavior.

Practice

Learning how to do something new always takes practice. Some of the skills in this book may be entirely foreign to you. For instance, our strategy for responding to verbal attacks includes mirroring, empathically reflecting back the other person's emotional message. If you're not accustomed to communicating in that way, it probably won't feel like a natural response. Moreover, even if you have experience with a certain behavior, that doesn't mean you're capable of using it effectively in every situation. Being skilled at mirroring the sadness of a close friend is no guarantee that you'll be able to mirror the anger of a disgruntled employee.

In the training programs in the next six chapters, you'll get to practice a variety of helpful communication behaviors that may not come naturally to you. You can use these exercises to build and strengthen new neural pathways. Follow the three principles we discussed earlier, making sure your practice is rewarding, intensive, and incremental:

- **Rewarding.** The experience of communicating more effectively can be a reward in itself. People often tell us that the strategies we teach leave them feeling much better than their old habits did. They're relieved to get a break from the resignation that comes from negative predictions or the frustration of endless complaining or yes-but arguments. When they use new, problem-solving behaviors instead, they feel more hopeful and empowered.

  You can also arrange to get immediate positive feedback when you perform new behaviors successfully. For many of the exercises in this book, we suggest working together with a partner. That person can let you know whenever you do something well, maybe saying "great job" or giving you a thumbs-up. Even more important is the feedback you'll get from their natural responses when you try a new behavior—such as the way they automatically relax and open up when you start building on their ideas rather than yes-butting them.

- **Intensive.** To bring intensity to your practice, do each skill-building exercise in chunks. Don't transform just one or two leading questions (or yes-buts, or complaints, or whatever you're working on) and then stop; keep going as long as it feels helpful. Repeat this kind of practice session as frequently as you can without getting burned out (daily if possible), continuing until the new skill begins to feel natural.

- **Incremental.** Practicing incrementally means not doing too many things at once, and proceeding gradually from simple tasks to tasks that are harder or more complex. Plan to do the exercises one at a time, not all in a single sitting. They steadily increase in difficulty throughout each training program, so you can start out with basic awareness-building activities and build up to challenging, interactive role-plays that simulate real, difficult conversations. (You may be surprised at how quickly a role-play exercise starts to feel real. Within a few minutes, most people find themselves reacting in the same way they would in the actual situation they're simulating.)

To maximize your chance of success, we recommend taking an incremental approach not just within each chapter, but also across the book as a whole. Don't attempt to change all your problematic communication habits simultaneously. Begin with one—preferably one that's relatively easy to change, not your most deeply ingrained pattern of thinking and talking. For example, suppose you have a strong tendency to complain, you grew up hearing everyone in your family complain, and your colleagues and friends complain to you on a daily basis. For you, the complaint exercises may not be the best place to start. You might try tackling another behavior first, and slowly work your way up to complaints. The good news is that any work you do in changing one habit will leave you better prepared to change other habits in the future. The habit-changing process (awareness, action, practice) stays the same. All you need to do is apply it to a different type of behavior.

Change and Stress

Have you ever had the experience of thinking you've successfully changed a habit, only to have it return with a vengeance when you're under stress? Perhaps you've managed to stop eating unhealthy snacks for a month, but the minute you get home from a brutal day at work, you start stuffing yourself. You might not even notice what you're doing; by the time your awareness sets in, you've eaten a whole bag of chips or half a pint of ice cream.

The same thing happens with communication habits. You might conquer your tendency to assign blame or make negative predictions in low-stakes, low-stress situations, but then slip right back into those behaviors when the pressure is high or your energy is low—when you've been up all night with the flu, your child throws a tantrum, or your boss dumps a last-minute assignment on you.

There's a reason for this sort of lapse: a stressed brain always tends to revert to using habitual pathways.[40] When we're feeling pressured or depleted, we don't have the mental resources we need to stay mindful and skillful. This means that when you're trying to change a habit, it's important to keep an eye on your stress level. Habit change is stressful as it is, since it forces you out of your comfort zone. When you add other external stressors to the built-in stress of trying something new, you're unlikely to be able to learn effectively. With that in mind, make sure you practice your new skills when you're feeling relaxed and energized, not tired or frazzled. Avoid trying to make too many changes at once, and don't get discouraged by the setbacks you're bound to experience from time to time.

The Promise and Potential of Your Changeable Brain

The promise of neuroplasticity is that the current state of a person's brain does not define the limits of their potential. People suffering from learning disabilities, OCD, stroke damage, or other brain-based problems can go a long way toward overcoming these conditions. In the same way, every one of us has the power to defy the limits of our habitual, unconstructive ways of communicating. We wrote this book to help you realize that potential for yourself. We'll start, in the next chapter, by introducing you to a very common and very unproductive way of handling conflict: the polite fight.

3

Polite Fights

"Rob and Amanda Parker were a very loving couple," their psychologist told us. "They weren't at each other's throats like many of the couples that I see. And yet they just couldn't find a constructive way to discuss the problems that were tearing them apart."

The past few years had been extremely stressful for the Parkers. Rob and Amanda had two healthy daughters (ages five and seven) but had always wanted a larger family, and their attempts to have a third child had ended in disappointment. Over the course of three years trying to conceive—including many aggressive and invasive fertility treatments—they had exhausted all possible options. Now, in addition to their grief, they were also struggling with the loss of romance in their marriage. Years of scheduling their sex life around temperature charts and surgical procedures had robbed them of any sense of spontaneity.

Ten months after their doctors had called an end to the fertility treatments, Rob and Amanda's relationship was growing more and more strained. This was easy to see when their psychologist, a colleague of ours named Mark Johnson, had them recreate one of their typical tough conversations. They'd been having this same "polite fight" on a regular basis:

Rob: *We used to make time to be together.*
Amanda: *But that was before we had kids and a house and bills to pay.*
Rob: *Of course, I know that. I'm not expecting us to be acting like we're dating.*
Amanda: *You say that, but you act like that's how I'm supposed to feel.*
Rob: *Don't you ever feel like you felt when we first got together?*

Amanda: *Of course, but you expect me to be ready for romance all the time, and that's just not realistic.*

Rob: *I'm not trying to pressure you. I'm just feeling this distance between us that I don't know how to handle.*

Amanda: *I feel distance too, but I don't think you understand how I'm feeling about not having a third child.*

Rob: *Don't you realize I'm upset by this too? I know it was you who had to go through all the procedures, but when things didn't work out, it was a loss for both of us.*

Amanda: *I know, but I don't think you know how this affects me. You expect me just to be over it.*

Rob: *I don't expect you to be over it, but that was almost a year ago.*

Amanda: *Sure, it was almost a year ago, but we don't even talk about it anymore. You act like it's all in the past, and I think about it every day.*

Listening to this conversation, Dr. Johnson recognized a familiar set of issues that arise for many couples. He refers to conflicts over romance and intimacy—often connected with the process of building a family—as the "common cold" of his counseling practice. However, as someone who'd been trained to take a behavioral approach to communication, he also understood that issues alone don't cause conversations to fail. When he looked at the specific communication behaviors that Rob and Amanda were using, it was obvious why they were having so much trouble. They had fallen victim to one of the most common conversation killers: the yes-but.

Communication Challenge 1:
Yes-But—the Great Divider

Although Rob and Amanda were saying different things, they were saying them in the same, unconstructive way. Almost every statement either of them made was a *yes-but*: a superficial, token agreement ("I know . . ." or "I don't expect you to be over it") followed immediately by a different idea ("but I don't think you know how this affects me" or "but that was almost a year ago"). We've all experienced the frustrating effects of yes-buts, whether they come from a child ("Yeah, but Mom said I could go!"), a friend ("A play could be fun, but tickets are so expensive"), or a supervisor

("That's a great idea, but it's not in our budget"). When we look at what yes-buts do to a conversation, it's no wonder they set us on edge and get arguments going.

The Problems with Yes-Buts

There are three distinctive problems caused by using yes-buts:

1. **Yes-buts send a mixed message.** Often people yes-but with the best of intentions, hoping to be diplomatic or make unpleasant news easier to hear. Disagreeing with someone directly (saying, "I see things differently" or "I'm not willing to do that") may seem too harsh or negative. It may sound more polite to say, "I can see how you'd feel that way, but . . ." The problem is that when someone does that, they're giving two conflicting messages at the same time, saying both yes and no. This doesn't make their message nicer. It just makes it harder for the other person's brain to process. Whenever someone gives us a contradictory message, it's almost impossible to hear both sides. As a result, we end up focusing on just one side—which leads us to the second problem.

2. **People hear only the "but."** Think about how you'd react if your friend told you, "I like your shirt, but that sweater doesn't match." Do you think you'd really hear the compliment on your shirt? In almost every case, what grabs people's attention is the disagreement: the "but" part of the message. It's human nature to notice differences rather than similarities. As a result, the "yes" part of the message—the part that shows some agreement, understanding, or common ground—simply gets lost.

3. **Any difference can become a conflict.** Yes-buts don't just heighten existing disagreements; they can actually create new ones. Consider what happened with Rob and Amanda. They were talking about two separate issues: (1) wanting more closeness and (2) grief over not being able to have another child. There's no essential conflict there. You can want closeness and still feel grief, or at least acknowledge that both of these experiences are valid. However, as the couple kept yes-butting, it started to seem as though one of them had to be right while the other one was wrong. Since neither person wanted to be wrong (who does?), they naturally kept arguing and the conflict continued to escalate.

The "But" Reflex

Nobody is a perfect communicator. We've all developed at least a few bad habits, many of them so automatic that we don't even notice them. This became very clear in one team of top executives that we trained. While observing one of their strategic meetings, we quickly noticed that whenever a particular person (call him Jim) spoke, he seemed to get resistance from others in the group.

To see what might be causing that resistance, we decided to track Jim's behavior. It turned out that every single time he made a comment, he started with the word *but*. He did this even when asking an otherwise neutral question ("But where do you think we can get this information?") or building on what someone else had said ("But let's see if we can get other departments on board with the idea."). All his "butting" made it sound as though he was continually opposing what other team members had said.

When we talked to Jim later, he said he had no idea he was communicating in this way. It was only by gaining that awareness— making his unconscious habit conscious—that he could start to do something different.

Yes-butting is one of the most reliable ways to get an argument going, whether you're speaking with just one other person or with a group. If the people you're talking to are the least bit competitive, they're likely to respond with yes-buts of their own. Before you know it, you can find yourself caught up in an endless ping-pong match of competing ideas. Yes-but communication is a leading cause of unproductive business meetings, as time that could be spent on collaborative decision making or problem solving is instead wasted on tedious arguments:

> *We need to invest in better technology.*
> *Yes, but we don't have the money.*
> *Of course there will be short-term costs, but over the long run we'll save money by being more efficient.*
> *That may be true, but we can't justify another expenditure right now.*
> *I know, but if we wait for the perfect situation, we'll never move forward.*

And so on. As the conversation continues, the two sides typically become increasingly rigid and polarized, to the point where it seems as though they have nothing in common.

While these sorts of polite fights are relatively civil compared to more heated arguments filled with insults and accusations, they are equally ineffective for resolving conflicts. Furthermore, a polite fight can easily escalate into something more serious. Getting stuck in a long, drawn-out back-and-forth debate is extremely frustrating. If it goes on for long enough, at some point people will probably start venting that frustration at one another, raising their voices and blaming each other for the problems they're facing. As the people get attacked, the real culprit—the group pattern of yes-butting—goes undetected.

The only time when yes-butting is likely to help someone reach their goals is when they're deliberately attempting to be provocative, and they don't care whether their message gets through to the other person. Think about cable news shows that pit liberal and conservative commentators against one another. You generally can't watch for more than a minute without hearing a yes-but. These discussions may not help to promote mutual understanding or agreement, but they're often highly successful at stirring up controversy, provoking strong emotions in the viewers, and increasing ratings.

The Upshot: When yes-but communication takes hold, any conversation can quickly turn into an argument, damaging relationships and making it hard to get anything done.

Skills for Managing Yes-Buts

Yes-butting is so common, at least in American culture,[1] that it affects all of us in one way or another. To avoid getting caught up in polite fights, you need to know both how to change your own yes-buts and how to respond effectively when someone yes-buts you. We'll teach you how to do that and also how you can effectively intervene in other people's yes-but conversations. For each skill, we'll follow our basic three-step program for behavior change:

1. Building awareness
2. Learning new behaviors (new actions to take)
3. Using repeated practice to turn those actions into habits

Transformation Skill: Controlling Your Own Yes-Butting

If you're someone who tends to yes-but a lot, learning how to do it less can make a huge difference in your communication. We've seen many people successfully kick the habit using the process that you're about to learn.

Transformation Step 1: Self-Awareness

The first step is to build your awareness of your own yes-butting. Be particularly alert in situations where you hear opinions or suggestions that you strongly disagree with. Notice if you start to feel tense or agitated—a natural response for most of us. Then see if you can track what's happening in your thinking. Are you listening to what the other person is saying and trying to understand their ideas, or are you busy coming up with counter-arguments? If your mind is filled with yes-buts, it will be difficult to avoid yes-butting out loud.

Almost all of us send mixed messages through yes-buts at least some of the time, even if we never use the word *but* (see the sidebar on "stealth-butting"). When you're just starting out, you may not realize that you yes-butted someone until a few hours or days after the conversation is over. With time, you'll find yourself noticing your yes-buts in the middle of a conversation. Eventually, if all goes well, you'll be able to stop yes-butting in time to turn things around before the discussion heats up.

Stealth-Butting

Some of the worst yes-but offenders are people who are convinced they never yes-but at all. Somewhere along the line they learned that "yes, but" was a bad thing to say, so they eliminated that phrase from their vocabulary. However, their yes-buts never truly went away. They just went underground, to reemerge as what we call *stealth-buts*. Stealth-buts don't contain the word *but* or even, in most cases, the word *yes*. But they still send a contradictory message and therefore have the same problematic effects as traditional yes-buts. Here are a few examples:

"Yes" variations	"But" variations
I understand where you're coming from . . .	. . . *however* . . .
I see your point . . .	. . . *nevertheless* . . .
That may be true . . .	. . . *on the other hand* . . .
I know that seems like the obvious solution . . .	. . . *still* . . .
You could say that . . .	. . . *only then* . . .
While that's one way to look at things . . .	. . . *have you considered* . . .
You're absolutely right . . .	. . . *it's just that* . . .
Sure . . .	. . . *and yet* . . .

Even "yes, and" can be a yes-but in disguise, as in, "Yes, I like your approach, and what we need now is something completely different." If you're arguing against what someone just said, simply changing *but* to *and* isn't going to erase the negative impact of your mixed message.

To help you in developing your awareness, you might ask a few people you trust to speak up when they catch you yes-butting (so long as they can do it respectfully, without being critical or blameful). One man we trained found his at-home mentors accidentally. After learning about yes-buts, he decided to teach the concept to his two sons, thinking this might help them to stop arguing so much with each other. What he didn't expect was that they'd start noticing how often he yes-butted them, which he soon learned was many times per day.

Transformation Step 2: Action—Build and Explore

Suppose you notice that you're about to yes-but and you manage to catch yourself in time. Now what do you do? Let's take an example. Your spouse suggests taking a two-week vacation, and you feel the impulse to say, "That would be nice, but my work schedule won't allow it." You hold back that comment, because you know that when you've yes-butted your spouse in the past, you've wound up in an argument. What do you say instead? You could just change the subject or try a noncommittal "Uh-huh," but then the important information you have would never get into the conversation.

Remember that every yes-but contains two separate messages: (1) an agreement (you'd really enjoy a two-week vacation) and (2) a different or competing idea (you can't imagine how you could take that much time off). The challenge is finding a way to communicate these ideas that makes it easier for the other person to hear them. You could do this in a variety of different ways; there's no single "right" strategy. What we'll teach you here is one method that we've found to be particularly effective, a strategy we call *build and explore*.

Build

Think of the build as expanding the "yes" part of your yes-but by putting more meat on the bones. Instead of saying a superficial, token "Yes" or "Sure" or "That would be nice," you mention three specific things about what you just heard that you genuinely like, agree with, or can add to. This may be difficult. When you hear a message you don't like, it can be hard work to see what's good or right about that message, rather than what's bad or wrong. In our vacation example, you might be tempted to keep bringing back your "but": "It would be really relaxing to go away for two weeks *if only I weren't so incredibly busy*," or "Yeah, long vacations are great *for people who have that kind of time.*"

Even if it seems easy to build once or twice ("One week isn't enough time to fully relax," "In two weeks I could make a big dent in that pile of books I've been meaning to read"), the next one might be a challenge. To think of a third build, you generally need to dig deeper and make a real mental and emotional shift—which is why we recommend doing it. It's this shift in mindset, away from resistance and toward genuine curiosity about the other person's ideas, that makes the building effective.

Once that shift happens, you might come up with a new idea that you hadn't considered before, such as, "With two weeks free, we'd be able to go someplace farther away, without worrying about the long flight or jet lag." And you might wind up feeling more supportive than you expected to feel about the idea you originally opposed. For instance, you might start to get really excited about taking a longer vacation, maybe remembering an old dream you had of taking an extended trip abroad.

Once you've sincerely built upon someone's idea, they're more likely to be receptive to what you say next. Typically, people will feel more relaxed and open to your ideas if you seem to be similar to them or on their side.

(Any idea that comes across as being too different or antagonistic will tend to provoke a defensive reaction.) Just remember that your builds need to be genuine. If you try to fake this strategy, without doing the necessary work to shift your focus from what's bad about the other person's idea to what might be good about it, your lack of sincerity will probably be obvious.

Signs of Success in Shifting from *Buts* to Builds

1. Did you notice your impulse to disagree when you heard the idea you didn't like?
2. Did you feel that impulse diminish as you worked to come up with three builds?
3. Did you end up with some genuine interest in the other person's point of view?

If you answered yes to any of these questions, you're making good progress.

Explore

So far, so good. You've fleshed out your "yes" with three sincere, specific builds. Now comes the tricky part: bringing in your concern—in this case, your worry about taking so much time off from work—without phrasing it as a "but." A good way to do that is to incorporate your concern into a broad (open-ended) question.[2] For instance, you might ask, "Do you have any ideas about how I could fit a two-week trip around my work schedule?"

To *But* or Not to *But*

When we teach about yes-buts in our trainings, people often raise the objection that yes-buts don't always cause problems. They make a good point. For instance, imagine your friend suggests meeting for coffee at four o'clock; you say, "I'd love to meet for coffee, *but* I can't get there until four-thirty"; your friend says that's fine, and the potential conflict is essentially over before it begins.

While it's impossible to know for sure ahead of time whether a yes-but will fuel an argument, there are two factors that make problems much more likely:

1. **The discussion is already confrontational, competitive, or hostile.** If the conversation so far has included yes-buts, criticism, or attacks (from you or the other person), the odds are good that your yes-but will only make things worse.

2. **You feel a sense of opposition or irritation.** If your yes-but is coming from an impulse to set somebody straight or oppose an idea you disagree with, it's likely to take the conversation in a negative direction.

In situations where one or both of these factors apply, you're better off not using a yes-but.

Consider what a difference this simple change could make in your communication. In a yes-but conversation, all your energy goes into arguing over who's right and who's wrong. By asking a broad question, you redirect that energy into constructive problem solving. This helps both you and the other person to stay open to new possibilities that you hadn't considered before. For example, you and your spouse might come up with a creative solution to your vacation dilemma. Maybe you'll think of a way to combine leisure travel with a work-related trip; do some work remotely while you're away; reassign one of your time-consuming projects; or fit in a few hours of overtime each week in the months before you leave. Not only will you avoid a fight, but you'll also increase the chances of getting what you both want—a nice long vacation that doesn't conflict with your work responsibilities.

Building and Exploring on a Charged Political Issue
While many yes-but arguments deal with practical decisions like planning a vacation, hiring a new employee, or making budget cuts, some of the most heated debates involve larger legal or political issues. Topics such as abortion, gay marriage, gun control, and defense policy challenge people's core beliefs and values. When you hear an opposing viewpoint on one of those issues, the temptation to argue may be almost irresistible. At a minimum, these sorts of conflicts can be very frustrating. In worse cases, they may seriously damage relationships, leaving colleagues, friends, or family members feeling alienated from one another.

The build-and-explore strategy gives us a more productive alternative. We'll demonstrate this by applying it to a controversial issue that often gets discussed in polarized, black-and-white terms: the tension between national security and human rights. In the following dialogue, Ruth is arguing for the importance of national security, in the context of airline travel, and Charles is arguing for the importance of human rights.

> **Ruth:** *National security concerns need to take precedence over individual human rights. The government should be able to do whatever it needs to in order to stop people from taking bombs onto airplanes.*
>
> **Charles:** *Yes, national security is important, but that doesn't make it okay to abandon our fundamental protections for individual human life and dignity. (Yes-but)*
>
> **Ruth:** *Sure, those are great ideals. However, when we're face-to-face with terrorist threats, that kind of idealism can put thousands or even millions of lives at risk. (Yes-but)*
>
> **Charles:** *It's easy to say that, but then you could use that argument to justify terrible human rights abuses! (Yes-but)*

And from here, the argument could continue indefinitely.

Now let's back up to the start of the conversation and see how it could go a little differently. Imagine that as Ruth makes her first comment, Charles notices his reaction and realizes he is about to yes-but. At that point, he might be able to shift his focus from the things he doesn't like about Ruth's opinion to some things he can genuinely agree with (i.e., his builds):

> **Ruth:** *National security concerns need to take precedence over individual human rights. The government should be able to do whatever it needs to in order to stop people from taking bombs onto airplanes.*
>
> **Charles:** *I agree with you that national security needs to be one of the country's top priorities, since attacks by terrorists can claim hundreds or thousands of lives. (Build #1)*
>
> *I also agree that we need to ensure the safety of our transportation systems—particularly airplanes, because they can be used to hit any target. (Build #2)*
>
> *I think we should all be prepared to tolerate some inconveniences in order to make this happen. (Build #3)*

Charles's next step is to ask a broad question that addresses his concern, while still leaving room for Ruth to give her opinion freely. This is where the real hard work comes in. It would probably be much simpler for him to think of leading questions[3] that back her into a corner, such as, "Don't you think the focus on security sometimes goes too far?" or "Don't we also have a responsibility to take human rights into account?" Here are a few examples of genuine broad questions Charles could ask:

- "Can you think of ways to help people see that their privacy is being protected, while still keeping air travel safe?"
- "Can you think of any ways in which protecting human rights might be compatible with promoting national security?"
- "Can you think of some steps the government could take to promote national security that don't infringe on individual rights, or that actually enhance those rights?"

What happens next is up to Ruth. Nothing Charles can do will guarantee a constructive response. However, by first telling Ruth where his opinions are aligned with hers, and then expressing his concern as a broad question rather than a "but," he's made it much more likely that she'll give serious thought to the issue he's raised.

We wouldn't expect that Ruth and Charles would end up in perfect agreement with each other. However, so long as neither person has radically extreme views—for instance, believing that anyone who disagrees with the government's policies should be put in jail, or that there should be no security at airports because it violates the right to privacy—there will be some areas of common ground. Exploring those together will give them a good shot at developing a certain level of mutual understanding and respect. They might even discover that they can learn something from each other.

Self-Butting

It's not just when we're talking to other people that yes-buts create problems. Many of us yes-but ourselves, replaying the same arguments over and over again in our heads.

A good example of this occurred in a communications seminar led by our colleague Claudia Byram. One of the participants was trying to go into business for herself and was growing increasingly frustrated. As she explained the thoughts she'd been having, Claudia recognized a pattern of chronic self-butting. Each time this woman came up with an idea for moving forward, her next thought was a "but": "I want to have a website up first, but I don't think I can get it finished for another few months"; "I really should have business cards, but I can't do that until I decide on a logo"; and so on.

Once Claudia taught her the build-and-explore strategy, her thinking became much more productive:

> I want to have a website up.
> That will give my business more credibility. (Build)
> I can get other people doing related work to link to my site. (Build)
> Clients will have an easier time finding me online. (Build)
> What can I do to help get a website up as soon as possible? (Broad question)
> I can do it in stages, starting out with a very simple version that just has my contact information and basic details about what I do. (Answer)

In the next seminar, a few weeks later, the woman announced that she had officially started her business. She reported that in addition to making her more effective, the new strategy had left her feeling less overwhelmed and more energized and optimistic about her new career.

Transformation Step 3: Practice

If you're ready to start working toward transforming your yes-buts, skip ahead to the Yes-But Training Program starting on page 48.

Response Skill:
What to Do When Someone Else Yes-Buts You

Even if you're someone who doesn't yes-but often, you're bound to find yourself in situations where someone else yes-buts you. Have you found a consistent, reliable, and effective way to respond? If not, keep reading.

Response Step 1: Awareness

Can you tell when you're being yes-butted? You probably notice something, but you may not fully understand what's going on. Say you've been suggesting lunch options to your friend, and he has a "but" for every idea: "I like that place, but it's too far away." "The food's good, but it's expensive." After a little while, you might start noticing that you feel irritated. The challenge is to do something constructive with that irritation, rather than simply venting it (snapping at your friend) or stifling it (trying to pretend you're not annoyed). See if you can take your irritation as a cue to get curious about what's happening in the communication. Once you realize that you're being yes-butted, you can choose how you want to respond. **To practice recognizing yes-buts, visit CTsavvy.com/YBquiz.**

Response Step 2: Action—Build and Explore (Again)

Did the build-and-explore strategy sound like something that would work for you in controlling your own yes-buts? If so, here's some good news: you can use the same method to respond to someone else's yes-buts. Think back to the argument between Charles and Ruth. Charles yes-butted first, but that doesn't mean he's the only one who could make a positive change. Just as he was able to build on Ruth's concerns about national security, Ruth could build on his concerns about human rights. For instance, she might say, "A lack of regard for human life and dignity is part of what makes terrorist attacks so appalling (Build #1). In trying to protect our society, we shouldn't abandon the basic principles that the society is based on (Build #2). Our country's respect for human rights is one of the reasons I'm proud to be a citizen (Build #3)." She could then follow up with a broad question, such as, "Given present-day fears about bombs on planes, if you were in charge of security screening at the airport, what would you do?"

Building and exploring could also help improve your conversation with your friend about lunch options. You might acknowledge and build on his concerns: "I think it's smart to give some thought to how far we want to drive and how much money we want to spend. I don't want this to be a big hassle or expense. I remember the last time we went out, we both thought the food was overpriced." Your broad question might be, "Can you think of any reasonable restaurants that would be easy to get to?" By responding in this way, you break the frustrating cycle of suggestions and yes-buts and open a door for constructive problem solving.

> **The Upshot:** At any point in a yes-but dialogue, switching to building and asking broad questions can help you understand other points of view, get your own viewpoint into the conversation, reduce everyone's level of frustration, and start to develop a collaborative solution.

Plan B: What to Do When You Can't Find a Way to Build

There may be times when someone yes-buts you and your reaction isn't another yes-but; it's just plain "No!" No matter how hard you try, you can't find anything you like or agree with in the other person's idea. In that case, it may work best to skip the building and go straight to a broad question to gather more information. You might ask, "Can you tell me more about why you think that?" or "Are there specific experiences that have led you to that conclusion?" Be sure to keep your voice tone neutral, without any harsh or sarcastic edge.

If someone's idea seems crazy, extreme, or stupid to you, that's all the more reason to respond with a question. There's a good chance that at least one of you has information the other person doesn't have. For instance, suppose you're discussing layoff decisions with a colleague, explaining what a tough time you're having. She says, "But you really should have gotten rid of David already," and this seems extreme and unfair to you. It's possible that your colleague knows something about David that you don't know. Instead of arguing with her, you could ask, "What makes you say that?" Just be sure that when you ask that type of question, you're genuinely interested in hearing the answer. Otherwise, your question may come out sounding like an accusation ("What makes you say THAT?").

If all else fails, if even broad questions don't seem to work, one other option is to clearly state your disagreement, saying "I disagree," "I have a different opinion," or "We may have to agree to disagree" (again, making sure your voice tone stays neutral). While this isn't as helpful as the other strategies for building mutual understanding, it does avoid the mixed message of a yes-but and therefore is less likely to get an argument going.

Response Step 3: Practice

If you're ready to practice the skills you need to respond more effectively to yes-buts, turn to the Yes-But Training Program on page 48.

Intervention Skill:
Turning Around Other People's Yes-But Conversations

Now that you know more about the drawbacks of yes-butting, you may start to notice when yes-buts are getting other people into trouble, and you may feel a desire to try to help them out. That can sometimes be risky, so before we teach you a strategy, a few warnings are in order.

- **Always start with yourself.** Before you can help other people change their behavior, you need to be able to change your own. Otherwise, you risk getting caught up in the very yes-but cycle you're trying to break. You may find yourself saying things like, "I know he started the argument, *but* that doesn't mean you have to continue it" or "Of course your idea is important; *however*, you're not expressing it in a useful way." Remember the father who tried to stop his kids from yes-butting each other, only to realize that he himself was the biggest offender? If you try to stop a yes-but with another yes-but, you'll not only lose credibility but also almost certainly fail.

- **Get permission.** When you decide you'd like to try an intervention, make sure that the people involved are willing to have you do that. You may be in a role that automatically gives you the authority to intervene (for instance, if you're working as a consultant or therapist). If you're not, ask the people for permission. Explain that you're noticing something that may be causing difficulty for them, and ask if they'd like to talk about it. If they say no, keep your mouth shut.

- **Focus on changing the communication, not the people.** We all sometimes judge people based on the way they communicate. When you meet people who do a lot of yes-butting, you might start to draw conclusions about their personalities, thinking that they're stubborn, selfish, arrogant, or oppositional. That kind of judgment will make it hard to avoid blaming them, which only creates more problems. It will also distract you from the real source of trouble: the yes-but communication pattern. You don't need to change anyone's personality to help change that pattern. In fact, you might find that improving the communication seems to resolve the personality conflicts. As one of our students told us, "After I stopped yes-butting, everyone around me suddenly got a lot nicer!"

Keeping those warnings in mind, let's now turn to our three-step process for coaching people out of a yes-but conversation.

Intervention Step 1: Awareness

Yes-but communication is everywhere. Once you get some practice listening for yes-buts, chances are you'll start noticing them all around you, in the conversations of colleagues, clients, friends, neighbors, family members, and even strangers. That's the easy part. It's when you try to make a difference in those conversations that you need additional skills to succeed.

Intervention Step 2: Action—Motivate, Invite, Redirect

Listening to a yes-but argument is the verbal equivalent of watching two people on opposite sides of a narrow doorway, both attempting to get through at the same time. Both of them are so busy pushing their own ideas forward that they don't leave space for what the other person is saying, and as a result neither of them ends up feeling heard. To resolve this frustrating impasse, someone needs to stand back for a moment and make some room. That doesn't mean just being quiet and waiting until it's their turn to talk; it means actively responding to the other person's ideas, to show that they really got the message. In the previous two sections, we discussed an effective way of doing this: building and asking broad questions.

When you're a part of the conversation, you can be the one who takes the initiative to start building. When you're not part of the conversation, and others are arguing, it's one of those people who needs to make the first move (with the other person following suit, to make sure each of them gets a chance to be heard and understood). To encourage this to happen, you can intervene in three ways:

1. **Motivate.** Motivate the arguers to try something different by helping them to see what's happening and what impact it's having. Ask them what they've been experiencing as they talk together, which will probably include frustration and a sense of not being understood. Then discuss what you think might be causing these problems. You might explain the concept of yes-buts, or just offer the metaphor of two people trying to get through a conversational doorway at the same time. Understanding the reasons for their frustration, and seeing a potential way out, can be a powerful motivator for change.

2. **Invite builds.** Point the way to a more constructive dialogue by inviting a shift from yes-butting to building. Either person can start by clearly stating the main idea they want the other person to understand. If the other person comes up with just one or two builds, or if the builds don't sound genuine, encourage them to keep going. Remember that it usually takes at least three builds to shift from resisting an idea to giving it serious consideration. Make sure the people take turns, so each gets a chance to have their point of view explored.

3. **Redirect nonbuilds.** At some point, possibly very early on, things are likely to start getting off track. If you hear another yes-but, interrupt the conversation and draw attention to it. You might point it out directly or ask the person, "Did you notice what you just said?" Then gently redirect them, asking them to either return to building or rephrase their objection as a broad question.

Dr. Johnson used this strategy to help the Parkers break out of the yes-but pattern we saw at the beginning of the chapter. When he talked to the couple about the way they were communicating, they were able to recognize that yes-butting wasn't getting them anywhere, and they were both willing to try something new. Rob offered to try building first, so Dr. Johnson asked Amanda to restate the idea she wanted her husband to understand.

> "I'd like him to acknowledge that not having another child is a major loss," she said, "and it makes sense to still be grieving over it."
>
> "I know this is a major loss," said Rob. "We thought all along we were going to have four or five children. Even though I know that we can still adopt, that wasn't the plan, not what either of us wanted. It's still really hard for me, too."
>
> At this point Amanda said, "I know you say it's hard for you, but it's harder for me."
>
> "Hold on, Amanda," Dr. Johnson said gently. "That came out as a yes-but. Instead of giving your evaluation of Rob's experience, can you ask him an open-ended question so he can tell you about it himself?"
>
> Amanda struggled for a few moments and then asked her husband, "Could you tell me more about why this is hard for you?"
>
> Rob nodded slowly. "It's hard because we have two daughters," he said, "and I always thought we'd have a son." He paused and took a deep

breath. *"It's hard because the problem may be me. It may be my fault you didn't get pregnant."* His eyes began to tear up. *"It's hard because I feel that I've failed, that I'm not the man you wanted me to be. It makes me worried that you want someone else who can do the one thing you want so much."*

At this point, both Rob and Amanda were in tears. She reached over and took his hand in hers.

This moment was a major turning point for the couple. For the first time in many months, they were able to experience loss and disappointment as something they both shared, with the potential to bring them closer rather than splitting them apart. As the conversation continued, there was no longer the same sense of opposition or competition.

When it was Amanda's turn to build, Rob asked if she could understand the issue he kept raising: feeling a loss of connection with her.

Amanda nodded. "I miss that too," she said. "I wish we could go back to the easy, spontaneous way we used to be with each other. I know things are really different now. I'm different now. I feel bad that I can't summon up the same passion and energy I used to have when we were first together."

"But that's okay," said Rob. "That's not what I'm asking for."

Dr. Johnson intervened again. "Rob, could you rephrase that idea as a build or a question for Amanda?"

"Oh, right," he said. "I did the 'but' thing, didn't I?" He thought for a moment. "I guess my question is, do you think there are any ways we can feel connected without having it be just like it was in the past?"

"Well," said Amanda, "actually, I do. Just now, as we've been talking, I've started to feel more connected to you than I have in a long time. If you could do more of what you've been doing here, letting me see the part of you that can understand the way I'm feeling, I think it would help me feel closer to you."

"I can do that," said Rob. "And for me, it's a relief to hear that feeling close still really matters to you. I'm feeling a lot more hopeful."

In fact, as Amanda and Rob began to communicate differently, both in their therapy sessions and on their own, they started to regain that sense of closeness and reconnect with the deep feelings they had for one another.

After three months, they were doing extremely well. They still had problems to deal with, but instead of yes-butting about them, they managed to solve them collaboratively by asking each other questions, listening to the answers, and figuring out ways to come to agreement.

Of course, their relationship didn't transform automatically as soon as they learned about yes-butting. But getting out of their yes-but cycle was a crucial first step. Only by redirecting their energy from arguing to solving problems—starting with the problem of understanding each other's feelings and points of view—could they work together to make positive changes in their lives.

> **The Upshot:** Even when people get stuck in a chronic, habitual yes-but pattern, skillful intervention from a coach, therapist, or facilitator can help get the communication back on track.

From Marriage to Meetings and Beyond

The yes-but intervention strategy—motivate, invite, and redirect—has applications far beyond couples therapy. When we work with organizations, we teach people to use the same sort of technique in their meetings. In one small company, we trained six individuals to be facilitators. Now, whenever anyone in a meeting (including the president) contradicts someone else's idea with a yes-but, a facilitator will immediately intervene and help get the conversation back on track. The strategy works just as well with kids, friends, neighbors, clients, and anyone else stuck in a yes-but conversation. While the content may vary greatly, the outcome is the same: less stress, fewer arguments, and greater potential to solve the frustrating problems that make us all want to yes-but each other sometimes.

Intervention Step 3: Practice

Now that you've learned all about yes-buts, it's time to begin the training program. Intervening in other people's yes-but conversations takes a very high level of skill. If you're interested in doing that, we recommend that you practice all of the exercises until the skills feel natural to you.

Training Program Guidelines

The guidelines below will help you get the most out of the training program that follows, as well as the other five training programs that appear throughout the book (at the ends of Chapters 4–8).

General Guidelines
- Do no more than one or two exercises in a single sitting, unless you've set aside a big chunk of time for an extended practice session with a partner or group.
- Practice at a time when you do not feel tired or stressed, to enhance your brain's ability to lay down new pathways.
- Don't get discouraged if you find the activities challenging at first. Think of your practice not as a quick fix, but as a long-term investment in improving your relationships and reaching your goals both at work and at home.

Working with a Partner
We recommend working with a partner when:

- Working with someone else would make the activities easier or more enjoyable for you.
- You could use feedback on whether you're doing the exercises correctly.
- An exercise is marked by this icon—**∞**—indicating that a partner is necessary or strongly recommended.

If you'd like to work with a partner, here are a few ways you might go about it:

- Find a friend or family member who's interested in learning communication skills, and set a regular time to practice together.
- Find a coworker who's interested in learning communication skills, and practice together after work or during your lunch break.
- Set aside time during a work retreat or team-building meeting for an intensive group practice session.

- If you belong to a group that does learning activities together, such as a book club or professional development team, devote one or more of your meetings to communication skills practice.

Whomever you work with, make sure you've all read the relevant chapter(s) before you begin.

Exercises

Yes-But Training Program: Managing Conflict Constructively

Basic Training: Building Awareness and Flexible Thinking

Exercise 1: Yes-Butting on Purpose ∞

Goals:
- Experience the effects of yes-butting on a conversation
- Increase your awareness of yes-buts (particularly stealth-buts)

Estimated time: 5–15 minutes

Together with a partner, practice having a conversation entirely in yes-buts. Start by stating an opinion—any opinion at all, from "It's too cold in here" to "That administration's tax policy destroyed the economy." Have your partner yes-but you, and then yes-but them back. Continue yes-butting each other for as long as you can. Get creative. See how many different ways you can say "yes" and "but" without using those words directly. (Refer back to "Stealth-Butting" on page 32 for alternative phrasing such as "yet," "however," "on the other hand," etc.)

When you're finished, talk with your partner about what the experience was like:

- Did you find it easy or difficult to phrase your comments as yes-buts?
- What did it feel like to yes-but, and to be yes-butted in return?
- How would you describe the quality of your conversation? For instance, was it effective or ineffective, engaging or dull, fun or frustrating?

Repeat this exercise as often as you'd like. Keep alternating who goes first, and start out with a different opinion each time. Building your skill with yes-butting intentionally will help increase your awareness of this behavior, so that you'll have an easier time recognizing yes-buts that occur naturally in your conversations.

Variation: Do the exercise on your own, thinking up yes-buts in your head, writing them down on paper, or even saying them out loud to yourself.

Exercise 1 Example

Starting opinion: We should go out to dinner tonight.

Yes-but #1: That would be fun. It's more expensive than staying in, though.

Yes-but #2: Sure, it will cost money, but we could go someplace reasonable like Joey's Pizza.

Yes-but #3: You're right that Joey's Pizza is cheap. However, it's not great quality food.

Etc.

Intermediate Training:
Deepening Your Yes-But Savvy

Exercise 2: Managing Your Mindset

Goal: Learn to reframe a tough issue as a joint problem to be solved, rather than a two-sided conflict

Estimated time: 5–10 minutes

Think of a practical issue in your life or work on which your opinion conflicts with someone else's. Describe the situation in two different ways:

1. As a conflict with two opposing sides, where you want one thing and they want another
2. As a joint problem you could potentially solve together, by taking into account both of your underlying concerns (the reasons why you each want what you want)

Then ask yourself, how does this second way of thinking change the way you might try to resolve your problem?

If you have trouble reframing your conflict as a joint problem, work together with a partner who can help you clarify your own underlying concerns, as well as what the other person's concerns might be.

Exercise 2 Examples

Example A

1. *Conflict:* I want to hire a new part-time employee, and my boss wants to use a freelancer instead.
2. *Joint problem:* We need a solution that will get the work done effectively and consistently, and that makes sense financially.

Change in how I might resolve this problem: After clarifying my underlying concern (getting work done effectively and consistently), I feel more open to considering a freelancer, provided that concern could be addressed.

Example B

1. *Conflict:* My husband wants to buy a sports car, and I want a minivan.
2. *Joint problem:* We're trying to balance the desire for a vehicle that's attractive and fun to drive with the desire for more interior space.

Change in how I might resolve this problem: I'm starting to consider other alternatives, beyond the two we've been discussing, that might give us both more of what we want.

Exercise 3: The Easy Build
and The Hard Build ∞

Goals:
- Increase your capacity to see both sides of a contentious issue
- Build skill at understanding opinions that you don't agree with, and at expressing that understanding to others

Estimated time: 10–20 minutes

Identify an opinion that you feel strongly about. It can be on any topic, from family plans to work conflicts to broader social and political issues.

Clearly state your opinion to your partner, and have them think up an opposing opinion. If you have trouble coming up with a strong opinion, choose one that you agree with from the list in the sidebar.

Competing Strong Opinions

Here are a few examples of opposing opinions that are frequent topics of yes-but debates:

1. Our meetings should be more tightly structured. (Our meetings should be less tightly structured.)
2. We need to freeze spending. (We need to spend more money.)
3. Our company's leaders are doing an excellent job. (Our company's leaders are doing a terrible job.)
4. Our country's leaders are doing an excellent job. (Our country's leaders are doing a terrible job.)
5. Women make better leaders than men. (Men make better leaders than women.)
6. Marijuana use should be legalized. (We need a no-tolerance policy on drugs.)
7. Abortion is a woman's choice. (Abortion is murder.)
8. The death penalty is a justified sentence for the worst crimes. (The death penalty is never justified.)
9. Our taxes are too high. (Our taxes are too low.)
10. The recent war was a terrible mistake. (The recent war was worth fighting.)

Now go through two steps:

1. *Easy Builds (on something you already agree with).* Find as many ways as you can to build on your own opinion. (Remember that a build expresses something specific that you genuinely like or agree with.) Your partner simply listens.
2. *Hard Builds (on an opinion that's different from yours).* Have your partner state the opposing opinion, and then build on that opinion as many times as possible. You don't need to agree with the opinion as a whole; you just need to identify a few aspects of the idea that you can see as being true, useful, or valuable. Make sure each build is sincere and

specific, not just, "You have a point" or "I could see how you'd think that." If you've picked a good subject to work with—something you feel strongly about—this should be quite challenging.

The next step is to do this exercise again, and again, and again. Keep picking new topics and thinking up sincere, specific builds. Take turns with your partner, and give each other feedback on how your builds come across.

Variation: Do this exercise on your own, writing your builds down on paper.

Exercise 3 Example

My opinion: We need a hiring freeze.

Opposing opinion: We need to hire more staff.

1. *Easy builds:* A hiring freeze would help us keep our expenses more manageable. Employee salaries are our greatest fixed cost, so that's a logical place to start making cutbacks. By freezing new hires now, we'll reduce the chances that we'll need to lay people off in the future.

2. *Hard builds:* I know several people have been putting in overtime, and hiring new staff would help ease the workload. I think the office ran more smoothly when we had a larger staff several years ago. I personally could use more administrative support to reduce my delays in responding to customers.

Exercise 4: Broadening Your Questions ∞

Goal: Build your skill at asking broad questions to gather useful information about plans or suggestions you don't like

Estimated time: 15–30 minutes

Begin by thinking of a suggestion or plan that you've heard recently, and that you strongly disagree with. (We've included a few examples in the sidebar to get your thinking started.) In this exercise, you'll think up questions to ask about that suggestion or plan. Your partner's job is to coach you through the process and write down the questions you come up with.

Suggestions or Plans You May Disagree With

- Your colleague's new marketing ideas
- A hiring decision your boss is about to make
- New government or company policies that seem unwise or unjust
- Spending cuts or tax hikes by your local or national government
- Your spouse's idea for a vacation destination, home improvement project, or major new purchase
- Your child's wish to purchase something that you think is too expensive or not age-appropriate
- Your relatives' plans for what to do with you over the holidays

Go through the following steps:

1. Identify the person who's responsible for making the suggestion or plan (the "Planner"), and think of a question you'd like to ask that person about their idea. State the first question that comes to mind.
2. Identify whether the question you came up with is broad, openly inviting the Planner to share their thoughts or opinions. If it isn't, come up with a different question that is broad. Then state your question out loud, and get your partner's feedback on your voice tone (which should be neutral, with no hostility or other negative feeling coming through). Once you've successfully stated a true broad question, go on to step 3.
3. Identify whether your broad question addresses the concern you have about the Planner's idea (the specific thing you don't like about their plan or suggestion). If it doesn't, come up with another broad question that does, and practice saying it out loud. Again, ask your partner for feedback on your voice tone and for any other help you need.

When you're done, switch roles with your partner. Keep taking turns so you both get opportunities to practice.

Variation: Do this exercise by yourself, recording your questions on paper. On steps 2 and 3, say the questions out loud, so you can practice keeping your voice tone neutral.

Exercise 4 Example

Planner: Daughter

What I disagree with: Her plan to go to a concert with her older friends

1. *First question that comes to mind:* Do you think I don't know what happens at these concerts?! (not broad)
2. *Broad question:* Why is it important to you to go to this concert?
3. *Broad question that addresses my concern:* If you ended up in a tough situation where people were drinking or doing drugs, what would you do?

Advanced Training:
Preparing to Apply the Full Yes-But Strategies

Exercise 5: Transforming Your Yes-Buts ∞

Goal: Build your skill at transforming your yes-buts into more effective communication

Estimated time: 15–20 minutes

Think of an opinion that you disagree with, on any topic, and work with a partner to do a two-step role-play:

Step 1: Unconstructive response
- Your partner states the opinion you disagree with.
- You respond with a yes-but, based on your primary concern (the main thing you don't like about the opinion).

Step 2: Strategic response
- Your partner repeats the same opinion.
- You respond with three builds, plus a broad question that incorporates your concern.

Be sure to practice both steps. Starting with a yes-but helps to clarify your primary concern, so you can address that concern with your broad question. When you're done, switch roles with your partner. We encourage you to practice as often as you can, until this new way of communicating comes naturally to you.

Variation: Do this exercise by yourself, either in your head, out loud, or on paper.

Exercise 5 Example

Idea I disagree with: Parents should be free to choose whether or not to vaccinate their children.

Step 1.

Partner: Parents should be free to choose whether or not to vaccinate their children.

Me: But if not enough children get vaccinated, there could be a resurgence of dangerous diseases. (Yes-but, based on my concern about the reemergence of dangerous diseases)

Step 2.

Partner: Parents should be free to choose whether or not to vaccinate their children.

Me: I agree that parents should be actively involved in making informed decisions about their children's healthcare. (Build #1) As a parent, it's important to me to be free to do what I think is best for my child. (Build #2) If I thought a particular vaccination posed a serious risk to my child's health, I wouldn't agree to it. (Build #3)

How can we protect against dangerous diseases like tetanus and whooping cough, while still giving parents enough control to do what they believe is right? (Broad question that incorporates my concern)

Exercise 6: Intervening in Other People's Yes-But Conversations ∞

Goal: Develop an ability to skillfully intervene in other people's yes-butting

Estimated time: 15–30 minutes

Intervening in other people's yes-but conversations requires a high level of skill. We recommend holding off on this exercise until you're adept at identifying yes-buts and using the build-and-explore strategy in your own communication.

When you feel ready to practice intervening, carefully review "Intervention Step 2," on pages 43–44. Then choose two individuals to practice with, preferably people who talk to each other frequently, and whom you know well (such as business partners who are friends of yours, or a couple you're close to). Tell them you're learning a new communication strategy, and ask if they'd be open to having you practice with them. If they say yes, go through the following process:

1. *Find a topic.* Have the people think of a very minor conflict that they've had trouble resolving. (Make sure it's nothing too serious—a disagreement about where to go for lunch or what type of movie to see, rather than a heated marital dispute or sensitive work issue.) Ask them to talk about the topic in the way they normally would, and listen for yes-buts. If you hear some, move on to Step 2. If not, ask them to choose a different topic.

2. *Motivate and invite builds.* Try the first two parts of the intervention strategy: motivate (bring awareness to the ways in which yes-butting is causing trouble for them) and invite builds (introduce the strategy of building on each other's ideas). Either person can start by stating the main idea they want the other person to build on. Aim for at least three genuine builds at a time, and have them take turns, so they both get a chance to have their point of view explored.

3. *Redirect nonbuilds.* Whenever the people get off-track, interrupt the discussion and gently guide them back to building or asking broad questions.

When the conversation is finished, get feedback from the people you were coaching. What was it like for them to shift from yes-butting to building? Did they become less frustrated or more frustrated? Were you able to interrupt the yes-butting without making them feel criticized or put down? Did they get any closer to solving a problem or making a decision?

Each time you practice this exercise, keep track of what you did that worked and what didn't work, so you can steadily increase your effectiveness. Wait until you feel fully comfortable with the strategy before you try intervening spontaneously in any yes-but conversations.

Want to learn more? Try more exercises at CTsavvy.com/YBexercises, plus the awareness quiz at CTsavvy.com/YBquiz.

4

Clairvoyant Readings

The story that follows comes from one of the coauthors' (Ben's) personal experience, so he'll narrate it.

It was a real loss for me to fall out of contact with Alan, but it was clear that he wanted nothing more to do with me.

When Alan and I first met at a conference, we hit it off instantly. We both did organizational coaching and consulting, and we found we had a lot to learn from one another. Over time, we developed a strong friendship and professional connection. Every month we spoke on the phone and coached each other on different cases we were working on. Whenever one of us was struggling with a difficult issue, in either our work or our personal life, we'd talk it through together and leave with insights and solutions we never could have thought up on our own. Overall, the relationship felt remarkably rewarding and supportive.

The turning point came about four years into our friendship. In one of our calls, Alan told me about an upsetting incident that had happened in a professional networking group he belonged to. Listening to his story made me angry. I thought he had been treated unfairly and deserved an apology. Feeling resentful on Alan's behalf, I spoke about the incident to another friend who belonged to that same group. This friend then raised the issue with the group leader, and eventually word got back to Alan that I'd been talking about his experience.

Alan called me up, furious—and rightly so. He had talked to me in confidence and expected I would keep the discussion between us. I apolo-

gized profusely but had the sense that it wasn't good enough. Clearly Alan was still upset. I worried that he would never again feel able to trust me. My fears were confirmed later that month. We had a date set for one of our mutual coaching sessions, and for the first time, Alan didn't call. I sent him an e-mail asking what had happened, and he didn't reply. I got the unspoken message: he had no interest in talking to me.

Over the next two years, my only contact with Alan was at the same annual conference where we had originally met. Although Alan wasn't rude or hostile, he made no attempt to engage me in conversation. The first year, when I said hello, he said hello in reply, but then kept on walking. The second year, even though we participated in a small workshop together, we did nothing more than exchange a few pleasantries. By that point, there was no doubt that Alan was still angry, and that I had little chance of restoring my friendship with him.

You may have noticed that we didn't include any dialogue in Ben's story. That's because in this case, the most influential communication was never spoken out loud. Ben wanted to restore his relationship with Alan, and, as we'll show later in the chapter, he could easily have done that. He simply didn't try—not because of what Alan had said to him, but because of what he kept saying to himself. He was convinced that he knew what was going on in Alan's mind. Consider some of his comments: "it was clear that he wanted nothing more to do with me," "I got the unspoken message," and "there was no doubt that Alan was still angry." All of these are what we call *mind-reads*. Without realizing it, Ben was allowing his mind-reads to ruin his friendship.

Communication Challenge 2:
Mind-Reads—Turning Friends into Fictions

When we mind-read, we state our assumptions about other people—what we imagine they're thinking or feeling—as though they're facts. Mind-reads may be simple statements about a person's psychological state ("Marilyn's tired," "Jim is still upset," "You're in a good mood today"); they may address someone's relationship with us or with others ("I can tell my boss is disappointed in me," "Adam clearly prefers working with Tom," "Our neighbors have a happy marriage"); or they may deal with any number of other topics ("You didn't enjoy that party," "I know Jack wants a raise," "He'd rather hire someone younger," "They're waiting for us to make the first move," and so on).

Mind-Reads as Weapons

A true mind-read is a relatively neutral comment that sounds like a statement of fact. Just as we might make a factual observation like, "Your eyes are bloodshot" or "He didn't shake my hand," we say, "You're clearly exhausted" or "He didn't feel comfortable with me." Sometimes, however, mind-reads take on a more personal, hostile tone:

- She thinks she's better than everybody else.
- Mark wanted this project to fail.
- Those doctors don't really care about their patients.
- It's clear you're not invested in this job.
- Obviously you'd rather go out with your friends than spend time with me.

This sort of accusatory mind-reading is a form of verbal attack. We'll discuss attacks in detail in Chapter 8.

Mind-reads get people into a lot of trouble. Have you ever talked to someone who seemed to believe they could read your mind? This can be extremely irritating, particularly when the person implies that they know you better than you know yourself, saying, "You don't really mean that," "You think you love her, but you're just infatuated," or "You don't realize how burnt out you are." The consequences of unspoken mind-reads (ones we say only to ourselves) can be just as serious. We may start to think, talk, and act in ways that are based more on imagination than on reality. That's exactly what happened with Ben and Alan.

When we rely too heavily on mind-reads, we are essentially populating our world with imaginary friends—not to mention imaginary coworkers, bosses, spouses, children, and so forth. These individuals may bear a strong resemblance to the real people they're based on, but important aspects of their personalities and emotional lives are created by our own minds. In the opening story, Alan became more and more of a fiction to Ben. The open-minded, compassionate person he knew appeared increasingly distant, closed off, and unforgiving.

Mind-reads are not always so negative. Some people may seem more generous, intelligent, and likable in our imagination than they would prove to be if we really got to know them. The problem is that, whether wicked or wonderful, imaginary friends aren't real.

The Upshot: When we treat our mind-reads as facts, we base our relationships on speculations, wishes, and fears rather than reality.

Where Do Mind-Reads Come From?

We don't typically go around making random assumptions about other people's thoughts and feelings; there are reasons behind our mind-reads. However, those reasons may have little or no connection to what's really going on. Mind-reading tends to be driven by ambiguity, shaped by personal bias, and supported by avoidance of direct questions. We'll describe each of these factors in detail below.

Ambiguity: How Mind-Reads Get Started

Mind-reads feed on ambiguity. When a person says or does something that is open to multiple interpretations, we jump to the explanation that makes the most sense to us. This often happens automatically, outside our awareness. We don't consciously reason, "Alex is looking out the window, which could mean that he's bored." We just think, "Alex is bored." Ambiguity creeps into communication in several ways:

- **Silence.** What does it mean when you ask a question and get no answer? Is the other person confused? Irritated? Afraid of saying the wrong thing? Or just carefully considering what you've said? What about when you get no response to an opinion, suggestion, joke, or personal story? Or when someone fails to reply to e-mail or voice mail messages? It's possible to read just about anything into silence.

Suppose the leader of a meeting makes a proposal and nobody responds. One observer of the meeting might assume this means that everyone agrees. Another observer might assume that everyone disagrees but is afraid to raise an objection. Someone else might conclude that no one really understood the proposal. We make these sorts of interpretations all the time, labeling silence in different situations as tacit support, patient listening, apathy, stonewalling, defiance, and so on. In the story that started this chapter, Ben interpreted Alan's silence as an expression of lingering anger.

- **Vagueness.** Sometimes words can be as ambiguous as silence. When a colleague says your latest presentation was "interesting," it's hard to tell whether that's a sincere compliment or a polite way of saying your ideas seemed bizarre. When your friend calls your new shoes "very unusual," you don't know whether she loves them or hates them. These vague comments fuel speculations about what the person really thinks. It's easy to slip into either a positive mind-read ("He was really impressed by my presentation") or a negative one ("She doesn't like my shoes but doesn't want to tell me").

- **Body language.** Not all communication is verbal. Aspects of our body language—including postures, gestures, facial expressions, and eye movements—can carry as much information as our words. Unfortunately, that information isn't always clear or consistent with the message we're trying to send. For instance, we know several people who've been told that when they're listening intently to someone, they tend to frown, tighten their jaw, or make other facial expressions that lead people to develop mind-reads that they're angry or judgmental.

- **Absence of voice tone.** Voice tone is a powerful force in communication. In fact, the tone we use frequently has a greater impact on a conversation than the words we say. There's a world of difference between the neutral remark "Remember that the meeting starts at 10" and the same words spoken with a snide or accusatory tone. And yet, in a written format like e-mail, both comments may look exactly the same. As a result, the sender's friendly reminder might get interpreted as an attack or a sarcastic jab. While e-mail is a great convenience, the ambiguity it creates can easily lead to misunderstandings. The same risks apply to text messaging and any other forms of electronic media that don't communicate voice tone.

More Dangers of Technology

The absence of voice tone is just one way in which technology can contribute to ambiguity. We experienced a different sort of problem on a conference call with one of our colleagues (whom we'll call Vicki). The issue we were discussing was a little touchy, and Amy noticed that she kept getting interrupted. Just as she began to speak, Vicki would start talking over her. As this pattern continued, an assortment of mind-reads ran through Amy's head: Vicki was irritated with her in general (she could imagine a few possible reasons why); she disliked the point of view Amy was expressing on this call; or maybe she felt so strongly about her ideas that she couldn't wait to get them in.

What was the real problem? Speakerphones. All of us were using them, and as a result, the first couple of words anyone said tended to get cut off. As a result, Vicki had no idea that she was interrupting. (In fact, her perception was that Amy kept interrupting her.)

Personal Bias: How Mind-Reads Take Shape

Once we're faced with an ambiguous message, what method do we use to interpret it? How do we fill in the blanks? In the case of mind-reading, we rely on what we already know, or think we know, which may or may not be relevant to the current situation. The information we draw on may include:

- **Personal tendencies.** When we're trying to understand how others think, feel, and act, the most obvious points of reference are our own thoughts, feelings, and actions. Suppose one of your coworkers recently dropped her only child off at college. If you've previously experienced "empty-nest syndrome," you might think, "That must be hard for her.

I'm sure she's lonely." If you had a different experience, you might think, "I'm sure she's relieved to have more time to herself."

You can also get into trouble by assuming that a particular behavior means the same thing coming from someone else as it would coming from you. For example, if you usually write chatty e-mails and send brief, impersonal messages only when you're annoyed, you might assume that someone who sends you a terse e-mail is feeling annoyed with you. It's possible that you're right but just as likely that you're wrong.

- **Worries and fears.** A good example of how worries generate mind-reads occurred recently when two of us (Amy and Ben) were leading a new training for the first time. The presentation included longer lectures and fewer interactive exercises than our other trainings, and we weren't sure how successful that format would be. Amy in particular was worried that people might get bored or overwhelmed trying to take in so much information all at once. When she saw a trainee fidgeting and shifting in his seat, she was certain that her fears were justified— this man's mind was drifting because she'd been talking for too long.

  As it turns out, the trainee was in fact distracted, but not for the reason Amy imagined. This person had a serious leg injury that made it painful for him to remain sitting. He didn't need the lectures to be shorter; he just needed to be able to stand up from time to time. When we asked the whole group to critique our new training format, we received nothing but compliments about the lectures.

- **Hopes and wishes.** We don't always imagine the worst. Sometimes we do just the opposite, seeing what we want to see. For instance, if you really want someone to like you, care about you, agree with you, or admire your work, the power of your desire might convert your wish into a mind-read: "Clearly Joel has feelings for me, but he's too shy to say so," "I know my friend has my best interests at heart," "My manager would never consider laying me off, because he knows I'm the best salesman he has." These mind-reads may make you feel good, and some of them may be accurate. But there's also a risk that they'll blind you to an unpleasant truth, perhaps leading you to ignore evidence that your friend isn't looking out for you, or that your boss is thinking of letting you go.

"He's Just Not That into You" and Other Relationship Mind-Reads

If you're tempted to mind-read your romantic partner, or potential romantic partner, there is no shortage of advice out there. Many books, articles, and websites will help fuel your speculations about your beloved's hidden intentions and desires, promising to reveal what all women or men really want, or to teach you foolproof ways to tell whether or not someone is fully committed.

The impulse to mind-read may be irresistible when attraction, love, and romance are on the line. Relationships bring up strong feelings that can amplify both hopes and fears. Have you ever talked to a friend in the early stages of dating who's developed an idealized view of their new partner? You get a picture of an individual without flaws, someone with exaggerated positive qualities ("She never thinks badly about anyone," "He's always looking out for other people"), who seemingly dropped down from heaven to be the perfect match for your friend ("We think exactly the same way," "We have the same values," "We care about all the same things"). When the partner turns out to be less than perfect, as all human beings are, that idealism may quickly dissolve into disappointment and disillusionment.

On the flip side of hopeful romantic mind-reads are those fueled by fears and insecurities ("I can tell she's still thinking about her ex," "He doesn't love me as much as I love him," "She's not attracted to me anymore"). All too often, these fearful thoughts never get discussed in an open, straightforward way. Either they come out as attacks ("You don't really care about me"), or they never get voiced at all.

It's not surprising that people find it hard to talk openly about such deep, personal worries. However, each mind-read that persists and doesn't get worked through creates an issue that the couple cannot talk about. These forbidden issues chip away at the couple's ability to build a truly close, authentic, intimate relationship, and to keep it strong over time. People who are getting divorced often say that the spouse they once knew so well started to feel like a stranger. That's a perfect description of what happens when mind-reads take over and open communication shuts down.

- **Stereotypes and generalizations.** Over the years, we all internalize certain assumptions about people in particular roles or with particular types of backgrounds or characteristics: "Lawyers are aggressive," "All only children are spoiled," "Men only care about one thing," "People who grow up poor have a better appreciation of money," and so on. In addition to the roles people consciously choose (minister, coach, CEO, Republican) and those they fall into automatically (sister, Hispanic, cancer patient), we may also categorize individuals into more subtle types of roles based on the way they communicate. For instance, we may start to see a particular person as a victim, steamroller, whiner, Pollyanna, or wet blanket. Have you ever thought to yourself, "I know the type" or "People like that are all the same"? These generalizations can easily lead to mind-reads about how "people like that" feel and think.

- **Hearsay and rumors.** Mind-reads can be contagious. If you hear from other people that your new neighbor is a snob, that idea may color all the interactions you have with him. When he turns down your invitation to a cookout, you might assume it's because he feels superior to you, rather than because he's shy, has strict dietary restrictions, or has a previous commitment for that day.

  If you have a tendency to share your speculations about someone else's intentions with other people you know, be careful about spreading your mind-reads (for instance, "The new salesman is trying to kiss up to the boss," "Alison is afraid of commitment," or "Frank is prejudiced against female leaders"). Your mind-read of someone may become that person's reputation—and reputations are very hard to shake.

- **Past experience with the person.** Established knowledge about a person—including what they've told you previously about their thoughts and feelings—is one of the more reliable sources of information. It's far from perfect, though. Do you ever change your opinion on an issue, or start to feel differently about someone or something over time? We'll bet you do. Other people do too. The more time goes by, the greater the possibility that what you used to know about somebody is no longer true.

- **Past experience with other people.** We may also try to understand people by comparing them to others we've known in the past: "She's just like my sister, always saying she agrees with me when it's obvious she doesn't" or "I've known plenty of employees like him. That type of person only feels motivated when there's a crisis." As with any other mind-reads, these sorts of thoughts are sometimes accurate and sometimes inaccurate. What they certainly are not is reliable.

Avoidance of Direct Questions: Why Mind-Reads Stick Around

While ambiguity and personal bias explain why we develop mind-reads, they don't explain why these assumptions are so persistent. There's no need for us to be stuck with them, since we could resolve them at any time by asking a direct question about what the other person is thinking or feeling. Instead of speculating ("He's angry," "He's disappointed about the decision we made"), we could just ask, "Are you angry?" or "Are you disappointed with this decision?" If we all did that, we could shed much of the pain, anxiety, and misunderstanding that comes from unchecked mind-reads. So why don't we ask these questions? There are a variety of reasons.

- **Lack of awareness.** As we mentioned earlier, mind-reading often happens automatically. Unaware that we're making assumptions, we feel as though we're perceiving something real—seeing a person's boredom in her facial expression, or hearing the resentment in her voice. Why would we bother testing something that we're certain is true? We wouldn't. And so we don't.

- **Fear of the answers.** Another common reason for avoiding direct questions is anxiety about what the answers will be. Maybe you'll learn that your positive mind-read is false: your boss actually isn't considering you for a promotion. Or maybe your negative mind-read is true: your spouse really does dislike your idea of vacationing with your parents. It might seem like basic common sense to not ask a question that might lead to an answer you don't like. On the other hand, not knowing something doesn't mean it's not true. Avoiding reality doesn't cause reality to change. Later on, in the skill-building section, we'll give you guidelines for deciding whether the benefits of checking out your mind-read outweigh the potential downsides of an unwelcome response.

- **Lack of trust.** If you don't already have a strong, trusting relationship with somebody, asking them about what they think or feel requires taking a risk. It's impossible to know what kind of response you'll get. The person may appreciate your directness, or they may feel uncomfortable, resentful, or annoyed. Lack of trust tends to make any new work team, social group, or romantic relationship a rich breeding ground for mind-reads. We're also more likely to mind-read if we distrust a person's motives or integrity. This can lead to a vicious cycle—the more we distrust someone, the more we believe our negative mind-reads, which leads to more distrust and less testing of our mind-reads, and so on. (The good news is that by working through your mind-reads, which you'll learn to do later in the chapter, you can start to rebuild trust and reverse this cycle.)

- **Group norms.** If you grew up in a family where mind-reading was the norm, it might never occur to you to check out your assumptions about other people. Or, you might ask more direct questions with your friends and colleagues but continue to mind-read your relatives. Most of us communicate a little differently in different contexts, responding to the dominant culture of each group or organization. In some organizations, it's commonplace for people to ask their coworkers, direct reports, and supervisors frank questions about their thoughts and feelings on work-related issues. In other organizations, such open questioning may seem shockingly out of place, particularly if it's directed toward a superior in the hierarchy. Norms regarding the sharing of personal information also vary across different countries.[1]

- **Active discouragement.** Sometimes people actively discourage us from asking about their thoughts and feelings. A boss might say, "It should be obvious why I think this is important. I shouldn't have to explain it to you." A spouse might say, "If you really loved me, you'd know why I got angry." Sometimes a parent will reward a child for mind-reading their feelings: "You're so perceptive; you can always tell when I'm upset."

Now, there's nothing wrong with paying close attention to what others say and do, and trying to get better at anticipating their responses. For instance, you might figure out that when your wife starts talking quickly, it usually means she's upset, or that when your boss says,

"That's one way to look at things," it usually means he strongly disagrees with an idea. However, there are always limits to what you can deduce from ambiguous messages. As you get more and more specific—making multiple leaps, from "She's upset" to "She's angry" to "She's angry with me" to "She's angry with me because I left dirty dishes in the sink"—you're less and less likely to be accurate.

> **The Upshot:** In ambiguous situations, mind-reads are a natural response, but they often cause problems when we mistake them for facts.

Skills for Managing Mind-Reads

Mind-reads are unavoidable. In ambiguous situations, we're bound to make some assumptions about other people, and others are bound to make some assumptions about us. They're also not inherently bad. If we had no ability to put ourselves in someone else's shoes, we'd have a hard time relating to them. But it's important to keep in mind that no matter how skilled we are at relating to another person, we can't know the exact thoughts running through their head. Moreover, many mind-reads stem less from empathetic attunement than from the sources of personal bias we discussed earlier (fears, hopes, past experiences, etc.).

Treating assumptions as facts can have tragic consequences. It's not uncommon for mind-reads to ruin friendships, end marriages, and create miserable work environments. If an inaccurate mind-read never gets questioned, it may endure for years. We may live our entire lives with false and sometimes painful beliefs about what the people around us think and feel. Consider the impact of believing "My father still hasn't forgiven me for selling the family business," "The tenured faculty have always looked down on me," or "My wife regrets marrying me instead of the man she was engaged to when I met her."

The goal of managing mind-reads is to develop skills to help limit their negative effects. In the following sections, you'll learn not only how to transform your own mind-reads but also how to respond effectively when other people express mind-reads of you or anyone else.

Some Tell-Tale Signs of Mind-Reading

Here are a few indications that your relationship with a particular person may be based more on your mind-reads than on reality:

- You spend more time talking to this person in your head than having real conversations with them.
- You spend more time talking about this person to other people than talking to them directly.
- It's not what the person says but what you think they're *not* saying that affects you the most.
- You often find yourself wondering what they think of you.
- You think this person is not telling you the whole truth.
- Many things they say bother you, even though the same comments wouldn't bother you if they came from anybody else.
- This person seems to think and react in exactly the same way as someone else you know or once knew.
- You think you often know what they're going through better than they do.

If more than two or three of these statements sound accurate, there's a good chance that the relationship you're thinking of is heavily influenced by mind-reads.

Transformation Skill: Trading Mind-Reads for Reality

In our experience, many of the communication behaviors we cover in this book are relatively well known. Whether or not a person has had any communications training, they usually have some familiarity with yes-buts, leading questions, complaints, and verbal attacks, even if they can't always identify them in conversation. In contrast, the concept of mind-reading is frequently new to people. One reason for this is that mind-reads tend to keep a low profile. Many of them are never spoken out loud, so they influence our communication in more subtle ways.

Another contributing factor is an issue we mentioned earlier: our mind-reads seem like facts to us. We may even view them as evidence of our keen perception or intuition. As a result, the odds are good that you've never before seen mind-reads as being a problem for you. Prior to picking up this book, you may never have heard the term *mind-read* or had any occasion to seriously question the assumptions you make about other people. If you mind-read a lot, the strategies in this section may help to bring positive change to many aspects of your life.

Transformation Step 1: Self-Awareness

A little self-awareness can go a long way toward counteracting mind-reads. Simply by seeing a mind-read for what it is—your own assumption rather than reality—you instantly begin to defuse its power. The first step is to start noticing the beliefs you have about other people's thoughts and feelings, and then ask yourself where those beliefs are coming from. Are they firmly grounded in real-world information, or are they based on gossip, hearsay, or your own worries or speculations? If you believe your boss is disappointed in you, is it because he said that in your performance evaluation, or because of the expression on his face the last time you talked? If you're sure your son doesn't want to come home for the holidays, did you hear that from him? Did someone else in the family tell you? Or did you jump to that conclusion because he hasn't bought his plane ticket yet?

After you've recognized that your belief about someone's unspoken thoughts or feelings is a mind-read, the next step is to acknowledge what that means: you might be wrong. This may be difficult to do. It's often tough to let go of long-held assumptions about the people in our lives, whether they have to do with a colleague's hidden agenda, a spouse's unspoken grudges, or a parent's silent regrets. Challenge yourself to admit that your assumptions could be inaccurate.

There's one final step in building your awareness. You haven't fully understood a mind-read until you've reflected on the effects it has on you, as well as what might change if you tested it against reality. See the sidebar below for detailed guidelines on doing an impact analysis.

Impact Analysis

To understand the impact of a particular mind-read, ask yourself the three questions that follow. As examples, we'll answer each question from Ben's point of view, in relation to his mind-read of Alan (as described at the start of the chapter).

Question 1: What is the impact of not testing the mind-read? Think about how your untested mind-read might be affecting the following five factors:

- **Your emotional state**
  (Ben: I feel sad and disappointed, and I get anxious whenever I see my former friend.)
- **Your self-perception**
  (Ben: I think a little less of myself for making a mistake that cost me a close friendship.)
- **Your perception of the other person**
  (Ben: I've started to see Alan as inflexible and unforgiving.)
- **Your relationship with that person, or with other people**
  (Ben: I've lost all contact with Alan.)
- **Potential opportunities in your life or work**
  (Ben: During our estrangement, Alan started his own business and began to collaborate more with other colleagues. I've missed out on the opportunity to be part of that network. I've also lost access to the expertise he shared with me in our peer coaching sessions.)

Question 2: What would be the impact of learning the mind-read is true?

(Ben: I think it would be hard to hear, but it would let me stop wondering about it and move on. It also might give me a chance to learn what I could do to regain Alan's trust.)

Question 3: What would be the impact of learning the mind-read is false?

(Ben: It would be a tremendous relief, and might help me regain the productive, fulfilling relationship we once had.)

Use the information you gather in your impact analysis to help you decide whether or not you'd like to test your mind-read. Here are three factors to consider (also see Figure 4-1 for a diagram of the decision-making process):

- **How much you care whether the mind-read is true.** Among all the mind-reads you have, there are sure to be many that don't affect you very strongly. For instance, you might believe that your colleague is

Figure 4-1. Decision Tree for Testing Mind-Reads

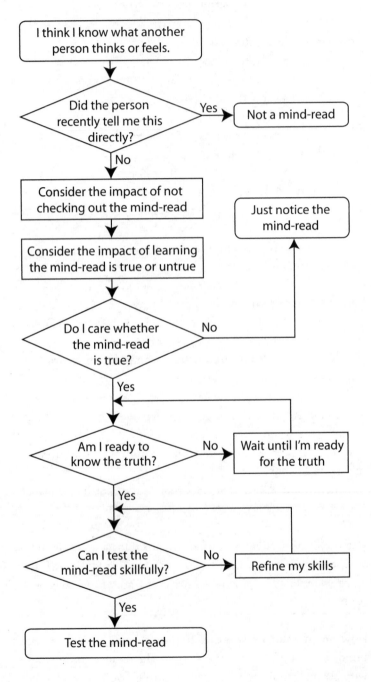

bored with her boyfriend, that your real estate agent would rather be a gardener, or that your neighbor doesn't like your dog. In cases like this where discovering the truth wouldn't make much difference to you, you might just want to notice that your assumptions may or may not be true, and leave it at that.

Other mind-reads have far more serious implications. You might worry that your new boss wants to replace you with one of his former colleagues, that your spouse is considering leaving you, or that your friend is very irritated with you. In these situations, you have compelling reasons to discover the truth—to potentially help save your job, your marriage, or your friendship, as well as to recover your own peace of mind. A good rule of thumb is that if knowing the truth could significantly change the way you act or the choices you make, you're probably better off knowing than not knowing.

- **Your readiness to know the truth.** When you imagine learning the truth about your mind-read, what reactions do you have? How do you think you'll respond if the answer you get isn't what you want to hear? If your mind-read is deeply personal or upsetting, checking it out is bound to cause an emotional shift. Instead of feeling the emotions created by your own assumptions, you'll feel the emotions evoked by reality.

On the positive side, people are often surprised at how much relief this brings. Even when the truth is upsetting, disappointing, or sad, having it out in the open tends to be less stressful than dwelling on an unspoken fear. It also frees up all the mental energy that's been going into worrying, allowing you to redirect your efforts into problem-solving. For instance, instead of continuing to worry that a colleague may have been offended by a comment you made, you can work toward repairing your relationship and finding ways to avoid causing offense in the future.

There's also a negative side, however. At times, learning what somebody actually thinks about you, or about the people and things that matter to you, can be extremely distressing. If you don't feel emotionally ready to face an unpleasant reality, by all means hold off asking about it until you feel more resilient. You might find it helpful to try taking the issue less personally (see the sidebar that follows).

Taking Things Personally

If you're feeling hurt by what another person thinks or feels, it's likely that you're taking things personally,[2] believing that what's happening is centered on you. In reality, someone else's thoughts or feelings give you information about them, not about you—even if they're talking about you or something you've done. Finding out that someone doesn't like your artwork tells you nothing new about your skill as an artist; it just tells you about that individual's personal taste. The same goes for people's reactions to your physical appearance, the way you laugh, your style of working, and so on.

Taking other people's behavior personally is a source of a great many mind-reads, such as "My daughter was snippy on the phone because she's mad at me" or "My friend was distracted during dinner because she was bored hearing me talk about my kids." We often fail to consider alternative explanations that have nothing to do with us: the daughter just had a fight with her boyfriend, or the friend was preoccupied with worries about her job. Thinking up alternative explanations for people's actions is a great antidote to taking things personally. We'll talk more about this topic when we discuss verbal attacks in Chapter 8.

- **Your ability to test the mind-read skillfully.** Checking out a mind-read isn't easy, particularly when it involves an emotionally sensitive topic. If you're too upset to raise the issue without yelling, bursting into tears, or having another strong emotional reaction, it's best to postpone the conversation until you feel calm enough to consciously choose what you say and how you say it. (If you find you can't control your emotional outbursts when discussing a particular topic, consider working through the issue with a coach or therapist.) Also make sure you've mastered the strategy for testing mind-reads, which we're about to explain in detail. Get as much practice as you need with the mind-reading exercises (starting on page 85), until you feel confident applying these skills.

Transformation Step 2: Action—Get a Reality Check

No matter how much insight you gain into your mind-reads, there's a limit to what you can figure out on your own. The information about whether your assumption is true or false doesn't exist in your own head; it lies within the person you're mind-reading. To get that information, you need to stop talking to yourself and get the other person in on the conversation by asking a direct question. Of course, asking a direct question doesn't guarantee a direct answer, but you can significantly improve the odds of getting a clear, useful response by being careful about when and where you have the conversation (your context) and how you have the conversation (your communication strategy).

Context

Choose your moment carefully. Some contexts are better than others for checking out mind-reads. For instance, we don't recommend starting this type of discussion in the midst of a work crisis, right before a big meeting, on your way out the door, or in an elevator. Try to have the conversation in a place that is relatively private, at a time when the other person isn't distracted or under stress. Never test a challenging mind-read by e-mail.

If your mind-read is related to a particular event or experience, don't wait too long to check it out. If you're worried that your sister didn't enjoy the dinner you cooked for her, talk to her while it's still fresh in her mind. If you wait three months before speaking up, she may not remember how she felt about the food.

Communication Strategy

The basic strategy for checking mind-reads has two parts:[3]

1. **State the thought you're having.** Be sure to keep your phrasing simple. Giving too much background will only complicate the issue and create confusion. Suppose you have a mind-read that a coworker disapproves of a recent hiring decision you made. Don't ramble ("I know I did ask for your input, but this was a complicated decision, and I wasn't sure how you'd react, or how I should talk to you about it . . ." and so on). Limit yourself to a single clear sentence ("I'm thinking you might be unhappy with the choice I made for this position" or "I've been thinking you may be disappointed that I hired Steve rather than Eric").

   Notice that by stating what you're thinking, you're expressing a fact about you, not about the other person. Avoid the temptation to talk about *them*, explaining all the things they've done that led to your mind-read: "You didn't respond to my e-mail announcing the decision. When I brought it up in the staff meeting, you were the only one in the group who didn't comment on it. During the hiring process, you kept telling me how great you thought Eric was." Those kinds of comments can easily come across as confrontational or accusatory.

2. **Ask a yes-or-no question.** When you're testing a mind-read, the basic question you want answered is whether that mind-read is true. Frame your question narrowly—for instance, "Is this true?" or "Are you feeling that way?"—so the only possible answers are "Yes" and "No." (If you ask a broad question like "What's happening with you?" or "What are your thoughts?" the yes/no answer you're looking for may get lost among other pieces of conflicting or tangential information: "Well, I guess I've felt that, but my feelings have changed over time, and I have mixed emotions about it . . .") After the person has responded, give yourself a few moments to take in their answer. Notice what it's like to have your mind-read confirmed or disconfirmed.

Table 4-1 gives several examples of how you might use this strategy to test a mind-read.

Table 4-1. Sample Wording for Testing Mind-Reads

Conversation with a . . .	Your Thought	Yes-or-No Question
Doctor	I'm concerned that you may be reluctant to tell me everything you know about my prognosis.	Are you holding back at all in what you're telling me?
Child	I'm thinking that you might be feeling bad about all the attention your little brother has been getting.	Are you feeling bad about that?
Coworker	Sometimes I think that when I play music in the office, it bothers you.	Does it?
Spouse	I'm worried that you don't trust me as much since you found out more about my past.	Do you sometimes think I'm not being honest with you?

After three years of living with his mind-read of Alan, Ben worked up the courage to test it. At the next conference he invited Alan to lunch, where they could have some quiet time to talk privately. Ben started the conversation by saying, "I want to see if we can clear the air a little. Ever since we had the conflict over the confidence I violated, I've had the feeling you're still mad at me. Are you?"

Alan looked confused. "No, I'm not mad at you," he said. "What confidence did you violate?" He couldn't even remember the conflict. When Ben reminded him, Alan explained that as soon as they'd talked it through, the issue was over for him. Then Alan revealed that he had a mind-read of his own: "I thought you were upset with me for missing our coaching session." Apparently he had responded to Ben's e-mail with an apology and an attempt to reschedule, and when he got no response (because Ben never saw the message), he assumed Ben was angry. As a result of their toxic mind-reads, both men had been awkward and cautious around each other, which each of them interpreted as evidence that the other person was holding a grudge.

In addition to the obvious benefits Ben gained by testing his mind-read—relief, reassurance, and the chance to restore a close friendship—he also used this situation as a learning opportunity. He thought back to the assumptions he'd made and asked himself why he'd been so convinced that his friend was still angry. What he realized was that he couldn't believe Alan had forgiven him because he hadn't fully forgiven himself. The main message he took away was a lesson that many people learn when they challenge their mind-reads: while these assumptions don't give us reliable information about other people, they often provide vital insights into ourselves.

What if You Don't Believe the Answer?

What happens if you check out a mind-read and don't believe the answer you get? The first thing to do is to notice that you have another mind-read, such as "Joan is lying to me" or "Frank doesn't trust me enough to be truthful." You may be right, or you may be wrong. The simplest option is to test your assumption in the same way you'd test any other mind-read. For example, you might say, "I'm worried that you don't feel comfortable giving an answer that might disappoint me. Is that true?"

If your doubt is based on specific facts, you might refer to those facts: "Once before, I yelled at you for giving me bad news. I'm thinking that now, you may avoid telling me bad news so I won't get upset. Is that true?" or "When you hesitated before answering my question, I thought you might be holding something back. Are you?" Be sure to keep your voice tone neutral and not accusatory.

If you've skillfully done all you can to encourage the other person to be forthcoming but still have a hard time believing them, consider the possibility that your own biases might be preventing you from recognizing the truth. You may find it difficult to trust what someone says because it contradicts your mental picture of that person. Letting new information sink in and change that picture can be difficult and unsettling. In our experience, when someone has done all the mind-reading checks they can and still doesn't believe the answers, there's a chance their hunch is right but also a very good chance that the other person is actually being truthful.

> **The Upshot:** When you do it skillfully, checking out mind-reads can bring both peace of mind and important data to help you make better choices in the future.

Transformation Step 3: Practice

If you'd like to practice transforming your mind-reads now, skip ahead to the Mind-Read Training Program starting on page 85.

Response Skill:
What to Do When Someone Else Mind-Reads You

The mind-reads you have of others aren't the only ones that can cause problems for you. Other people's mind-reads of you can do just as much damage. Being able to respond skillfully to these assumptions can help you avoid unnecessary conflict and misunderstanding in all areas of your life and work.

Response Step 1: Awareness

Once you start looking for mind-reads, they're not hard to spot when they come up in conversation. Someone might tell you, "It's obvious that you're unhappy" or "I know you think this is a reckless idea." **To practice recognizing mind-reads, visit CTsavvy.com/MRquiz.**

More difficult to detect are mind-reads that go unspoken. You can sometimes get clues about a person's mind-reads from their behavior; they may start acting in ways that don't make sense or seem out of character for them. For instance, if they start acting apologetic or defensive for no apparent reason, they may have a mind-read that you're angry or judging them in some way. Or, if they ask you repeated, probing questions—such as "Are you sure you're okay?" or "Are you sure you don't mind?"—they may have a mind-read that there's something specific that you're not saying.

Of course, as we emphasized in the last section, you can't know for sure what somebody is thinking (including whether they have a mind-read) without asking a yes-or-no question and getting an answer. For example, you could say, "I'm getting the impression that you think I'm upset" or "I get a sense that you're not sure I mean it when I say I don't mind," followed by a yes-or-no question: "Is that true?" Be sure to wait for an answer.

Once a mind-read is out in the open, you have a chance to respond to it. This is a valuable opportunity, particularly if the mind-read is inaccurate. Learning about someone's distorted perceptions of you allows you to correct those distortions by bringing in new, more accurate information. Resist the very natural impulse to get defensive, which will likely discourage the person from disclosing what they're thinking. Instead, welcome the chance to get the truth out on the table.

Response Step 2: Action—Clarify, Clarify, Clarify

Since mind-reads thrive on ambiguity, one of the most effective countermeasures is clarity. When someone has a mind-read of you, there are three important pieces of information to clarify: what the mind-read is, where it's coming from, and whether it's true or false.

Content of the Mind-Read

First you need to get clear on the exact content of the mind-read. A good way to do this is to use a paraphrase, followed by a yes-or-no question. For instance, say your manager tells you he's reassigning a particular project because it's clear that you regret taking it on. You could say, "It sounds like you got the impression that I'm sorry I took on this project. Is that right?" In a personal context, a friend might say she doesn't enjoy going out with you after work because you judge everything she does. You could say, "It feels like whatever you do, I have a judgment about it. Is that right?"

This specific type of phrasing—a paraphrase plus a yes-or-no question—simultaneously accomplishes two goals: ensuring that you understood what the other person said, and showing the person that you were really listening.

Origin of the Mind-Read

Next, find out what's driving the person's assumption. Even the most far-fetched mind-reads come from somewhere. Ask a broad (open) question like, "What have I done that gives you that impression?" or "What do I do that makes you feel that way?" Make sure it's a real question and not an accusation ("What on earth gave you that idea?"). The person's answer will give you important information about the impact your words and actions are having on them. In the work situation, your manager might mention that you complained several times about your frustration with the project. In the personal discussion, your friend might remind you of critical comments you made about men she met in bars while you were out together.

Accuracy of the Mind-Read

Now comes the moment of truth (literally). Is the person's mind-read true? Is it false? Is just part of it true? Don't automatically jump to an answer: "I'd never regret a work opportunity" or "Of course I'd never judge you." Take a moment to consider the issue, and then respond honestly.

If the mind-read is false, clearly state your true thoughts or feelings. Be careful to keep the focus on you, not on the other person. Don't say, "You're wrong" or "That's not true." In talking to your manager, you might say, "I don't regret taking on the project. Although I'm finding it challenging, I'm learning a lot." Then ask a follow-up question to get the person's perspective on the issue you're discussing—for instance, "Is it still an option for me to keep the project?"

If the mind-read is true or partly true, acknowledge that, and then ask a follow-up question. You might tell your friend, "I do have strong opinions about your relationships with men," and then ask, "Would it be better for our friendship if I waited to express my opinions until you asked for them?"

By clarifying the reality, whatever that is, you help the other person to make a better decision. Your manager may or may not change your work assignment, and your friend may or may not continue going out with you after work. Either way, they make more informed choices.

Note: If someone states a simple mind-read that you immediately recognize as being true, you might not bother clarifying its content or origin and instead skip straight to confirming that it's accurate. For instance, if your spouse says, "You really don't like this new paint job" and that's true, you might just say, "You're right, I don't."

Strategy for Clarifying a Mind-Read of You

- **Clarify the content.** State a paraphrase and ask a yes-or-no question.
- **Clarify the origin.** Ask a broad question.
- **Clarify the accuracy.** Correct the mind-read (if false), confirm it (if true), or do a combination of both (if partly true), and then ask a follow-up question.

Note: If it's immediately clear to you that the mind-read is true, you can just acknowledge that and skip the rest of the strategy.

The Upshot: When you respond to other people's mind-reads of you with openness and honesty, you help to build relationships that are based on reality rather than fears, wishes, or speculations.

Response Step 3: Practice

The exercises starting on page 85 will help you build the skill to respond more effectively to other people's mind-reads of you.

Intervention Skill:
Coaching Other People through Mind-Reads

Intervening in a mind-read is a little different from intervening in the other types of communication discussed in this book. Typically, you'll intervene in conversations where someone is talking to a third person (yes-butting them, asking them leading questions, complaining with them, etc.). With a mind-read, the third person is usually not in the room; you're just hearing about them. Therefore, instead of facilitating a two-person discussion, you'll be doing one-on-one coaching.

> ### A Word of Caution about Mind-Read Coaching
> To coach another person through testing a mind-read, you need to be prepared for the possibility that they'll get an answer that's difficult to hear. Having a positive mind-read disconfirmed (the person they like really isn't attracted to them) may destroy a dearly held hope or fantasy. Having a negative mind-read confirmed (their father really is disappointed in their choice of career) may turn a worrisome speculation into an upsetting reality. Don't try coaching someone if you're not able to respond skillfully to the grief, disappointment, anger, and other strong feelings they may wind up experiencing. Also, it's best not to intervene in mind-reads unless you have clear authority to do so, either because of your formal role (coach, mentor, therapist, etc.) or because the other person has explicitly asked for your help.

Intervention Step 1: Awareness

As you build your awareness of mind-reading, you might be surprised at how frequently it crops up in everyday conversations. For instance, a colleague may mention that his manager thinks he's incompetent, or a friend may say that her husband feels bored with his life. Often people reveal mind-reads when they're asking for communication advice. We hear that all the time in questions like, "What do you do when you can tell your employee isn't willing to change?" or "How can I establish my authority with someone who clearly doesn't respect female leaders?"

Without an understanding of mind-reads, we'd just take these comments at face value. The challenge is to recognize that the person is giving assumptions rather than facts, and then find out where those assumptions are coming from. Ask them, "Did he tell you that's how he felt?" or "Did you hear that directly from her?" If the answer is no, you might ask a question to find out how this person's mind-read is affecting them: "How does having this thought affect your relationship with your manager/husband/employee?"

Intervention Step 2:
Action—Guiding a Mind-Read Transformation

If the mind-read has a significant impact, it's probably worthwhile to bring it to the person's attention, either introducing the term *mind-read* or explaining the idea in a more general way. One strategy is using a paraphrase to reflect back what they've told you (for example, "What I'm hearing is that your husband hasn't said he's bored, but you believe that he is, and that belief is making you anxious"). You might also ask them to imagine (1) what it would be like to get confirmation that their belief is true, and (2) what it would be like to learn that it's false.

You may have noticed by now that the process we're describing follows the steps in the mind-read decision tree (see Figure 4-1 on page 72). The goal is to help the person decide whether or not they want to test their mind-read. If they do want a reality check, you can teach them the strategy we described earlier in this chapter: choosing an appropriate context and then testing the mind-read by stating that thought and asking a yes-or-no question (being sure to take time to take in the answer).

We recently had the opportunity to help one of our friends (call her Tracy) to challenge a troubling mind-read that was interfering with her work. Three months earlier, a small consulting company had hired her as an editor on an extensive project that would take nearly a year to complete. Now, after a conflict with the company owner (Paul), she was feeling so bad about the project that she was tempted to drop it altogether. "He thinks I'm overcharging him," she said, "and I don't want to work for someone who doesn't trust me or value what I do."

Tracy came into conflict with Paul during a phone conversation about her expenses. She had found a few books that she thought would help her do a better job on the project, and she wanted the company to buy them for her. When Paul said no, she pushed back, explaining that other companies she'd worked for had always covered these sorts of expenses. Paul stayed firm in his refusal, and they ended up in an argument. As Tracy explained to us, she was fine with dropping the issue of the books but was upset about other comments Paul had made. He kept referring to the size of her bills, saying, "That's a lot of money. I'm paying you so much to do what you're doing. I don't know anyone who's paying as much for editorial work as I am."

In Tracy's mind, there were only two possible reasons why Paul would say those things: either he thought she was being dishonest and overbilling him, or he thought she was incompetent and slow, so the work was taking longer than it should. After the phone call, she felt shaken and began to doubt herself. She looked back through her records and saw that the charges she'd billed were right in line with her earlier estimates. She thought Paul was judging her unfairly but wasn't sure how to bring up the topic without starting another fight.

When we explained the concept of mind-reads to Tracy, she was able to see that she had some untested assumptions about Paul. Although she still believed those assumptions were accurate, she acknowledged that she might be wrong, and she decided she'd rather know the truth than go on worrying. If it turned out that Paul did think she was dishonest or incompetent and would not reconsider that judgment, she'd talk to him about stopping work on the project.

Tracy did a good job of testing her two mind-reads, stating them in a nonaccusatory way ("I'm worried that you think I'm overcharging you" and "I'm worried that you think I'm working too slowly") and asking whether each one was true. In fact, both were entirely off-base. Paul didn't have any problem with the rates Tracy was charging or the hours she was working. What bothered him was that she kept arguing about a relatively insignificant sum of money. His comments were meant to show the contrast between what he was paying Tracy (tens of thousands of dollars) and the cost of the books (less than a hundred dollars). To him, her continued arguing showed that she didn't appreciate how much business he was giving her—a mind-read on his part, which Tracy reassured him was not true. With their mind-reads cleared up, both Tracy and Paul felt much better about their professional relationship and were happy to maintain Tracy's role as editor on the big project.

> **The Upshot:** By guiding someone through the same process you'd use to test your own mind-reads, you can help them avoid anxiety, misunderstandings, and unnecessary conflict.

Intervention Step 3: Practice

Intervening in other people's mind-reads can be challenging, particularly when they're thoroughly convinced that their assumptions are true. Before you attempt to do this, use the exercises that follow to build your awareness and skill. As with all the strategies in this book, we encourage you to become adept at managing your own communication first (in this case, skillfully testing your own mind-reads and responding to other people's mind-reads of you), and only then move on to coaching.

Exercises

Mind-Read Training Program:
Knowing What You Don't Know

The impact of mind-reading varies greatly from person to person. We've met people for whom it's hardly ever a problem. Whenever they're wondering what's on someone else's mind, they simply ask. On the other end of the spectrum, some people's lives are dominated by mind-reads, to the point where they spend much of their energy worrying about what everyone around them thinks and feels. If you are a heavy mind-reader, you might find all of the exercises in this section relevant to your life. As always, do only those exercises you find helpful.

For general guidelines on how to get the most out of each training program, review "Training Program Guidelines" in Chapter 3, on page 47. Note that this icon—∞—marks exercises for which we strongly recommend working with a partner.

Basic Training:
Building Awareness and Flexible Thinking

Exercise 1: Mind-Read Inventory

Goals:
- Clarify your mind-reads by putting them into words
- Gain insight into any systematic biases in the assumptions you make about other people

Estimated time: 8–15 minutes

Start to identify your own mind-reads:

1. Make a list of at least five people who have played an important role in your personal or professional life, whether that influence has been positive or negative.
2. List as many mind-reads as you can for each person. Remember, a mind-read is something you think you know about a person's thoughts or feelings that they haven't explicitly stated to you. For each mind-read, ask yourself:

    •   What specifically do I believe the other person is thinking or feeling?
    •   How certain am I of this mind-read, on a scale from 1 to 10 (1 is not at all certain, 10 is absolutely positive)?

It may help to record your answers in the form of a table. (See Table 4-2.)

Table 4-2. Sample Mind-Read Inventory

Mind-Read	Level of Certainty
Person I'm Mind-Reading: Joe (brother)	
He thinks I should spend more time with our parents.	9
He's proud of me for going back to get my master's degree.	6
He feels ashamed about dropping out of school.	7
Person I'm Mind-Reading: Kevin (boss)	
He thinks the management is treating our department unfairly but doesn't feel like he can say that to us.	5

3. When you've written up mind-reads of several different people, see if you notice any patterns. For instance:

    •   Are your mind-reads mainly negative, mainly positive, or an even mix of both?
    •   Are there systematic differences between your mind-reads of women vs. men? Coworkers vs. friends vs. family members? People of higher status (such as your boss) vs. those of equal or lower status?
    •   Do you have the same mind-read about several different people?

- Do your mind-reads tend to open up or close down future opportunities for effective communication?

Consider what these patterns might tell you about the ways you tend to think about the people and relationships in your life.

Exercise 2: Impact Analysis ∞

Goals:
- Build awareness of how a particular mind-read has affected your thoughts, feelings, relationships, and other aspects of your life
- Compare the potential impact of checking out the mind-read to the impact of not checking it out

Estimated time: 15–25 minutes

Working with a partner, go through the following steps:

1. Pick a mind-read that you'd like to understand better, and tell it to your partner.
2. Your partner asks you the questions in the Impact Analysis sidebar (presented earlier in the chapter on pages 70–71) and records your answers.
3. Talk with your partner about what you both learned.
4. Switch roles, and repeat the process as often as you like.

Variation: Do this exercise on your own, writing down your answers and reflecting on what you've learned.

Exercise 3: Real-Time Tracking

Goal: Deepen your understanding of how your mind-reads affect your daily conversations

Estimated time: 5–10 minutes daily

At the end of each day, think back to any challenging, awkward, or frustrating conversations you had (whether in person or by phone, e-mail, or text). For each situation, write down your answers to the following questions:

1. What was the context?
2. Did I have any mind-reads (assumptions about what the other person was thinking or feeling)?
3. If so, how did those mind-reads affect my conversation?
4. How might things have gone differently if I didn't make those assumptions, or if I tested the assumptions I had?
5. Did I recognize my mind-reads before doing this exercise? If so, when?

Variation A: Instead of doing this exercise daily, do it every week or every month, thinking back to all the difficult conversations you can remember during that time. Answer the five questions above about each of those conversations.

Variation B: If you're able to notice your mind-reads soon after a difficult conversation, do this exercise right at that moment.

Exercise 3 Example

1. **Context.** Telling my boss my ideas about the Zipcor project.
2. **Mind-reads.** She's getting impatient with me. She isn't interested in what I'm saying.
3. **Effect on the conversation.** I got nervous and stumbled over my words.
4. **How things might have gone differently.** I could have asked her whether the information I was giving was useful to her, or if there was other information she wanted instead.
5. **When I recognized my mind-reads.** A few hours later, when discussing the situation with a colleague.

Intermediate Training:
Deepening Your Mind-Read Savvy

Exercise 4: Acknowledging Alternatives ∞

Goals:
- Build awareness of the characteristic ways in which you tend to interpret people's behavior
- Increase your ability to view a situation from multiple perspectives

Estimated time: 10–30 minutes

One way to help counteract mind-reads is to consider possible alternative explanations for people's behavior. We recommend doing this with a partner:

1. Read through the situations below, and jot down the first explanation that comes to mind for each. (Have your partner write down their ideas separately.)

    •   Soon after you loaned your brother some money, he fell out of contact with you.
    •   Your coworker hasn't congratulated you on your recent promotion.
    •   You met someone you liked at a party and e-mailed them several days later but got no response.
    •   Whenever you raise the issue of going on vacation, your spouse changes the subject.
    •   Your daughter doesn't talk to you about her boyfriend anymore.
    •   Your supervisor sends you an e-mail saying, "Call me right away when you get in."
    •   Your friend often stares at your new ring.
    •   During a staff meeting, one of your employees keeps looking at his watch.
    •   One of your students asks many more complex, technical questions than anyone else in the class.
    •   One of your instructors directs more challenging questions to you than to anyone else in the class.
    •   When you explain your new idea to a business associate, she says, "That's interesting. I need some time to think about it."
    •   The leader of a group you belong to holds an event and invites most people in the group, but you don't get an invitation.

2. Compare your explanations with your partner's, and see if you notice any consistent themes. For instance, did either of you tend to think the best of people ("He's probably busy working, trying to earn back that money"), think the worst of people ("He has no intention of paying me back, so he doesn't want

to talk to me"), or think the worst of yourself ("I must have said something to upset him")?

3. Working together, brainstorm as many different explanations as you can for each scenario (skipping any that don't interest you).

Variation A: Repeat this same exercise with real situations in your life. What have people said or done that led you to mind-read them? What are some alternative explanations for their behavior?

Variation B: Do this exercise on your own, without a partner.

Advanced Training:
Preparing to Apply the Full Mind-Read Strategies

Exercise 5—Transforming Your Mind-Reads ∞

Goals:
- Develop skill at testing your mind-reads against reality
- Make preparations to test specific mind-reads in your life

Estimated time: 15–25 minutes

Pick a real mind-read you have of somebody in your life, find a partner to role-play that person, and work through the following steps:

1. Give a clear statement of your mind-read, followed by a yes-or-no question. (For instance: "I sometimes think you're unhappy with the salary you're making. Is that true?")
2. Your partner answers yes.
3. Repeat steps 1 and 2, this time with your partner answering no.
4. Talk together about how things went. Ask your partner:

   - Did your mind-read come across as a statement about you and your concerns rather than as an accusation?
   - Was your message simple and clear?
   - Was it clear to them that you wanted a yes-or-no answer?
   - Did you seem open to hearing the truth, whatever it was?

Also talk to your partner about your experience:

- What was it like to state your mind-read out loud and ask a direct question about it?
- What was it like to hear that your mind-read was true?
- What was it like to hear that it was false?

If your initial attempt didn't work well, keep trying until you're satisfied with the result.

5. Ask yourself whether you want to test your mind-read in reality. If you do, plan out a good time and place for having the conversation. We always recommend starting with relatively easy, low-stakes mind-reads. Don't have the first mind-read you test be about your boss's ethics violations or your spouse's affair. As you become more comfortable with the process, you can gradually build up to more and more challenging topics.

6. Switch roles, working through one of your partner's mind-reads.

Want to learn more? Try more exercises at CTsavvy.com/MRexercises, plus the awareness quiz at CTsavvy.com/MRquiz.

5

Catastrophe Forecasts

The Parks County School Committee's bargaining team knew they had to find a way to make their next negotiation with the teachers union less disastrous. In all their recent attempts, they'd come to the table with good intentions of reaching a fair agreement, yet left with nothing to show for it but confusion, anger, and humiliation.

The reason for their failure was no mystery. His name was Bob, and he'd been the union president for the past two years. Bob had a reputation for being outrageous and unpredictable, stopping at nothing (including threats, taunts, and lies) to throw the other side off balance. And clearly, his tactics were working. Accustomed to calm, rational deliberations, the bargaining team had no good response to Bob's inflammatory comments. They always ended up on the defensive, unable to keep the conversation focused on the facts and proposals they had so carefully prepared.

Whatever ideas the school negotiators put forward, Bob's responses seemed grossly out of proportion. After they'd suggested that his proposed health insurance plan was too expensive, he'd launched into a tirade, proclaiming that he wasn't going to stand for teacher bashing. Then he'd shown up at a school committee meeting with one hundred of his teachers and their children, all waving signs with accusations of union busting.

The negotiators knew they needed outside help. They called in Beulah Trey, an organizational psychologist, to help them plan a more effective response. As the planning session began, Beulah asked them to start the discussion on their own, so she could observe how they were approaching the problem. It didn't take long for the conversation to get heated, though not because there were strong differences of opinion. In fact, everyone seemed to be in full agreement about what would happen in the next negotiation:

"You know he'll make it sound as though we're trying to deny the right to organize."

"He's such a liar!"

"If we try to present the facts, he'll just laugh and make sarcastic jabs. How are we supposed to respond to that?"

"We can't. Either we let him win or we resort to the same tactics he uses, which will undermine our own integrity."

"It's a disgrace! This isn't a real negotiation. He's making a mockery of the whole process."

"It's so wrong. And it's the students who will lose out in the end."

After only ten minutes of talking, the mood was split between outrage and resignation. Even before the negotiation began, it felt like a lost cause.

What went wrong with this conversation? The team's stated goal was to influence what *could* happen, by planning. But they spent all their time and energy deciding what *would* happen, by predicting—specifically, negatively predicting. They didn't just predict what Bob would do (imply that they were trying to deny the right to organize, then mock any facts they gave); they went on to predict two possible results (either Bob would win, or they'd sacrifice their integrity) and the ultimate outcome (the students would lose out). Faced with this seemingly inevitable reality, it's no surprise they wound up feeling angry and hopeless.

Communication Challenge 3: Negative Predictions—Making Our Fears Our Reality

When we make negative predictions, we treat our worries and fears about the future as if they're facts. We state with certainty, "We'll never meet this deadline," "This damage will cost a fortune to repair," or "There's no way the president will approve our plan."

The most obvious problem with negative predictions is that they cause unnecessary misery. As we worry about what will happen later, we start to react as though the dreaded event has already occurred. For example, say you're predicting, "Steve will be late and we'll miss the train to the client meeting." The odds are good that long before the train arrives, you'll already be feeling irritated with Steve. You may have a long conversation with him in your mind, lecturing him about how irresponsible he is and how much trouble he's caused. Then maybe you'll think ahead to the meeting, imagining your embarrassment at walking in late and having to apologize to your client. If you jump even further into the future, you might picture losing the client, losing your job, telling your family that you lost your job, and so on. Before you know it, you're experiencing the anticipated agony of weeks, months, or years of problems, all based on an imagined chain of events that may never get started.

In the opening story, we saw how the Parks County school administrators worked themselves into a near frenzy through negative predictions. They felt all the anger that went along with hearing taunts and lies, plus all the disappointment of experiencing a major failure, even though none of those things were actually happening at that moment.

Another problem with negative predictions is that they are frequently self-fulfilling. There are two primary ways this can happen. First, these predictions cause anxiety, fear, anger, and other strong emotions that interfere with whatever it is we're trying to accomplish. Have you ever been so nervous about failing an exam that you couldn't focus on the test? Or been so worried about an interview going badly that you were anxious the entire time (thereby making the interview go badly)?

If you bring negative expectations into a tough conversation, you may end up acting in ways that elicit the very responses you're trying to avoid. For instance, a friend of ours remembers worrying for weeks about an upcoming meeting, afraid of how her boss would respond to her analysis of some recent financial losses. By the time the meeting came, after many sleepless nights, this woman was an emotional wreck. As a result, the tone of her presentation was defensive right from the outset. It's no surprise that within minutes, her boss got upset and started criticizing her.

The other way negative predictions become self-fulfilling is by stopping us from taking steps to achieve a better outcome. This was clear in the case of the school negotiation. Not only did the group's catastrophizing take up time and energy that could have been used for constructive planning; it also made planning seem hopeless. Convinced that things would go badly and that nothing they could do would help, they saw no reason to try.

The Pitfalls of Personal Predictions

One particularly thorny type of negative prediction involves telling someone else about their future thoughts and feelings: "You're going to be mad when you see this," "You're not going to like my idea," "I know you'll be disappointed with the food here." That kind of statement can be extremely annoying. It's bad enough to have someone tell you what you're thinking or feeling right now, as if they're telepathic. (We covered this in the mind-read chapter.) Having them predict your future mental state suggests not only telepathy but the gift of prophecy as well—quite a presumption.

A prediction such as "You won't like this" can easily become self-fulfilling. Whatever you say next, the person is predisposed to notice what they don't like about it. In addition, these types of remarks may come across as judgmental. If you tell your colleague, "You won't like this plan," he may hear an implied criticism: "You're closed-minded" or "You never like new ideas." If you tell your girlfriend she's going to get upset, she may take that to mean, "You're overly emotional" or "You're too sensitive." With any of these predictions, you're sending at least one potentially irritating message: "You're predictable."

Negative predictions can be particularly damaging when a whole group (like the school bargaining team) agrees that they're true. In many situations, having other people agree with you is a good thing. There's less conflict, it's easier to make decisions, and—let's face it—it just feels good to hear someone else say you're right. When it comes to negative predictions, however, agreement is probably the last thing you need.

Shared agreement with a negative prediction often has a contagion effect, leading to escalating worry, fear, and even group panic. A clear example of this occurred in a group of graduate students working toward a post-doctoral degree in educational consulting. As part of their program, they were assigned to spend two weeks training and mentoring teachers in a poor, inner-city public school in a largely African-American neighborhood. In preparation for this task, the program leader asked the trainees to imagine what it would be like when they first arrived at the school, and to talk together about the challenges they'd face.

None of the trainees had relevant experience to draw from. They were all from white, middle-class, suburban backgrounds and had never worked with a population that was so different from them racially and socioeconomically. In the absence of real data, they relied on their imaginations and conjured up worst-case scenarios: confrontations with verbally aggressive, physically imposing male teachers who resented the presumption that people from the ivory tower of academia had anything to teach them. The more the trainees talked, the more they scared themselves with increasingly frightening predictions. When the time came to report to the school, they were very anxious.

Reality proved them entirely wrong. The teachers were friendly and welcoming, and the things they were angry about were the same kinds of things the trainees/mentors were angry about: lack of supplies, lack of support for underachievers, lack of teacher training in new curricula, and so forth. Men and women alike were grateful for any help they could get to improve the results in their classrooms. This experience taught the trainees a useful lesson about the danger of relying on ungrounded assumptions about the future, though not before those assumptions had caused them a great deal of anxiety and distress.

> **The Upshot:** Negative predictions cause unnecessary suffering and also increase the chances that our fears will come true.

What About Positive Predictions?

Since negative predictions have negative effects, you might imagine that positive predictions would have positive effects. In truth, negative and positive predictions are more alike than different. Whether we say, "We'll never finish" or "We'll finish in no time," "We'll make a fortune" or "We'll lose everything," we're still talking about an imagined future as if it were real.

Positive predictions cause less short-term fear and anxiety than their negative counterparts, but they can be every bit as damaging to a planning or decision-making process. Often it takes work to achieve the results we want, and both types of predictions tend to discourage us from doing that work—either because a good outcome seems impossible (so there's no point) or because a good outcome seems inevitable (so there's no need). Positive predictions also carry the added risk that if they don't come true, we're caught off-guard by an unpleasant surprise.

Typically people make positive predictions with good intentions, wanting to reassure themselves ("Next time I know I'll make the sale"), reassure others ("Your symptoms are bound to resolve soon"), keep people motivated ("If we work hard, we'll win this contract"), or simply create an upbeat environment ("We'll all have a great time!"). They may get frustrated when others don't share their optimism. It's not uncommon to hear arguments between negative and positive predictors: "Everyone will love this idea!" "Karen won't like it." "She'll come around." "It will take weeks to convince her." And so on. These battles of warring assumptions can go on indefinitely. There's no way for either person to win, because it's impossible to be right about the future when it hasn't happened yet (though that doesn't stop anybody from saying "I told you so!" when a prediction comes true).

Why Do We Expect the Worst?

If making negative predictions is so bad for us, what leads us to do it? One answer is that it shields us from something that can seem even worse: uncertainty. The future is inherently uncertain, and living with uncertainty can feel uncomfortable, even unbearable. Predictions give us a sense of control by creating the illusion that we know what will happen.

Of course, a prediction doesn't have to be negative. We can also make positive predictions, as described in the sidebar above. There are three factors that may bias people toward pessimism (negative predictions) rather than optimism (positive predictions): attempts to manage emotions, reliance on fixed ideas, and generalizations from past experiences.

- **Attempts to manage emotions.** People often have a sense that if they prepare for disappointment in advance, by worrying about it, it won't hurt so badly when it finally happens. This is the rationale behind "bracing yourself" for bad news or criticism. In reality, rehearsing the negative feelings you expect to feel almost never makes the actual experience any easier. All it does is make the bad feelings start earlier and therefore last longer.

- **Reliance on fixed ideas.** Sometimes our expectations are driven by fixed ideas about how the world works, including both general rules of life ("Nice guys finish last," "Nothing good comes easily") and more specific beliefs that hit closer to home ("This company never rewards innovation," "All my romantic relationships end badly"). These beliefs frequently include mind-reads, which you learned about in Chapter 4. For example, a prediction that your coworker will resent your promotion may stem from a mind-read that she really wanted that job, that she thinks you're incompetent, or that she sees you as kissing up to the CEO.

- **Generalizations from past experiences.** When people are convinced that their negative predictions are true, it's often because they're generalizing from bad experiences they've had in the past. Clients sometimes tell us, "This isn't a prediction, because it's based on facts" or "I've been in this same situation before, so I know what will happen." It's this type of generalization that led the school bargaining team to imagine their upcoming meeting as a repeat performance of others they'd had before.

The reality is that no two situations are exactly the same. Take the example of asking for a raise. If your last request for a pay hike was rejected, you might predict that making the same request a year later would bring the same result. But any number of things may have changed during that year. Perhaps the company's financial situation has improved, or your supervisor has gained an increased appreciation for your work. Moreover, it's possible that you didn't communicate effectively the first time, so just stating your request in a different way could get you a better response. If you fail to consider these possibilities and simply accept your negative prediction as a fact, you'll probably do the one thing that guarantees your request won't get approved: you'll keep it to yourself.

> **The Upshot:** There are strong motivating forces behind our negative predictions, which can give them a powerful hold over us and leave us convinced that the future we fear is inevitable.

Skills for Managing Negative Predictions

Like all the other behaviors described in this book, negative predictions come more naturally to some individuals than to others. Even if you don't use them much yourself, you can probably think of people in your life who do. Whether you're a chronic worrier, an eternal optimist who hates it when others catastrophize, or a person who falls somewhere in the middle, you'll find strategies in this section designed to help you take a more constructive approach to the future.

Transformation Skill: Confronting an Uncertain Future

Negative predictions have a lot in common with mind-reads. Both involve constructing an imagined reality by treating our speculations as facts. However, as soon as we start considering strategies, it's clear that there's one crucial difference. Unlike with a mind-read, the accuracy of a prediction is not only unknown; it's unknowable. In Chapter 4, we showed how you could test mind-reads by asking people what they're thinking or feeling. There's no analogous test for negative predictions. You can't just ask the future what it has in store for you. You need a different set of skills, still starting with awareness, but moving on to new ways to come to terms with reality.[1]

Transformation Step 1: Self-Awareness

Do you ever find yourself dwelling on something bad that might happen ("I'll never get that job," "Katherine won't agree with me," or "Bill will drop the ball on our big project")? Think about a specific event or piece of news that you anticipate with a sense of fear, dread, or resignation. Chances are, you're treating your worry about the future as if it's a fact, destined to happen. That is a negative prediction.

Before you can find an alternative to your prediction, you need to get clear about exactly what you're expecting to happen. Suppose you feel anxious about giving a negative performance evaluation to a man who reports to you. Ask yourself, what bad outcome are you imagining? Are you expecting him to be hurt? Defensive? Angry? Are you afraid that you'll be too harsh, or not firm enough? State your worry clearly: "He'll get depressed and I'll feel guilty" or "He won't take any responsibility for what's not working." Then you're ready to move on and start challenging that assumption.

Transformation Step 2:
Action—Gathering Facts and Choosing a New Direction

When we make negative predictions, we create imagined facts that disconnect us from reality and prevent us from taking constructive action. An effective antidote is to do the opposite: gather genuine facts that help us reconnect with what's real, and then use those facts to guide our actions.

Gathering Facts

There are three important types of facts to consider: facts about the future, the past, and the present. We'll relate each of these to the same negative prediction: "I'm going to mess up my big speech."

- **Fact about the future.** There is only one critical fact to recognize about the future: that it is unknown, not yet decided. Accepting this fact is the first, and often most important, step in working through a negative prediction. It may also be one of the most difficult. If you're convinced your prediction will come true (for instance, if you feel no hope at all about your upcoming speech), it's hard to admit that you might be wrong.

  Questions to ask yourself: Can I know what's going to happen in the future? (Note: The truth is that no one knows for sure what's going to happen until it happens. Accepting this is a necessary step to take before you can do any more work on a negative prediction.) Am I aware that I'm treating my prediction about the future as though it were already true?

- **Facts about the past.** If your negative prediction is based on past experiences, you'll probably be able to remember plenty of facts that support that prediction, but you'll likely overlook others that don't support it. This is because the state of mind you're in affects the type of memories you recall. In general, people remember more happy events when they're happy, more upsetting events when they're upset, and so on.[2] The worry or fear generated by negative predictions will tend to elicit more worrisome or fearful memories. Therefore, if you're feeling anxious about your speech, it will likely be easy to recall other anxiety-provoking events—like losing your place during a talk and being criticized by your manager—but harder to recall instances when you've presented yourself well and received positive feedback.

In addition to overlooking past successes, you may also forget about the specific factors that contributed to less successful outcomes. For instance, you might vividly remember the humiliation of stumbling over your words in a previous speech but forget all the events that preceded it: having the flu and being up half the night coughing; filling in at the last minute for another colleague who was supposed to give the speech; or feeling so stressed that you procrastinated and didn't practice the speech until the night before.

To keep your memories more balanced, see if you can get curious about what new information you can learn from the past. It may be useful to get coaching from a friend who can help jog your memory. For example, you might ask a colleague if you're forgetting anything about the circumstances of a previous presentation.

Questions to ask yourself: Have I had any positive experiences in past similar situations? When I've had negative experiences in similar situations, what factors contributed to those outcomes?

- **Facts about the present.** What do you really know about your current situation? Related to your speech, you might consider the amount of time you have left to prepare, the resources available to you, information about the group you'll be speaking to, and so on.

As we suggested in the previous section, pay particular attention to facts you might tend to overlook. It's common to focus on the similarities between your current situation and others that ended badly but overlook the ways in which it's different. You might notice that just like a previous failed speech, this one deals with highly technical subject matter, but might forget that this time you know the material better and are speaking to a less technically savvy audience. It's also common to focus on factors that you can't control, such as the fact that your boss's boss will be present for your speech. You may need to be reminded about the factors you can control and the various options that may increase your chances for success, like the potential to get help from an executive coach or from a colleague who gives presentations frequently.

Keep an eye out for pseudo-facts like mind-reads or broad generalizations. For a mind-read (such as "My colleague doesn't want to spend time helping me prepare"), you can use the skills from Chapter 4 to test whether your assumption is true. For generalizations, try to replace your interpretations ("I'm no good under pressure") with more specific data ("When I feel pressured, I get anxious and have trouble concentrating"). (Notice that data can help guide you to useful next steps—in this case, finding ways to reduce your anxiety—while fixed interpretations leave you stuck with the status quo.)

Also be on the lookout for relevant facts you simply don't know, and then track them down if you can. Not sure whether you can get temporary clerical help for the work that's taking you away from researching your speech? Go ahead and ask. Don't know how long it will take you to review 30 documents of background material? Review a couple of average-length documents and time yourself. You might be surprised at all the facts you don't have and how many of them you can gather if you try.

Gathering data won't tell you for certain what the future holds, but it can give you a much more realistic sense of what's likely to happen. Often, the outcome we fear is possible but not probable. You might be killed on your next domestic plane flight, but the odds of that happening are one in 14 million;[3] your next report might take a month to finish, but all previous reports have taken you two weeks; you might freeze and forget your opening lines, but it would be the first time in 15 public speaking engagements.

Questions to ask yourself: What is different about my situation now, compared to similar past situations that ended badly? What factors in my current situation might impact the outcome I'm worried about? Which of those factors can I influence or control? What resources and options do I have? What relevant facts am I missing, and how can I gather those facts?

Selective Memory and Biased Thinking

When we have a negative prediction, we tend to:

- Remember negative past experiences but forget positive past experiences

- Remember bad outcomes but forget about the contributing factors that led to those outcomes
- Notice the similarities between the present and the past but overlook the differences
- Focus on factors we can't control rather than those we can
- Mistake pseudo-facts for real facts
- Mistake possibilities for probabilities

Maintaining a Fact-Finding Frame of Mind

It's much easier to gather useful facts when you're feeling relatively calm rather than in the midst of a full-blown panic. There may be times when you try to consider the facts of your situation but feel too anxious or agitated to focus. If this happens, take a break. Don't force yourself to concentrate. You may find it helpful to do something that relaxes you, whether it's going for a run, doing yoga, meditating, listening to music, or just taking some deep breaths.

If you start out relatively calm but begin feeling anxious as you go through the fact-gathering process, check to see if you are retoxifying your mind with more negative predictions. For instance, as you're remembering facts about a past failed speech, have you gone back to thinking about what might go wrong this time ("If I do that badly again, I could lose my job, and then I'd be unable to pay my mortgage . . .")? When you become aware of this cascade of catastrophizing, label what's happening ("These are negative predictions") and notice that your distress is coming directly from those thoughts. Ask yourself, "Can I know what's going to happen in the future?" If you can face the reality that you can't, you'll probably find that your distress starts to diminish. When you feel less stressed and pressured, your fact-finding will be much easier and more effective.

Choosing a New Direction

A negative prediction acts like a black hole, a place where our time and energy go to die. The worry and anxiety it causes can take up huge portions of our mental space. When we recognize that a prediction isn't real, we can start to reclaim all that energy and send it in a more constructive direction, guided by the facts we've discovered. There are two primary options: planning for action and managing uncertainty.

- **Planning for action.** While we can never have complete control over the future, we can often have a strong influence on the events that concern us. After you've gathered your facts, concentrate on the ones that offer you choices, and translate those facts into options for action. What opportunities do you have to get more help or more information, communicate more effectively, or make better decisions than you did in the past? What steps can you take to prevent the outcome you fear and make the outcome you want more likely? Consider your big speech. In the time that you'd otherwise spend imagining your future failure, you could do research, prepare notes, practice, and get feedback and coaching.

  Sometimes, it may also be smart to do some contingency planning. Suppose you were hired by an accounting firm on the condition that during your first year, you pass the CPA (Certified Public Accountant) exam. Knowing that more than half the people who take this test fail it,[4] you may want to devise a backup plan. If you don't pass the first time, when will you take it again? How many chances will you get? Just be sure you don't focus so much on your Plan B and Plan C that you neglect your Plan A, which in this case means doing everything you can to pass on your first attempt.

  Questions to ask yourself: Knowing what has happened in the past, what could I do differently this time? What steps can I take to help prevent the outcome I fear and make a better outcome more likely? Are there any contingency plans I want to put in place?

- **Managing uncertainty.** You're probably familiar with the Serenity Prayer, generally attributed to theologian Reinhold Niebuhr: "God grant me the serenity to accept the things I cannot change; courage to change the things I can; and wisdom to know the difference." So far, we've been talking about the things you can change. However, there will always be some things that are entirely out of your control: Your supervisor has already decided which employees will get laid off, and you're just waiting to hear the news. Or you've taken a blood test and need to wait a week for the results to come in. In these situations, our basic recommendation is the same as Niebuhr's: acceptance.

  True acceptance means not jumping to either a negative prediction ("I'm going to lose my job") or a positive prediction ("I know my job is safe"), but instead acknowledging the reality of uncertainty ("I don't know whether I'll lose my job or not"). Try to acknowledge the uncertainty not just of the immediate outcome you fear but of what might happen after that. Watch out for hidden assumptions embedded in your thinking, such as "If I lose this job now, I'll be out of work for a year" or "If I'm diagnosed with this disease, I'll never have a happy, fulfilling life." Even if one of your short-term negative predictions comes true, that doesn't mean your longer-term predictions are destined to happen.

Many people find it extremely challenging to sit with uncertainty,[5] particularly when the stakes are high. Some turn to meditation or other spiritual practices, while others prefer more physical approaches, like going for a run or getting a massage. You might find it helpful to talk with a therapist or sympathetic friend about your situation, or to not talk about it at all, distracting yourself by getting immersed in other things. Whatever method you choose, coming up with an effective way to deal with uncertainty—instead of creating the illusion of certainty by making predictions—will serve you well in many aspects of your life.

Question to ask yourself: If I'm finding it difficult to sit with uncertainty, what can I do right now to help myself?

The Antidote to Negative Predictions: Asking Questions

We've taught you three productive alternatives to making negative predictions: gathering facts, planning for action, and managing uncertainty. With each of these, we've listed one or more potentially helpful questions to ask yourself. For easy reference, we've collected all those questions together in the sidebar that follows.

Questions to Undo Negative Predictions

Questions for Gathering Facts

- Can I know what's going to happen in the future?
- Am I aware that I'm treating my prediction about the future as though it were already true?
- Have I had any positive experiences in past similar situations?
- When I've had negative experiences in similar situations, what factors contributed to those outcomes?

- What is different about my situation now, compared to similar past situations that ended badly?
- What factors in my current situation might impact the outcome I'm worried about?
- Which of those factors can I influence or control?
- What resources and options do I have?
- What relevant facts am I missing, and how can I gather those facts?

Questions for Planning
- Knowing what has happened in the past, what could I do differently this time?
- What steps can I take to help prevent the outcome I fear and make a better outcome more likely?
- Are there any contingency plans I want to put in place?

Question for Managing Uncertainty
- If I'm finding it difficult to sit with uncertainty, what can I do right now to help myself?

> **The Upshot:** Although you can't control the future, you can make conscious choices about the ways you think, act, and manage your time and resources in the present—which not only gets you back in touch with reality but also may help prevent the outcome you fear.

Transformation Step 3: Practice
If you'd like to start building your skill in transforming negative predictions, skip ahead to the training program starting on page 114.

Response Skill:
Responding to Predictions That Others Present as Facts

As you get a better sense of the pitfalls of negative predictions and the benefits of transforming your own, you'll likely become more sensitive to their influence on the people around you. The guidelines in this section will help you respond constructively when others present their predictions as facts.

Response Step 1: Awareness

When somebody is making a negative prediction, they generally won't announce that that's what they're doing ("Let me tell you what I'm predicting," or "Here's what I'm pretending to know about the future"). Instead, they'll either present their assumption as a fact ("This is going to be a disaster") or just talk about how worried or anxious they are.

Think about people you know who express a lot of fear or anxiety, or who seem resigned to things not going their way. In your conversations with them, try to identify the specific predictions they have. If they don't state them directly, you might want to ask questions to get clarification. For instance, if your friend says, "I'm dreading my next meeting with my boss," you could ask, "Is there something in particular you're afraid he's going to say?" or "What are you worried will happen?" The goal of this questioning is not to teach the other person something but to increase your own understanding of what's going on. **To practice recognizing negative predictions, visit CTsavvy.com/NPquiz.**

Just as important as noticing what others do is noticing how you react. Does listening to these predictions make you feel anxious, concerned, or annoyed? Do you tend to downplay the person's concern ("I'm sure it will be fine"), agree with the concern ("Yeah, that will be awful"), blame the person for thinking that way ("You're always so pessimistic"), or try to solve their problem for them ("You should have someone else in the meeting for moral support")? In order to be helpful to them, you need to be able to neutrally observe how they're talking, without getting drawn into the content of what they're talking about.

In many circumstances, increasing your own awareness may be all that you do. Be careful not to assume that the other person needs or wants you to help change their thinking. When someone believes a negative prediction, that prediction is part of their reality, and disrupting another person's reality is not something to be done lightly. Unless you're in a role (such as a coach or a therapist) that automatically gives you authority to work with their communication, don't intrude on a negative prediction without an invitation. If you're not sure what kind of response the person is looking for, ask, "How can I be most helpful to you as you think through this problem?" If they simply want to vent and have you hear how upset they are, stick to listening and being empathetic. If they want you to take a more active role in helping them, you can move on to Step 2.

Response Step 2:
Action—Shifting Focus and Asking Questions

After you've worked through your own negative predictions, you know the basic process for helping someone else work through theirs. The key is asking questions, both to gather facts and to make plans for the future. However, before the other person can benefit from that strategy, they need to do one more thing: realize that their negative prediction is a thought, not a fact. Otherwise, why would they bother with the strategy? If things are predestined to go badly, facts and plans won't help.

To come to that realization, the person needs to shift their attention away from their external problem (such as the meeting they think will go badly or the money they're sure they'll lose) and onto their internal problem (their assumption that they can predict the future about the meeting or the money). If they're not used to analyzing their own communication, this change in focus may feel jarring. Before moving forward, ask whether they're willing to step back from the issue and look at the way they're thinking and talking about it.

Once the person has agreed to talk about their communication, you can bring their attention to particular things they've said (like "I know this meeting is going to go badly" or "I'll never get that money back"). Ask how those thoughts are affecting them. When they treat the bad outcome as inevitable, how do they feel? What happens to their ability to problem solve? Invite them to read the first part of this chapter, or just explain the basic concept of a negative prediction. It may be helpful to share your experiences in working through your own negative predictions. If they're open to trying a new way of thinking, guide them through the series of questions in the sidebar that follows. (These are the same questions you've used to transform your own negative predictions, just adapted for talking to someone else.)

Questions to Undo Another Person's Negative Predictions

Questions for Gathering Facts

- Can you know what's going to happen in the future?
- Are you aware that you're treating your prediction about the future as though it were already true?
- Have you had any positive experiences in past similar situations?
- When you've had negative experiences in similar situations, what factors contributed to those outcomes?
- What is different about your situation now, compared to similar past situations that ended badly?
- What factors in your current situation might impact the outcome you're worried about?
- Which of those factors can you influence or control?
- What resources and options do you have?
- What relevant facts are you missing, and how can you gather those facts?

Questions for Planning

- Knowing what has happened in the past, what could you do differently this time?
- What steps can you take to help prevent the outcome you fear and make a better outcome more likely?
- Are there any contingency plans you want to put in place?

Question for Managing Uncertainty

- If you're finding it difficult to sit with uncertainty, what can you do right now to help yourself?

Organizational trainer and consultant Fran Carter gets many opportunities to respond to negative predictions from her clients. In one instance, a junior-level manufacturing supervisor (we'll call him Ed) mentioned his desire to hire a new employee for his team. "I want to make a proposal," he said, "but it will never go through. The executives won't listen. They won't even bother answering me." With Fran's help, Ed came to realize that his negative predictions were holding him back from working toward the change he wanted. He agreed to try switching to gathering data and making plans.

First, he thought back to past situations where his requests for additional staff hadn't been answered. As he recalled the facts about how he'd communicated, he realized that he hadn't actually made any specific requests. He'd just complained: "We're so understaffed here," "There's far too much work for a team this size," "We don't have enough people to perform this function," and so on.

With Fran's coaching, Ed planned a different way to present his ideas. He decided to put together a document including a detailed analysis of the pros and cons for making the hire. He also added a request that whatever the decision, he receive a response within a week. The result? Not only did the executives respond; they immediately approved the hire.

The Upshot: Through skillful questioning, you can help steer a conversation away from distressing predictions and toward productive goals and plans.

Response Step 3: Practice

Responding effectively to someone else's negative predictions is challenging, particularly if you have a strong tendency to react in an unproductive way. Before you attempt the response strategy, we recommend doing as many of the exercises (starting on page 114) as possible.

Intervention Skill:
Turning Around Negative Predictions in a Group

Negative predictions can be contagious, spreading to another person, a small group, or even an entire organization. Fortunately, the same approach you learned for talking with a single individual can also be effective in talking with a group, whether it's a group of two or two dozen. As always, make sure you've developed a high level of skill in your own communication before you try intervening with others.

Intervention Step 1: Awareness

Shared group predictions may be the easiest type to spot, so long as you're not caught up in them yourself. When people get on a roll catastrophizing together, it affects the whole emotional climate of the conversation. The more people talk about the future, the greater the feeling of fear, resignation, anger, or whatever other emotion their predictions are generating. When you notice this sort of phenomenon, pay attention to the specific comments people are making. What precisely are they predicting is going to happen?

Intervention Step 2: Action—Shifting Group Focus and Asking Group Questions

With groups, as with individuals, the first challenge is shifting the focus away from what's being discussed and onto how it's being discussed. Make sure you have enough authority in the group to make this type of intervention. That authority may come from your role as a leader or facilitator, from your relationships with each person, or from a group culture in which every individual is empowered to intervene in the group's process of working.

Start by bringing people's awareness to the way they've been talking about the future. Ask if they remember the specific things they've said, like "We're going to miss our deadline" or "Our budget will never get approved." Do they realize they're talking as if a negative result is inevitable?

Then ask the group how this type of communication is affecting their ability to solve their problems or reach their goals. If they've been talking for a fair amount of time and haven't accomplished anything, it should be clear to them that something isn't working and that a different approach might be helpful. (That's a good reason to wait a little while before intervening, rather than interrupting the first negative prediction you hear. Wait to see if the group naturally gets back on track, in which case the problem disappears, or if it veers further and further off course, in which case the problem becomes obvious to everyone.) The same questions you used for working through individual negative predictions, in the sidebar "Questions to Undo Another Person's Negative Predictions" on page 109, can help with a group as well.

Negative Prediction Detection System

Your skilled intervention can make a big difference in a group discussion that's been dominated by negative predictions. But what
happens when you leave? If the group has a strong tendency to
negatively predict, people are likely to slip back into that habit.
Lasting change requires not one intervention but many, repeated
over time.

One way to solve this problem is to create a new role in the
group: negative prediction monitor. In every important meeting,
someone takes responsibility for monitoring the communication
and bringing attention to any negative predictions. The same person can do this over several meetings, or everyone can rotate. In
this way, the group develops the capacity to self-correct, heading
off catastrophizing before it derails the conversation.

Think back to the school negotiating team we introduced at the start
of this chapter. Their conversation was dominated by predictions that the
union president (Bob) would use disruptive tactics and that as a result, their
suggestions would get ignored and the whole process would break down.
After about 10 minutes, the consultant (Beulah) interrupted the discussion
and reminded the group of their goal: planning negotiation strategies. The
negotiators recognized that they hadn't made any progress toward that
goal, and when Beulah explained the concept of negative predictions, they
were able to see why. They were more than willing to try something different to help themselves move forward.

As the group focused on the facts of their past negotiations, they
started to remember details that they had previously overlooked. In particular, they realized that Bob's behavior seemed to follow certain patterns.
He wasn't constantly on the offensive, exploding into angry outbursts;
rather, his agitation seemed to develop gradually. When things started
to head south, there were some obvious warning signs—he began talking
more loudly, with an edge in his voice, and started gesturing more and
more wildly with his hands. There was also a predictable pattern in the
school negotiators' responses. Each time Bob showed aggression, they
would become increasingly upset, lose track of their rational arguments,
and put all their energy into defending themselves.

Using this new information, the negotiation team was able to do some contingency planning. While they couldn't change Bob, they could change the way they responded to him. This time, they decided, as soon as they observed any signs of trouble, such as a rising voice tone or waving hands, they would call a break and strategize together before coming back to the table. (Under the rules of the negotiation, they had full authority to call a break at any time, another fact that hadn't occurred to them as they were making predictions.) Then, when the talks resumed, they would begin by summarizing the points Bob had made (so he would know they'd heard him and therefore wouldn't feel compelled to keep saying the same things) as well as the points they had made (so their ideas wouldn't get forgotten).

Once the team had finished planning their response to Bob, there wasn't much left to say about him. They were able to let that issue rest and move on to discussing the substantive issues of the negotiation, refining their proposals and practicing the arguments they wanted to make. By the end of their meeting, they had clear plans both for handling possible setbacks and for making the best possible use of the time they had to speak.

The results were better than anyone in the group had expected. Although there were several instances where Bob got agitated and raised his voice, they stuck to their plan of calling breaks, taking time out to strategize, and giving summaries. In addition to helping them to calm down and refocus their energy, this also seemed to leave Bob a little calmer and either more able or more motivated to have a rational discussion. Throughout the process, the school negotiators felt much more sure of themselves and their arguments than they had in the past. And by the end of the meeting, the two sides had identified more points of agreement than they had the last three times they'd met.

The Upshot: With the right type of intervention, you can help an entire group shift from fruitless catastrophizing to taking an active role in getting the outcome they want.

Intervention Step 3: Practice

If you'd like to be able to use this strategy in your life or work, start building your skills now. The exercises that follow will help prepare you to intervene in a clear, insightful, and effective way.

Exercises

Negative Predictions Training Program: Separating Facts from Fears

If reading this chapter made you realize that your head is full of negative predictions, you may find many of these exercises helpful. If you have the opposite tendency, leaning toward unrealistic hopes, feel free to adapt some of the exercises for positive predictions.

> For general guidelines on how to get the most out of each training program, review "Training Program Guidelines" in Chapter 3, on page 47. Note that this icon—**OO**—marks exercises for which we strongly recommend working with a partner.

Basic Training:
Building Awareness and Flexible Thinking

Exercise 1: Tracking Fears and Realities

Goals:
- Clarify your negative predictions by putting them into words
- Get a more objective perspective by tracking how your predictions affect you, as well as whether or not they come true

Estimated time: 10–20 minutes

Start putting words to your worries. Think about worries you have about what will happen with your work, family, friends, health, personal or professional development, or any other aspect of your life. Consider both short-term predictions (about what will happen in the next few days, weeks, or months) and longer-term predictions (about the more distant future).

For each worry, ask yourself:

- What exactly am I predicting will happen?
- How certain am I of this prediction, on a scale from 1 (not at all certain) to 10 (absolutely positive)?
- How has this prediction been affecting my thoughts, feelings, and actions (including both what I do and what I don't do)?

Write down your answers and come back to them later, after the event you predicted either happens or doesn't happen. Then ask yourself:

- Did my prediction come true?
- Have the effects of my prediction on my thoughts, feelings, and actions been helpful?

It may help to record your responses in the form of a table. (See Table 5-1.)

Table 5-1. Tracking Fears and Realities

Prediction	Level of Certainty	Effects on My Thoughts, Feelings, and Actions	Did It Come True?	Have the Effects Been Helpful?
When our company lease comes up for renewal, the landlord will raise the rent by 10% or more.	7	• Thoughts: Mentally rehearse arguments with landlord • Feelings: Anxiety, anger • Actions: Stay up late worrying about finances, call around about other office spaces	Yes	Learning about other office spaces: helpful Other effects: not helpful
The dinner party next Friday will be boring.	8	• Thoughts: Imagine the boring party, plan excuses for leaving early • Feelings: Irritation, helplessness • Actions: Complain to colleagues and family about the party	No	No

Variation A: Instead of coming up with many predictions in one sitting, keep a running list. Each day, list any predictions you've made in the past 24 hours, together with your level of certainty about them and the effects they're having on you. Also note any past predictions that have come true, or failed to come true, during that time. Ask yourself whether the effects of those predictions have been helpful or unhelpful.

Variation B: Try a quick, simple version of this exercise. Don't worry about tracking your thoughts, feelings, and actions. Just list your negative predictions, your levels of certainty, and, when the time comes, whether or not each one came true.

Exercise 2: Your Habitual Response to Negative Predictions

Goal: Become aware of how you tend to respond to negative predictions
   and whether or not that response is useful
Estimated time: 5–10 minutes (at various times during your daily life)

Start noticing the situations where you hear other people making negative predictions. You might find that you hear them most from particular individuals, such as a great-aunt who's always worried about her health, or a neighbor who seems to worry about everything. There might be certain work contexts—perhaps a monthly budget meeting, or even every meeting—where the atmosphere tends to be filled with a sense of apprehension or doom.

What is your instinctive reaction in these circumstances? Do you agree and join in the catastrophizing? Do you give reassurance that everything will be okay? Do you just feel hopeless and shut down? Or is there something else you do or say? Noticing what you habitually do is the first step to being able to do something different.

Try keeping a record of your responses. For each prediction you hear, make a note of how you felt, what you did or said, and how the other person or people responded to you. (See Table 5-2.)

Table 5-2. Responses to Predictions

Prediction I Heard	How I Felt	What I Did or Said	How Other(s) Responded to Me
I know I'll get a bad grade on this exam.	Concerned	You'll do great. (Positive prediction)	Arguing

Intermediate Training:
Deepening Your Negative Prediction Savvy

Exercise 3: The Experience of Predicting, Fact-Finding, and Proposing ∞

Goal: Notice any emotional shifts that occur when you move from predicting the future to finding facts and making proposals
Estimated time: 15–20 minutes

In this exercise, we ask you to make negative predictions on purpose, and then switch to using other types of communication. Team up with a partner, pick a situation you're worried about, and go through the following steps:

1. **Predictions**
   - Make negative predictions about the situation for one minute, while your partner listens.
   - Talk with your partner about how your predictions affected both your emotional state and their emotional state.

2. **Facts**
   - State facts about the situation for one minute. Your partner listens and provides coaching if they notice you making predictions instead of stating facts.
   - Talk with your partner about the effects on your emotions.

3. **Proposals**
   - Generate at least five proposals for what you could do in this situation, while your partner listens and provides coaching if they notice any predictions.
   - Talk with your partner about the effects on your emotions.

4. **Debriefing**
   - Talk with your partner about any similarities and differences in your experiences of the three types of communication.

At the end, switch roles, so your partner tries the three types of communication while you listen and provide coaching.

Exercise 4: Reasons and Remedies

Goals:
- Gain insight into specific factors that contributed to past negative experiences
- Practice strategies to minimize the chances of similar bad experiences happening in the future

Estimated time: 8–15 minutes

Go through three steps:

1. Think of a previous bad experience that you're afraid might happen again in the future.
2. Write down as many factors as you can think of that may have contributed to the past negative outcome.
3. Pick one or two of those factors that you can control or influence in some way, and brainstorm strategies for making a positive change.

Repeat this exercise several times with different negative experiences from the past.

Variation: Work together with a partner who can brainstorm with you.

Exercise 4 Example

1. **Bad experience from the past.** The last time I presented a proposal to a client company, several individuals asked challenging questions that I wasn't expecting. I got flustered, stammered, and left feeling humiliated.
2. **Contributing factors.** Not finishing the proposal until the previous day; general anxiety about public speaking; mind-reads that people at that company don't respect me; not being prepared to answer those specific questions; not fully understanding the questions.
3. **Two factors I can influence.** (1) Anxiety—I can take the public speaking training our company offers and also build my confidence by practicing future presentations ahead of time with a colleague I trust. Working together, we can think about possible questions that people might raise and then practice how I'd answer them. (2) Understanding the questions—If I'm not sure whether I understand a question, I can ask the person for clarification before I give an answer.

Advanced Training: Preparing to Apply
the Full Negative Prediction Strategies

Exercise 5: Transforming Your Negative Predictions ∞

Goal: Build skill at transforming your negative predictions into more constructive forms of communication

Estimated time: 15–20 minutes

Think of a negative prediction that's worrying you, and find a partner to help you work through it. That person has two responsibilities:

1. Asking you the questions in the sidebar "Questions to Undo Another Person's Negative Predictions," on page 109, to prompt you to gather facts and engage in planning
2. Helping you stay on track (for instance, making sure you're sticking to facts, rather than assumptions, and keeping an eye out for facts that you might be overlooking)

Your job is to thoughtfully answer the questions.

When you're finished, talk with your partner about your experience. Did you think or feel differently about your negative prediction after answering this series of questions? What might you do differently in the future, as a result of going through this process? Then switch roles, so you coach your partner through transforming one of their negative predictions. Repeat the exercise as often as you like.

Variation: Do this exercise on your own, asking yourself the list of questions.

Want to learn more? Try more exercises at CTsavvy.com/NPexercises, plus the awareness quiz at CTsavvy.com/NPquiz.

6

Question Traps

The only thing more dramatic than Ricardo Garza's rise to success and influence was the speed with which it all seemed to be falling apart. Ricardo had been the pride of the HG Biotech sales division, a superstar with an entrepreneurial spirit, keen intuition, and a wealth of creative ideas. Given his outstanding performance as an account executive in Latin America, he'd been the natural choice to lead the company's push to develop a major new market in Europe. He was quickly promoted to sales director and charged with assembling a team to manage this initiative.

At first, there was every indication that Ricardo would excel in his new role. His reputation and charisma helped him attract an impressive group of talented, independent-minded managers—entrepreneurial mavericks much like himself. These executives respected Ricardo's accomplishments and also liked him as a person. Some considered him a friend. Together, they should have made an unstoppable team. None of them would have imagined that after just six weeks, more than half the group would be threatening to quit, placing the whole initiative (not to mention Ricardo's career) in jeopardy.

What went wrong? To Ricardo, it seemed clear that the managers he'd hired were unwilling to accept direction from him. It's not that he was looking for blind followers; on the contrary, he'd made it clear to the team that he valued everyone's input and wanted an open dialogue. However, he did need some cooperation in order to get things done, and all these people did was argue with him. The managers themselves saw the situation quite differently. While they still liked Ricardo personally, they experienced him as a dominating and controlling leader. In theory he might want collaboration, but in practice he just pushed through his own agenda.

Knowing that something needed to change, and change quickly, Ricardo called in Claude Marchessault, a leadership coach who'd worked with other executives in the company. When Claude sat in on one of the team's meetings, he saw exactly how they were getting derailed.

For the first 15 minutes, Ricardo was the only one who spoke. Prior to the meeting, he had drawn up a diagram showing several different market segments, together with strategic business alliances the team was developing in those areas. Now he circled a spot on the diagram, saying, "This is where our main focus needs to be, yes?" After a momentary pause, he went on, "Here's what's happening with these customers. . . ." Ricardo proceeded to give a detailed analysis, stopping periodically to ask, "Isn't that right?" Primarily he addressed the group as a whole, but every so often he'd turn to one individual and ask, "Don't you think?" or "Wouldn't you agree?" Receiving no response, he'd say, "Okay, then" and continue talking.

Only when Ricardo had finished and sat down did the other team members speak up. All of their comments pointed out problems with what their leader had said: "That's what we thought a week ago, but it's not quite accurate." "Sure, you've identified one important point of focus, but there are several others you haven't considered." "What you're saying applies to our traditional alliances, but some of our new partnerships don't fit that mold."

As Claude observed these interactions, it was easy to see why the managers saw Ricardo as domineering, as well as why he saw them as rejecting his leadership. It was also easy to see which dysfunctional communication pattern lay at the root of their problems.

Communication Challenge 4: Leading Questions—a Question and Answer All Rolled into One

Alert readers who remember the lessons of Chapter 3 may have recognized what the managers did to contribute to the communication breakdown: they were all yes-butting. But what was it that triggered this arguing? What was their leader doing?

What Ricardo Garza intended to do was facilitate an open dialogue. Often a good way to do that is to ask questions, and he did ask quite a few. The problem was the types of questions he asked: "Yes?" "Isn't that right?"

"Don't you agree?" All of these questions encourage competition, rather than collaboration, because all of them are *leading*.

Many people find leading questions extremely frustrating. When someone uses this type of communication, they're doing two different things at once: giving their own opinion and asking you for a response. The "right" or expected response is to agree with their opinion. Suppose your aunt says, "Aren't these fruitcakes delicious?" Her opinion is "These fruitcakes are delicious," and the expected response is yes. Or maybe your manager says, "It won't be a problem for you to work overtime today, will it?" Clearly the expected response is no.

Leading questions have two components embedded within them:

- An opinion
- A question

The opinion makes it clear what the "right" response to the question is.

Being asked a leading question puts you in a bind. If you give the "right" answer, you may feel like you've been coerced or manipulated, even if that answer was truthful. Even if you don't mind working overtime, you may still resent the way your boss asked you about it. The other option is to give the "wrong," unexpected answer ("Actually, I think this cake is too dry" or "Yes, working overtime would be a problem"). This might feel risky. You might believe that the person doesn't really want an honest answer, or that they can't hear it without getting angry, offended, disappointed, or defensive. And you might be right.

In addition to the problems they create on the receiving end, leading questions also cause trouble for the people who use them. Typically this type of communication happens unconsciously. In our training and coaching, we hear a lot of people use leading questions, and in almost every case, they have no idea they're doing it. Often they sincerely want an honest response, and they're dismayed to realize that people feel pressured to agree with them. This type of pressure tends to provoke one of two opposing reactions: defiance or compliance. The managers in our opening story became defiant, asserting their divergent viewpoints with yes-buts. A compliant response—agreeing inauthentically, because that's what seems to be expected—can be even more problematic.

The compliance elicited by leading questions may be particularly damaging for individuals in leadership positions, who are already at risk of not getting truthful information. As the authors of *Primal Leadership* explain, high-level leaders are often subject to *CEO disease*: "the information vacuum around a leader created when people withhold important (and usually unpleasant) information."[1] Business leaders can be intimidating, simply because of their position and power (including their power over the jobs of their employees). It's no wonder people are afraid to disappoint or upset them. This same effect can happen in any situation where one person has more power or authority than the other—for example, with a doctor and patient, parent and child, or teacher and student.

Leading questions exacerbate this problem. Imagine that a CEO asks his manufacturing team, "You're all set to meet this customer's deadline, right?" Who wants to be the one to say, "No, we're running three weeks behind"? If nobody has the nerve to give the "wrong" answer, there may be serious negative consequences for the team, the customer, the leader, and the organization as a whole.

The combination of leading questions and compliance masks conflicts rather than resolving them. In the short term, the communication may seem highly efficient—people reach decisions quickly, without any debates or disagreements. The problem is that if those decisions aren't based on reality, they're not sustainable over the long term. They may also generate resentment, leading to a lack of follow-through or even outright sabotage of supposedly agreed-upon ideas. Leaders who mistake forced agreement for true consensus may get a nasty shock when the plans they pushed through start falling to pieces.

One final drawback of compelling agreement through leading questions is that it discourages innovation and imagination. When you block the free flow of ideas, it's difficult for new, creative solutions to emerge.

Although leading questions are generally counterproductive, in some situations they serve an important purpose. One clear example is legal cross-examination. Think of the courtroom dialogue in *Perry Mason*, *Law and Order*, and other legal dramas. Hostile witnesses frequently face aggressive barrages of questions, like "Isn't it true that Mrs. Jones filed for a restraining order against you? Isn't it true that you wanted her dead?

You went to her house that night, didn't you?" In this situation, leading questions suit the lawyer's purpose perfectly. The implied "right" answer is exactly what they want the jury to hear.

Don't All Questions Lead?

The short answer is yes. To some extent, all questions lead by pointing in a certain direction. You can think of a question as a funnel, channeling information into a conversation. Different types of questions (see the following sidebar) create different types of funnels.

Four Types of Questions

The questions that people ask fall into four general categories.[2] Only the first two (broad and narrow) serve the real purpose of a question: asking for new information. The other two (leading and righteous) take the form of a question but have entirely different effects on a conversation.

1. **Broad questions.** Open-ended questions that invite others' thoughts, conclusions, opinions, or proposals.
   What's the best way to reduce our debt? How do you think we should respond to this applicant? How should we spend our next vacation? Why do you think those problems keep happening? Where could we find the money to fund this program?

2. **Narrow questions.** Direct, specific questions asking for facts or for yes/no or either/or answers.
   Do you think this is a good idea? Is it shorter to go by Route 1 or the turnpike? Which of these two products is cheaper to produce? How many people will be in the class? Who was the seventh president of the United States?

3. **Leading questions.** Opinions in question form, implicitly seeking agreement rather than new information—or, in some cases, seeking no answer at all.
   Isn't this a great plan? It's really hot today, isn't it? Do you really think that? Don't you think he's the best candidate? Wouldn't you rather have breakfast before we go out?

4. **Righteous questions.** Attacks in question form, expressing blame, indignation, or outrage.
   Do you think I like working day and night? Do you ever think of anyone but yourself? Does he have any idea how stupid he sounds? What's the matter with you?! What were you thinking?!

The largest possible funnel is a broad question. If you ask your coworker, "What are your thoughts about the upcoming merger?" you're defining the topic of discussion (the merger), but you aren't putting any limits on what they might say about that topic. Even the somewhat narrower question "What do you think is the greatest challenge we face with the merger?" is still broad, since there are any number of opinions the person could give in reply.

A narrow question such as "Do you think the merger is a good idea?" or "When will the merger be announced publicly?" provides a much smaller funnel. The possible answers are now strictly limited—in these cases, to either yes or no, or to an isolated piece of data. With a leading question, the funnel is even smaller. When you ask, "Aren't you nervous about the merger?" or "Don't you think it's a good move for the company?" you leave room for only one acceptable answer: agreeing with you. (The alternative is to disagree and risk a confrontation.) With some leading questions and all righteous questions (like "Can you believe they let this happen?!"), you're not asking for an answer at all. Essentially, the funnel is completely blocked.

The ability to use questions to set the direction of a conversation is an essential leadership skill. For instance, if you're trying to encourage people to think creatively and generate new ideas, you'll want to use plenty of broad questions. If you're trying to pin down specific pieces of data, you'll want to use narrow questions. And most of the time, if you want to get an honest, straightforward answer, you'll want to avoid asking questions that are leading or righteous.

The Upshot: While broad and narrow questions play a useful, important role in many conversations, leading questions often don't get genuine answers and frequently cause trouble.

Skills for Managing Leading Questions

So far we've primarily been focusing on the effects of leading questions in professional contexts. However, this type of communication is just as powerful, and just as damaging, in personal relationships. Wherever you encounter leading questions, whether at work, at home, or in other areas of your life, you'll find skills in this section to help encourage a more open dialogue.

Transformation Skill:
Taking the Push Out of Your Questions

All of us ask questions, and all of us sometimes fail to get accurate information. Often the most important information we can receive is something we don't want to hear: a disagreement with our ideas, challenge to our perspective, or objection to our plans. If you find that you frequently don't get that type of information, the strategies we're about to describe may be important for you to learn.

Transformation Step 1: Self-Awareness

To stop yourself from asking leading questions, you first need to have an awareness of them. Read through the "Spotting Leading Questions" sidebar on the next page and see if you recognize any expressions that you tend to use (like "Don't you think?" or "Wouldn't you say?" or "Right?"). If you're not sure, we recommend that you ask someone who's close to you and whom you trust to tell you the truth—someone who isn't reluctant to give you difficult feedback (as a subordinate employee might be).

For instance, you might ask a coworker, "When I ask for your reactions to my ideas, do you feel like I'm open to hearing your opinions, or do you feel pressure to agree with me?" Or you might ask your spouse, "When we're making plans and I ask what you want to do, do I come across as really wanting to hear your answer? Does it ever feel like I just want you to do what I want to do?" Be sure to avoid asking leading questions such as "You tell me the truth, don't you?" or "I don't pressure you, do I?"

If you learn that you do come across as leading, ask what you do to give that impression. What words do you typically use? Also, you can invite the person to speak up in the future when they hear you use a leading question. You'll probably find that it's easier for somebody else to notice how you're communicating than for you to notice it yourself. (Just be careful not to get defensive or hostile, punishing the person for doing what you asked.)

Children tend to have great radar for this type of communication. If you have a child old enough to understand the concept of leading questions, try making them an offer: every time they catch you using one, you'll give them a quarter or some other reward. Kids usually jump at the chance to point out their parents' mistakes. As a side benefit, they wind up with useful knowledge about effective communication. Some of the people we've coached have been amazed at how much they've learned in this way (not to mention how many rewards they've had to hand over!).

No matter whom you enlist to help build your awareness, you'll gradually get better at noticing your own leading questions. Eventually you'll reach the point where you can stop yourself before you use one and try a new approach.

Spotting Leading Questions

There are several identifying features that can help you spot leading questions.

Aren't, Don't, Isn't, and Other Leading Lead-Ins

The most obvious giveaway that a question is leading is that it starts with a negative contraction like *aren't, don't, isn't, can't, won't*, or *wouldn't*: "Don't you just love this dress?" "Can't you come a little early?" "Won't it get too cold?" Sometimes negative contractions come at the end of sentences, in little mini-questions like "Isn't it?" or "Wouldn't you say?" These transform simple statements of opinion into leading questions: "The president made a great point, don't you think?" "We should buy now, shouldn't we?"

Right?

An even shorter version of the mini-question is simply saying, "Right?" or "Yes?" For instance: "You're on top of this, yes?" "He's the most qualified candidate, right?"

Really, Truly, Honestly

In a subtler form of leading question, the asker's opinion comes out through words like *really, truly,* or *honestly:* "Do you *really* think people will buy that product?" "Is that *truly* what you want?" "Do you *honestly* believe John will follow through this time?" It's obvious to the listener what the "right" answer is ("No, I don't think people will buy that product," "No, that isn't what I want," "No, I don't believe John will follow through").

Transformation Step 2:
Action—Separate Your Opinion from Your Question

The first challenge in rephrasing a leading question is figuring out what you want to communicate. Remember that a leading question combines two separate components: an opinion and a question. You may want to state both of these, or just one or the other.

Sometimes, when the stakes are low and you don't need anyone else's feedback, you might want to give only your opinion: "I think the landscapers did a nice job." "I thought the acting in that play was great." "I think I look better with short hair." At other times, you might want to follow your opinion with a request for the other person's perspective. You can do this using either a broad question ("I think this cherry pie is delicious. What do you think?") or a narrow question ("I think the first offer sounds like the best deal. Do you agree?").

Both of those options are less problematic than asking a leading question (like "Don't you think the first offer sounds best?"). However, if you're looking for an entirely unbiased response, we recommend leaving out your opinion and moving straight to a question. After you've told somebody what you think, they may feel uncomfortable expressing a different opinion. This is particularly true in situations where your opinion holds a lot of weight. If you tell someone who reports to you that you like the first offer, they may be hesitant to tell you they prefer the third one. You're better off asking, "Which of these offers do you think sounds best?" (narrow question) or "What are your reactions to these offers?" (broad question).

Table 6-1 gives five different examples of leading questions and options for rephrasing them in the form of opinions, narrow questions, and broad questions. The options you choose may vary depending on the context, the

Table 6-1. Sample Wording for Rephrasing Leading Questions

Leading question 1: Wouldn't it be great to hold the leadership retreat at my beach house?
Opinion: I think it would be great to hold the leadership retreat at my beach house.
Follow-up question: Do you agree? or What are your thoughts?
Narrow question: Do you think it's a good idea to hold the leadership retreat at my beach house?
Broad question: Where do you think we should hold the leadership retreat?
Leading question 2: Our new website is too complicated, isn't it?
Opinion: I think our new website is too complicated.
Follow-up question: Do you agree or disagree? or What do you think?
Narrow question: Do you think our new website is too complicated, too simple, or just right?
Broad question: What do you think about our new website?
Leading question 3: This medication has been working well for you, hasn't it?
Opinion: From looking at your chart, it seems like this medication has been working well for you.
Follow-up question: Is that right? or Is there anything I'm missing?
Narrow question: Is this medication working well for you?
Broad question: How is this medication working for you?
Leading question 4: You'll visit us over the holidays, won't you?
Opinion: It would be great to have you visit us over the holidays.
Follow-up question: Would that work with your schedule?
Narrow question: Are you planning to come visit over the holidays?
Broad question: What are your plans for the holidays?
Leading question 5: You're not planning to wear that shirt to Grandma's party, are you?
Opinion: I think it would be nice if you wore a dress shirt to Grandma's party.
Follow-up question: Do you have a clean dress shirt you could wear? or What do you think?
Narrow question: Are you planning to change your shirt before Grandma's party?
Broad question: What are you planning to wear to Grandma's party?

person you're talking to, the subject you're talking about, and your own personal preferences.

By transforming his leading questions, Ricardo Garza helped to rescue his sales team from the brink of collapse. When coach Claude Marchessault described the communication pattern he'd observed, Ricardo was able to see how his own behavior had fostered conflict rather than open dialogue.

He was eager to try a new strategy. What would work best, he concluded, was to first state his opinion and then ask a broad question like, "What's your thinking on this?" or "Does anyone have a different opinion?" or "Do you have anything else to add?"

At Ricardo's invitation, Claude also did some coaching with the group as a whole. The managers realized that they'd been reacting more to the way their leader was talking than to the content of what he was saying. In fact, even in their yes-butting, they rarely disagreed with what he said; they were just bringing in new information that he didn't have. After Ricardo made a commitment to asking broad questions rather than leading questions, the managers committed to stating their ideas without the "buts" that made them sound like objections or criticism.

This relatively simple change, from leading questions and yes-buts to broad questions and straightforward answers, made a tremendous difference for the group. Freed from the frustration caused by their dysfunctional communication, they were able to focus their energy on what they did best: market analysis and sales strategizing. They began to live up to their potential as a group, developing into a high-performance team that capitalized fully on the knowledge and skills of all its members.

The Upshot: By separating your leading question into two parts, your opinion and your question, you greatly increase the chances that one or both of those messages will get heard—which in turn makes it much more likely that you'll achieve the result you want.

Before we conclude this section, we want to offer one note of caution: while Ricardo experienced no significant downside to transforming his leading questions, that isn't always the case. When you make the shift to asking direct broad or narrow questions, you need to be prepared to hear answers that you might not like. In our experience, most people prefer to face reality by getting honest answers rather than being surrounded by yes-men (or yes-women). Still, it can be distressing to learn that other people don't agree with you, particularly if you've been assuming that they do. If you don't feel ready to hear the truth about a particular issue and you don't have a compelling reason to ask for it, you can always decide to not ask a question at all.

Transformation Step 3: Practice

If you'd like to get started practicing skills to transform your leading questions, skip ahead to the exercises starting on page 137.

Response Skill: What to Do When Questions Lead You

When someone asks you a leading question, it may seem as though there's no good response—you can either give in and agree or disagree and risk starting a conflict. Fortunately, there are strategies you can use to get out of that bind.

Response Step 1: Awareness

After reading our descriptions of leading questions, you may already have begun thinking of situations where you hear a lot of them. You may recognize phrases like "Don't you think" or "Can't we" as something that your friend, child, or boss always tends to say. If you haven't thought of any examples yet, try doing that now. Think back to past situations where you've felt pressured to agree with someone, or said yes when you really wanted to say no. See if you can identify the particular comments that have made you uncomfortable. Do they include leading questions? **To practice recognizing leading questions, visit CTsavvy.com/LQquiz.**

You might also begin to notice leading questions in the media—in movies, advertisements, and television and radio shows. Many ads and marketing materials are full of leading questions: "Aren't you tired of paying high prices?" "Wouldn't it be great to have silky smooth hair?" "Don't you want to meet the woman of your dreams?"

Pay attention not only to how those questions are phrased but also to how you habitually respond. When you hear a leading question in an ad or a political argument, does it sound persuasive to you or just annoying or manipulative? When people in your life ask you leading questions, are you more inclined to agree or disagree with what they say? Different people have different tendencies. Some automatically agree, even if that agreement isn't sincere, while others automatically disagree.

Seeing Pushy Questions, Not Pushy People
Throughout this book, we've encouraged you to focus on people's behaviors (what they say and how they say it) rather than on what's happening inside them (their motivations, intentions, or personality traits). When

somebody uses leading questions, it can be easy to see them as being pushy, closed-minded, or domineering. If you don't respond effectively, you might also start seeing yourself as a pushover or helpless victim. Shifting your attention to behavior provides a more constructive perspective.

One of our coaching clients (Susan) used this perspective to help work through a family conflict. At the time, she was seven months pregnant and living with her husband in a two-bedroom condominium in the Boston area. For the past several years, Susan's younger cousin Anne had come to stay at the condo whenever she visited the city. Anne had several close friends in Boston, but they all had tiny apartments with no room for her to stay.

Susan assumed her cousin knew that this arrangement would have to change. They had talked weeks ago about her plans to convert the guest room into a nursery, and she couldn't imagine handling both an infant and a houseguest. As a result, she was taken aback during their next phone call when Anne said, "This doesn't mean I can't visit, does it? I'll still be able to stay with you, right?" As Susan struggled to think of a response, Anne continued, "I'm happy to sleep on the couch, and I can help out with the baby. Won't that be fun?" Susan stammered a noncommittal reply and got off the phone feeling anxious and angry.

When Susan first talked to us, she described the issue as a personality problem: her cousin was pushy and insensitive. She was also mad at herself for not being assertive enough to set a clear boundary. Changing focus from people to behavior made a big difference for her. Once she recognized that Anne had asked leading questions, which always put the listener in a bind, she understood why she'd had so much trouble responding. This helped her to stop being so hard on herself. It also helped to diminish her anger at Anne. She could see her cousin's behavior as reflecting a lack of communication skill rather than bad intentions or a flawed personality.

As Susan prepared for their next conversation, she no longer felt an impulse to make Anne realize she was wrong ("You just don't understand what it means to have a baby"). Instead, she decided to describe the problem as a simple misunderstanding ("It sounds like we have different expectations about what will happen once the baby is born").

Susan's awareness of leading questions soon paid off in another, unexpected way. She became skilled at detecting this sort of communication, and in our next coaching session, she reported a revelation. After an argument with her husband, she realized that what had started the conflict was a series of leading questions. This time, though, the questions weren't directed at her. She was the one who had asked them all.

Response Step 2: Action—Reframe, Reflect, and Respond

Earlier in this chapter, you learned to rephrase your own leading question by separating your opinion from your question. When someone else asks you a leading question, you can help them make that same separation. Figure out how to reframe their message—as an opinion, a question, or both—and then reflect it back with a paraphrase. This gives you the power to choose which part of the message to focus on.

Suppose you tell your doctor that you'd like to try switching to a new medication and she says, "Don't you think you should wait a few weeks?" Here are three different ways to reframe and reflect that leading question:

1. **Focus on the opinion.** Paraphrase the person's opinion, and then check your understanding: "It sounds like you think I should wait a few weeks. Is that right?"
2. **Focus on the question.** Paraphrase the question, and then check your understanding: "You want to know if I think it's better to wait a few weeks. Is that right?"
3. **Focus on the opinion and the question.** Paraphrase both the opinion and the question, and then check your understanding: "It sounds like you think I should wait a few weeks, and you want to know whether I agree. Is that right?"

What you do from that point on is up to you. If you've brought attention to the person's question (with option 2 or 3), you'll probably want to respond to it in some way. You can either answer it directly ("I'd prefer not to wait") or else explain why you're not answering it ("I don't know enough yet to answer that question" or "I want to hear your thoughts before I make a decision"). If you've focused only on their opinion (option 1), you don't need to share your own opinion at all. Instead, if you'd like, you could ask them to clarify their perspective ("Could you tell me why you think that?").

> **The Upshot:** Although a leading question puts you in a bind, you have the power to get out of that bind by choosing which part of the message you reflect and respond to.

What if This Strategy Doesn't Work?

There may be times when you diligently attempt each variation of this strategy but get only negative reactions. For example, in talking with your boss, no matter which part of her leading question you paraphrase, she immediately responds with hostility. The most likely cause is that you're not doing what you think you're doing. There are two common ways people go off the rails when they paraphrase:

1. **Negative emotions leak out.** If you feel anxious, defensive, or angry when you use this strategy, those feelings are probably leaking out in your voice tone. As a result, instead of giving a clear, neutral paraphrase, you're primarily communicating how upset or uncomfortable you are. This often provokes a strong negative reaction from other people.

   If you are feeling reactive, notice whether you have any mind-reads (such as "She doesn't want to know what I really think") or negative predictions ("If I answer truthfully, she'll get angry"). Recognize that these are products of your own thinking, not facts about reality. You might review the steps of the transformation strategies described in Chapter 4 and Chapter 5 to help challenge your assumptions.

   We also strongly recommend practicing the strategy with people you feel comfortable with (such as close friends or family members) before trying it with someone who poses more of a risk (such as your supervisor or a major client). Until you've had some practice, any new strategy is likely to feel a little awkward, which can make you sound nervous or unsure.

2. **The paraphrasing sounds artificial or mechanical.** For your paraphrase to be useful, you need to demonstrate that you understood the other person's message, not just that you heard the words they said. In some situations, it's more effective to rephrase someone's idea in your own words rather than repeating exactly what you heard. Particularly when you're new to this skill, a word-for-word paraphrase may end up sounding like robotic parroting, which can annoy people.

   If you find that people get annoyed when you paraphrase them, get more practice before you try again. Work through some of the exercises in the training program that help build this skill, particularly Exercise 3 (page 139). You may find it useful to work with a mentor or coach who can give you feedback on how you're coming across.

Response Step 3: Practice

Just reading about how to respond to leading questions is no guarantee that you'll act differently the next time you hear one. It takes practice to use this strategy effectively. If you're ready to start, skip ahead to the exercise section starting on page 137.

Intervention Skill: Turning Around Other Conversations When You Hear Leading Questions

The leading questions in your own conversations aren't the only ones that can have an impact on you. If one of your employees uses them with their staff, there may be repercussions for your company. If your spouse uses them with your children, there may be repercussions for your family. If you do mediation, facilitation, or counseling work with couples or groups, your clients' leading questions may affect their ability to make decisions and resolve conflicts. For people who encounter these situations frequently, the ability to skillfully intervene can be invaluable.

Intervention Step 1: Awareness

Once you're able to identify leading questions when they're directed at you, you shouldn't have too much trouble noticing them in other situations. If you don't immediately recognize the phrasing (hearing a "Wouldn't you agree" or "Isn't it true"), your first clue might be a general impression. For instance, as you're observing a meeting, you might become aware of a vague sense of discomfort or unease. You might begin to view the leader as domineering and observe that nobody raises any objections to her ideas. Whenever you suspect that people are saying yes when they mean no, try to notice the types of questions that are being asked.

Intervention Step 2: Action—Refocus and Invite Reframing

In the response strategy section, we showed you one way to help separate the two parts of someone's leading question: paraphrase the opinion, the question, or both. This is a fairly indirect method. Since your purpose is to improve the conversation, not to teach the other person something, there's no need to draw attention to how they're communicating; instead, you can keep the focus on the topic of discussion.

Here we're going to discuss a more direct intervention you can use if you have permission or authority to be in a teaching or coaching role. When you hear someone ask another person a leading question, you can refocus the discussion and invite them to reframe their ideas:

1. **Refocus.** Bring the person's awareness to their communication by pointing out that you hear two different things in what they're saying: an opinion and a question. Ask if they are aware of both of these parts. If they aren't, you might paraphrase each one, so it's clear what you're referring to.

2. **Invite reframing.** Ask them what they'd like to bring into the conversation—just their opinion, just their question, or both—then invite them to do that. If they want to say both their opinion and their question, ask them to give their opinion first. Listen carefully to their question, and give coaching if it comes out leading or unclear.

As an example, suppose you've been hired to do communication consulting with a group in a research lab. One of the senior researchers (Jeff) reports, "All the data right now support my original hypothesis," then says to a more junior colleague (Ellen), "You'd agree with that, right?" You might intervene and say, "I'm going to interrupt, Jeff. I'm hearing two things in what you're saying: an opinion and a question. Are you aware of both parts?" If he says yes, ask which of those he wants to bring into the conversation—the opinion, the question, or both. Wait for his answer, and then invite him to continue, providing coaching if he gets off track. (If he were to say no, you could provide a paraphrase: "Your opinion is that all the data support your hypothesis, and your question to Ellen is whether or not she agrees.")

This technique, working with a real leading question at the moment when it's asked, creates a powerful learning opportunity. However, it's a very direct approach and can feel confrontational, so we don't recommend using it outside of teaching or coaching contexts. Also, if there's any edge of judgment or irritation in your voice tone, the intervention can backfire and lead the other person to argue with you instead of learning from the experience. If you're not confident that you can stay neutral, calm, and nonjudgmental, steer clear of this strategy until you've had more practice.

One additional caution: whenever you help someone transform a question that's leading into one that's more direct, the result may be an answer that is unexpected and unwelcome. In our lab example, Ellen might say that her latest findings put Jeff's hypothesis in doubt, and as a result Jeff might get angry or defensive. Don't open the door to a potential conflict unless you're confident in your ability to turn it into a learning situation.

> **The Upshot:** Even if a leading question isn't directed at you, you can still use your skills to help diminish its negative effects on the conversation.

Intervention Step 3: Practice

These strategies aren't complex, but they're far from easy. We recommend getting as much practice as possible with the exercises that follow.

Exercises

Leading Questions Training Program: Taking the Pressure Off

If you've realized in the course of this chapter that you frequently ask leading questions, that revelation may have come as an unpleasant surprise. It can be upsetting to learn that you do something that inhibits open dialogue and makes it difficult for people to give you honest answers. However, we encourage you to see your new awareness as very good news. The more leading questions you use, the more you'll benefit from changing this one behavior. And while it always takes practice to change an old habit, the basic strategy for transforming leading questions is simple. In most cases, you'll still ask a question; all you need to do is replace one type of question with another. This single change can make a tremendous difference in your ability to get accurate information about what the people around you are thinking and feeling.

For general guidelines on how to get the most out of each training program, review "Training Program Guidelines" in Chapter 3, on page 47. Note that this icon—∞—marks exercises for which we strongly recommend working with a partner.

Basic Training: Building Awareness and Flexible Thinking

Exercise 1: Leading in Sales

Goal: Increase your ability to detect leading questions
Estimated time: 1–5 minutes (at various times during your daily life)

Now that you know more about leading questions, increase your awareness by seeing how many of them you can spot in your daily life. Pay particular attention in any situation where someone is trying to sell you something, whether it's a TV ad selling shampoo or a politician selling an idea. The use of leading questions to cross-examine a witness is another type of selling: selling an argument to a judge or a jury. Listen for these any time you watch a legal drama. Keep a running list of various leading questions you hear or read throughout the week.

Exercise 2: Question Dissection

Goals:
- Develop skill at discriminating between leading, narrow, and broad questions
- Develop skill at rephrasing leading questions as more effective forms of communication

Estimated time: 8–15 minutes

Read through the leading questions below, and rephrase each of them as (1) an opinion, (2) a narrow question, and (3) a broad question. You don't have to match the exact meaning of the original question or use the same words; just try to capture the general idea. We give our suggestions in "Exercise 2 Solutions" on page 143, at the end of the Exercises section. If you find it very easy to come up with opinions and narrow questions, feel free to skip right to the broad question.

1. Isn't this an interesting chapter?
2. Wouldn't it be best to get more opinions before making a decision?
3. You're not going to say that to him, are you?

4. Do you *really* believe you can finish preparing in three hours?
5. Don't you think that was a great movie?
6. There's no reason for production to be delayed, is there?
7. You don't see any problems with this exercise, do you?
8. Won't that be too expensive?
9. Do you *honestly* think the committee will approve your request?

Variation: Team up with a partner, first doing the exercise separately and then comparing and discussing your answers.

Exercise 2 Example

Aren't these beautiful flowers?
Opinion: I think these are beautiful flowers.
Narrow question: Do you like these flowers?
Broad question: What do you think about these flowers?

Intermediate Training:
Deepening Your Leading Question Savvy

Exercise 3: Paraphrase Practice ∞

Goals:
- Increase your ability to paraphrase ideas with accuracy and ease, in preparation for paraphrasing leading questions
- Experience the difference between a word-for-word paraphrase and one that's rephrased in the speaker's own words

Estimated time: 8–15 minutes

Together with a partner, go through the following steps:

1. Your partner states an opinion, preferably one that you strongly disagree with. The opinion can be on any subject—politics, religion, family or relationship issues, child-rearing, etc.
2. Paraphrase that opinion in two different ways:

   - Using the same words your partner used
   - Changing the words but keeping the meaning the same

3. Get feedback from your partner about how effective you were. Was each paraphrase both accurate (capturing the intended meaning) and sympathetic (conveying interest without any skepticism or negativity)? If not, keep trying until you're successful.
4. Talk with your partner about which version of the paraphrase each of you preferred, and why.
5. Switch roles, and repeat as often as you like.

Exercise 3 Examples

Example A

Opinion: President X did a great job managing the economy, considering the state it was in when he took office.

Paraphrase 1: You're saying President X did a great job managing the economy, considering the state it was in when he took office.

Paraphrase 2: You're saying that given how bad the economy was before, President X did really well at managing the situation.

Example B

Opinion: I think dogs make much better pets than cats, because they're more friendly to people.

Paraphrase 1: You think dogs make much better pets than cats, because they're more friendly to people.

Paraphrase 2: When it comes to pets, you really prefer dogs to cats because cats aren't very friendly.

Correction from partner: That's not quite right. Try again.

Paraphrase 2 (second try): When it comes to pets, you prefer dogs to cats because dogs are friendlier.

Exercise 4: Dissecting Real Questions ∞

Goals:
*   Increase your ability to rephrase leading questions from your own life as more effective forms of communication
*   Increase your ability to plan effective ways to ask others for their opinions

Estimated time: 10–30 minutes

This exercise is similar to Exercise 2, but this time you'll work with questions from your own life. Practice with a partner who can help you if you get stuck. There are three different versions of the exercise; you can choose to do all of them, or pick just one or two. Whichever version(s) you use, switch roles at the end so your partner gets a chance to practice, and repeat the activity as many times as feels useful.

Version 1: Your Leading Questions
1. Think of a leading question you've asked in the past, and tell it to your partner.
2. Rephrase the question as an opinion, a narrow question, and a broad question.
3. Talk with your partner about which type of communication each of you thinks would have worked best in your situation.

Version 2: Other People's Leading Questions
1. Think of a leading question that someone has asked you.
2. Rephrase that question as an opinion, a narrow question, and a broad question.
3. Talk with your partner about which type of phrasing each of you would have preferred to respond to.

Version 3: Questions You Haven't Asked Yet
1. Think of an issue that you'd like to get someone else's opinion on.
2. Come up with three different ways to ask for that opinion: a leading question, a narrow question, and a broad question.
3. Talk with your partner about which of these comes most naturally to you, and which one each of you thinks would be most useful.

Variation: Do this exercise on your own, writing your ideas down on paper.

Advanced Training: Preparing to Apply the Full Leading Question Strategies

Exercise 5: Responding to Leading Questions ∞

Goal: Build your skill at responding effectively to leading questions
Estimated time: 15–30 minutes

In this exercise, your partner asks you a leading question, and it's your job to respond. Think of a leading question that you've had trouble responding to in the past, and tell it to your partner. (If you can't think of one, use any leading question that you find challenging.) Then role-play the conversation in three different ways:

1. **Focus on the opinion.** Your partner asks you the leading question. You paraphrase the opinion embedded in the question, and then ask, "Is that right?" Wait for your partner's response.

2. **Focus on the question.** Your partner repeats the leading question. You paraphrase the embedded question and ask, "Is that right?" Wait for your partner's response, and then answer the question.

3. **Focus on both the opinion and the question.** Your partner repeats the leading question again. You paraphrase both the embedded opinion and the embedded question and ask, "Is that right?" Wait for your partner's response, and then answer the question.

Get your partner's feedback on how each of your responses comes across, and talk together about which one seems most effective. If you're not satisfied with any of your first attempts, keep trying until you can settle on a response you like. Then switch roles, so your partner gets a chance to practice. Repeat the exercise as often as you like, either in one sitting or over several days, weeks, or months. This activity can be challenging, so don't worry if it takes many tries for the new skills to start feeling natural to you.

Exercise 5 Example

Leading question: We all agree that Steve is the best candidate, right?

1. **Focus on the opinion.** I'm hearing that you feel we've come to consensus that Steve is the best candidate. Is that right? (Partner answers.)

2. **Focus on the question.** You're asking if we're all agreed that Steve is the best candidate. Is that right? (Partner answers.) Answer to the question: I don't think we're totally in agreement. Some people have expressed reservations that we haven't addressed yet.

3. **Focus on both the opinion and the question.** I'm hearing that you feel we've come to consensus that Steve is the best candidate, and you're asking if that's true. Is that right? (Partner answers.) Answer to the question: In fact, that's not true. Some people have expressed reservations that we haven't addressed yet.

Exercise 2 Solutions

The solutions given below aren't the only possibilities. There are a variety of equally good answers, so don't worry if the ones you came up with are different from ours.

1. **Isn't this an interesting chapter?**
   Opinion: I think this is an interesting chapter.
   Narrow question: Did you find this chapter interesting?
   Broad question: What's your reaction to this chapter?
2. **Wouldn't it be best to get more opinions before making a decision?**
   Opinion: I think it would be best to get more opinions before making a decision.
   Narrow question: Have you collected all the information you want to have before making a decision?
   Broad question: What kind of information do you think is most important for helping you make this decision?
3. **You're not going to say that to him, are you?**
   Opinion: I don't think you should say that to him.
   Narrow question: Are you planning to tell him that?
   Broad question: How are you planning to talk to him about this issue?
4. **Do you *really* believe you can finish preparing in three hours?**
   Opinion: I don't believe you can finish preparing in three hours.
   Narrow question: Have you done this type of preparation before in three hours?
   Broad question: How are you planning to use those three hours of preparation time?
5. **Don't you think that was a great movie?**
   Opinion: I think that was a great movie.
   Narrow question: Did you think that was a good movie?
   Broad question: What did you think about the movie?

6. **There's no reason for production to be delayed, is there?**
    Opinion: I don't think there's any reason for production to be delayed.
    Narrow question: Do you see any reasons for production to be delayed?
    Broad question: What factors might affect the production schedule?

7. **You don't see any problems with this exercise, do you?**
    Opinion: I don't think there are any problems with this exercise.
    Narrow question: Do you see any problems with this exercise?
    Broad question: What aspects of this exercise do you think are most effective and least effective?

8. **Won't that be too expensive?**
    Opinion: I think that will be too expensive.
    Narrow question: Is there money in our budget to cover that expense?
    Broad question: How can we arrange to cover that expense?

9. **Do you *honestly* think the committee will approve your request?**
    Opinion: I don't think the committee will approve your request.
    Narrow question: Are you confident about getting approval from the committee?
    Broad question: What factors do you think will encourage the committee to approve your request?

Want to learn more? Try more exercises at CTsavvy.com/LQexercises, plus the awareness quiz at CTsavvy.com/LQquiz.

7

Gripe Cycles

Five years after taking over the family business, Sarah and Theresa Banks were feeling totally overwhelmed. Their parents had run a clothing store together for two decades, and when they died—just three months apart—the sisters had been determined to keep the business in the family. Professionally, they'd been successful. While they'd never earned huge profits, they'd made a comfortable living despite tough economic conditions that forced many local stores to close. On a personal level, though, they were suffering.

In addition to being sisters, these women were also best friends. Both in their thirties, they shared a love of travel and the outdoors, and they often took long hiking trips together with a group of mutual friends. Or, rather, they *used* to take long hiking trips, before they took over the store. In recent years, neither of them had taken more than two days off at a time. They were just too busy working. By the time they called in a communications coach (coauthor Anita Simon), their business completely dominated their relationship. They no longer felt like close friends, just business partners. In Theresa's words, "We've always thought that being family helped our business to succeed. Now it feels like this business is causing our family—what's left of it—to fall apart."

The problem wasn't one of conflict. Unlike many family members who do business together, the sisters rarely fought. They were in perfect agreement on what their main problem was: working too much, without enough down time. They also seemed to agree on what they could do about it: nothing. As Anita listened to them talk, she got a clear picture of a bad situation they felt powerless to change.

"We're like an old married couple," said Sarah. "We don't do anything fun anymore."

"I know," said Theresa. "It's hard to see all our friends still out traveling, knowing we can't go with them."

Sarah sighed. "It seems like all we do is work. We're too young for this."

"I'm just so tired and overwhelmed. We put in so many hours that I don't have energy to do anything else. It's been months since I've done any of my artwork, or even read a book."

"I'm fed up with being in the store all the time," said Sarah, "but I know we have to be. And you work even more than I do."

"I know it's not good," said Theresa. "It's like we're trapped here. Sometimes I wish we didn't care about this stupid store. We could close up for a while and go away and just forget about it."

Sarah shook her head. "That will never happen," she said. "It just won't work."

Communication Challenge 5: Complaints

As you were reading through the dialogue between the two sisters, did the tone of their comments sound familiar to you? Did you recognize the hopeless, resigned, and frustrated feeling of the conversation as something you encounter in your own life and work? That sense of hopelessness is a defining feature of one of the most common unproductive forms of communication: complaints.

The main message coming through in complaints is that some aspect of our life is unfair, too much, or not enough, and there's nothing we can do about it. The voice tone is whining or frustrated, and sometimes resentful. We may complain about our work ("We never get anything done in these meetings"), our home life ("All I do all day is clean up after the kids"), traffic ("Driving in this city is such a nightmare"), the weather ("This heat is unbearable"), or anything else we don't like. When we complain, we're taking a passive role, talking as though we're helpless victims of our circumstances.

A few isolated complaints here and there are usually nothing to worry about; after griping for a little while, we refocus our energy to do something useful about whatever is bothering us. The real trouble begins when we move into a repetitive, self-perpetuating cycle of complaints, either on our own or together with somebody else. That's what happened with the sisters in our opening story—one complaint led to another, and then another, and another, reinforcing the sense of hopelessness and resignation.

Complaining Complaints versus Noncomplaining Complaints

The term *complaint* means different things in different contexts. In this book, we're using it to describe a frustrated or resentful way of talking about situations that feel unfair, overwhelming, or burdensome. This is quite different from other senses of the word, in particular formal complaints (official allegations of ethical or legal wrongdoing) and customer complaints (reports of specific problems with products or services). When people talk about someone *complaining*, the meaning they have in mind is usually the same as what we're discussing here. When they talk about *filing* or *reporting* a complaint, they're usually referring to neutral, factual statements, which are much more likely to communicate information effectively.

In some cases, more than one meaning applies. For instance, some customer complaints also meet our definition of a complaint. A customer at a restaurant might whine to the manager, "The service was so slow, we were absolutely starving, and now it's late and we have to pay our babysitter overtime," and so on. Note that the person could just as easily communicate their displeasure by giving a fact ("It took an hour for my food to arrive") or a feeling ("I feel really disappointed with my experience here").

Repeated complaining leads to two sets of problems: practical and emotional. The practical problem is that complaints act as a substitute for taking productive action. Expressing our displeasure in this way focuses our attention outward (on what's wrong with our situation) rather than inward (on what we might do to make things better). For instance, griping about how cold it is in your office doesn't get you any closer to turning up the heat or putting on a sweater.

There are also emotional consequences. Have you ever been in a group where everyone complains together for minutes or hours (or days or years) on end? Or listened to a friend go on and on about everything that's wrong with their job or their relationships? When a cycle of complaints gets going, the feeling of frustration and resignation can be highly contagious.

Partly as a result of this emotional contagion, it's hard to respond effectively to someone who's complaining. Complaints tend to elicit one of three unhelpful responses:

1. **Joining.** Getting drawn into the sense of hopelessness and adding to the ongoing litany of complaints ("I know, the working conditions are terrible here; they don't appreciate anything we do").
2. **Arguing.** Trying to change the other person's attitude by contradicting them ("It's really not that bad") or using yes-buts ("Sure we're in a tough situation, but it's bound to get better soon").
3. **Trying to help.** Attempting to solve the person's problem by proposing solutions ("You should talk to your manager" or "Why don't you raise the issue in our next meeting?").

The first response (joining) may give some satisfaction to the person who's complaining, at least at first. You're validating their point of view about how bad things are, and, as the saying goes, misery loves company. However, while complaining together can build a sense of solidarity and closeness, it also tends to reinforce feelings of helplessness and passivity. Joining in someone's complaints about a problem doesn't do anything to help solve it.

Arguing with the person isn't any more productive. When someone tells you things are bad, simply insisting that things aren't so bad is unlikely to be persuasive. Still, for many people, the most natural response to complaints is a yes-but or a contradiction. We sometimes see this in couples. Whenever one partner says, "We never get any fun time alone together," the other automatically says, "Sure we do" or "But we had fun at the party last weekend." At this point, the person with the complaint usually argues back—"You just don't get it" or "That's not the same"—and the argument continues on from there.

The third type of response (trying to help) may at first sound much more promising than the other two. It can seem like a constructive thing to do: when someone complains about a problem, you offer a helpful proposal to fix that problem. In reality, when a person is complaining, proposals from somebody else usually aren't helpful at all.

Remember that complaining is associated with a passive, victimized mindset, a sense that bad things are happening and there's nothing anyone can do to help. By suggesting that something *will* help, you're telling the person that they're wrong—which makes this response similar to the second one (arguing). Don't be surprised if you end up in an argument, as the other person feels compelled to convince you that the situation really is hopeless and all your suggestions are bound to fail. And they may have a point. Your suggestions may not be very useful. Since you're not the one with the problem, you're not in the best position to know how to solve it.

Meeting a complaint with a proposal often leads to a vicious cycle:

- "I'm so exhausted." (Complaint)
- "Why don't you stop and rest for a while?" (Proposal)
- "There's just so much I need to do." (Complaint)
- "How about resting for 10 minutes?" (Proposal)
- "I can never relax if I know I have to get right back up." (Complaint)
- And so on.

Notice that we can't blame the failure of this exchange just on the complaints or just on the proposals. Neither type of communication is inherently bad. The problem is the repeating, unproductive pattern that both speakers are contributing to (complaint-proposal-complaint-proposal). If this pattern continues, we can expect the two of them to grow increasingly frustrated. For the person making proposals, it's frustrating to keep making an effort to be helpful, only to have every well-intentioned suggestion get shot down. For the person complaining, it's frustrating to have someone keep talking as if they can solve the problem, while giving advice that doesn't actually help.

> **The Upshot:** Communicating in complaints tends to block problem solving, perpetuate a sense of hopelessness, and elicit responses from others that fail to help, or even make things worse.

The Secret to Understanding Complaints

Complaints are deceptive, diverting our attention from the true sources of trouble. When we hear a coworker griping about the delays in their production schedule, we tend to get focused on those delays. With the sisters in the opening story, it's tempting to get focused on the long hours they're spending at the store. But in order to really be helpful, we need to shift focus away from what's being complained about and back onto what's happening for the individual who's complaining. The secret to understanding complaints is recognizing two underlying issues: (1) the person wants something (which is often unclear, even to them), and (2) they feel powerless to get it.

> There are two issues underlying any complaint:
>
> 1.   The person wants something
> 2.   They feel powerless to get it

These same two issues are at the heart of any complaint, whether it's about work-related stress, chronic health problems, barking dogs, or ungrateful children. Until those issues get addressed, the odds are they'll keep generating more and more complaints. You'll learn strategies for addressing those issues effectively in the sections that follow.

Skills for Managing Complaints

Complaining is so common that you're bound to encounter it in some area of your life, whether or not you do it frequently yourself. The goal of managing this type of communication is not just to stop the complaints but to resolve the underlying issues that are driving them. The best way to start is to gain an understanding of your own complaints.

Transformation Skill: Shifting from Passivity to Action

Transforming your own complaints can bring significant payoffs, both emotionally (freeing you from feelings of frustration, resignation, and helplessness) and practically (helping you take action to change things that aren't working and get more of what you want).

Transformation Step 1: Self-Awareness

When you find yourself in a situation you don't like, do your thoughts tend to move toward complaining ("This is awful") or problem solving ("I wonder what I can do to make things better")? For many of us, complaining is the natural response. Challenge yourself to notice when you get caught up in complaints. Be alert for times when you feel discouraged or frustrated, and pay attention to how you're communicating, either out loud or in your thoughts to yourself. Is your tone of voice (or thought) whiny or resentful? Do your words imply that the bad situation is never going to change?

It might be easier for another person to notice what you're doing than for you to notice it yourself. Consider asking someone close to you to speak up (respectfully, of course) when they hear you complain. Ask for this feedback only if you really want to receive it, knowing that it might be difficult to hear. It can help to tell the person exactly what you'd like them to say (for instance, "I think that was a complaint").

Once you recognize that you're complaining, you have an opportunity to step back and change your mindset—realizing that before you solve your external problem (the hassles or stresses you're complaining about), you need to solve your communication problem (the way you're thinking and talking about your hassles or stresses). Specifically, you need to stop complaining and try doing something different, such as the strategy we're about to describe.

Transformation Step 2: Action—Asking Yourself What You Want, Then Asking How You Can Get It

Remember the two issues that underlie complaints? When you're complaining, there is (1) something that you want, together with (2) a sense of being helpless to get it. A powerful antidote is to ask yourself two questions: (1) "What do I want?" and (2) "What proposal can I make to help get that to happen?"

This strategy helps to shift your mindset from that of a victim to that of a problem solver. Finding out what you want replaces feelings of dissatisfaction or resentment with focus on a clear goal, and making proposals replaces passivity and helplessness with active effort. A natural side-effect of this process is an increase in hope: the sense that nothing can be done about a problem starts to dissolve when you begin actively doing something about that problem.

Strategy for Managing Complaints

- Ask yourself what you want
- Make a proposal for how to get it

Depending on the nature of your complaint, you may need to repeat the strategy several times before you find a solution that feels right (see the following sidebar). The idea is to persist for however long it takes to discover what you want and make a satisfying plan for achieving it. You may also find it helpful to have a friend walk you through the questions rather than just thinking them through yourself.

Tip of the Iceberg

Often we complain about trivial things that are merely the tip of a larger iceberg of irritation and distress. For this reason, when you start working through a complaint, it's likely that the first one or two wants you identify will be superficial. It may take a bit more digging to get to your true underlying hopes and desires.

For instance, say you're complaining about your commute. You might realize that you want to be able to avoid rush hour traffic by starting and ending work later (proposal: ask your supervisor if you can adjust your hours). On a deeper level, you might wish for more freedom in scheduling your time, so you don't need anyone's approval for the specific hours you work (proposal: talk to your supervisor about arranging a more flexible schedule). Going even deeper, you might discover that what you really want is greater autonomy to choose the projects you work on and the way that work gets done (proposal: explore the potential to transition to a different job). When you pursue a deep, thoughtful inquiry into what you want, minor complaints can sometimes lead to life-changing decisions that transform your life and work.

Once you start to transform your complaints, you might find that they stop draining your energy and begin to play a constructive role in your life. When you discover that you're complaining, take it as a cause for hope and even excitement. A complaint tells you that there's something you want, which means there's a chance you just might get it—making your life that much better than it was before. One woman we trained, an instructor in alternative health modalities, transformed her complaint "I never get to see my friends and family in Canada, except over Christmas when it's cold" into a want ("I want to visit Canada during the summer") and a proposal ("I'll look for opportunities to work in Canada during the summer"). As a result, she discovered several options for paid teaching engagements in Canada and now spends six weeks out of every year traveling, teaching, and visiting the people she cares about in her home country.

Table 7-1, on the following page, shows various examples of how complaints might get translated into wants and proposals.

Troubleshooting the Complaint Strategy

If your first attempts at using the complaint transformation strategy don't get you the results you want, check to see if one of the following factors is getting in your way:

- **You're focusing on others rather than yourself.**
  Problem: You can't think of any helpful proposals, because what you want depends on other people changing.
  Example: You've been complaining about the way your friend changes plans at the last minute. You want her to be more reliable, but you don't have the power to change her.
  Solution: Refocus on what you want for yourself, not what you want from anyone else. Ask yourself what would be different *for you* if the other person changed. What would you have then that you don't have now? And how could you find another way to achieve that same goal? In the situation with your friend, you might realize that your main goal is avoiding the disappointment of looking forward to going out and then ending up with nothing to do. One way to achieve that is to make backup plans of other fun things you can do if your friend cancels.
- **You have negative predictions or mind-reads.**
  Problem: You can think of a proposal but still feel helpless because you're sure that it won't work or that someone else doesn't like the idea.
  Example: You want a raise and realize you could ask for one, but you're certain your boss would say no because he thinks you haven't earned it. (See the sidebar on page 155 for a more detailed, real-life example.)

Table 7-1. Various Complaints Translated into Wants and Proposals

Complaint	Underlying Want	Possible Proposals
Our life is so boring. We just sit around and watch television every night.	I want to spend more time going out and having fun with you.	• Buy season tickets to a good theater. • Set aside one night every week to go out. • Ask to be included when friends with more active social lives make evening plans.
We never get anything done in these meetings.	I want to leave each meeting with a clear understanding of what we decided and what will happen next.	• Volunteer to lead a discussion at the end of every meeting to summarize the group's decisions and identify action steps. • Ask for advice from a colleague who runs effective meetings.
The work they have me doing is so mindless a robot could do it.	I want to do work that is meaningful to me.	• Volunteer to take on more challenging tasks. • Suggest alternative, more efficient ways to accomplish simple tasks. • Explore other job opportunities inside and/or outside your organization.
With all the construction going on, it's so noisy that it's impossible to work.	I want to be able to work without distractions.	• Buy a set of noise-cancelling headphones. • Make plans to work off-site or work during hours when there's no construction being done.
We have so much junk cluttering the counters that I can never find the bills and other important mail.	I want to be able to easily find important pieces of mail when I need them.	• Pick a location to file important mail that's separate from the rest of the mail and other pieces of paper. • Suggest setting aside time once a week for each person in the family to organize their mail and recycle anything they don't want.
All anyone does around here is complain.	I want my interactions with coworkers to leave me feeling better rather than worse.	• Use the strategy for transforming complaints to start complaining less. • Teach the strategy for transforming complaints to coworkers. • Use the strategy for responding to complaints (coming up in the next section).

Solution: Notice that you have a negative prediction or a mind-read (or possibly both). Remember that this is an assumption coming from your own thinking, not a fact about reality. If you have trouble believing that your assumption might not be true, try the full strategy for transforming negative predictions (see Chapter 5, page 99) or transforming mind-reads (Chapter 4, page 69).

Mind-Read and Negative Prediction Paralysis

Sometimes mind-reads and negative predictions prevent us from taking simple actions that could easily solve the problems we're complaining about. Our favorite example of this occurred in one of Anita's workshops. During lunch, a participant (Joan) had stopped at a nearby clothing store. After the workshop resumed, Joan realized she'd left her very expensive coat in the dressing room. "Oh no," she blurted out. "It's gone!" Anita asked what was wrong, and Joan explained. "Anybody could walk away with that coat," she said. "There's nothing I can do. By the time I go back, it will probably be gone."

Anita asked Joan if she could use this situation as a teaching example. When Joan agreed, Anita asked her what she wanted. "I want my coat," she answered. Anita then asked what she could propose that might help. Joan's first proposal was to stop thinking about it.

"Try again," Anita encouraged her. "Is there anything else you could do?" "Well," said Joan, "I guess I could go back and get my coat if it's still there. But I've already wasted class time talking about this, and everybody's getting irritated. Leaving now will make things worse." (Notice how her mind-read led to a negative prediction that discouraged her from taking action.)

Anita asked Joan to test her mind-read by getting data about what the other participants were actually thinking. As she did that, she was visibly moved to learn how far off-base she'd been. Not only were the other participants not mad; they were getting worried about her coat too. When Joan returned from the store 10 minutes later, coat in hand, they all cheered.[1]

- **You're focusing on superficial issues.**
  Problem: You come up with a proposal to solve your immediate problem but still don't feel hopeful about your situation as a whole.
  Example: You develop a plan to help your assistant minimize the errors in his reports, but this doesn't solve the larger problem of his failure to meet your expectations.
  Solution: Repeat the strategy. Ask yourself, beyond the original issue you identified, what do you really want to have happen? Then make a proposal for achieving that broader change. Continue to go deeper, coming up with wants and proposals again and again, until you feel satisfied with your results (for instance, until you feel that your proposal addresses the big picture of your assistant's performance).

You Can't Always Get What You Want, But if You Try the Complaint Strategy, You Just Might Find . . .

- You see the ways in which your own thinking has been holding you back
- You feel less helpless and more empowered to start making positive changes in your life
- There's more than one way to get what you really want and need

---

The Upshot: When you transform your complaints into actions, you greatly increase your chances of getting what you really want.

Transformation Step 3: Practice

We've told you a lot about the benefits of transforming your complaints into positive actions. If you'd like to start working toward that now, turn to the exercise section starting on page 163.

Response Skill: Responding to Other People's Complaints

How do you usually respond when somebody complains to you? Do you get irritated with them? Join in the complaining? Offer helpful suggestions?

Most people's habitual responses are not very useful. The good news is, you can apply what you've already learned about complaints to help make these conversations much more productive.

Response Step 1: Awareness

Complaints are one of the easiest types of communication to recognize. Often the first signal you'll get is a shift in your own frame of mind. As you listen to the other person complain, you might notice an impulse to help. When you see someone you care about having problems and you think of a solution they seem to have overlooked, the urge to share that solution can be almost irresistible. Alternatively, you might feel your energy start to wane or find yourself getting annoyed. For some people, hearing others complain is extremely irritating.

The clearest giveaway of a complaint is that the person's voice tone is whining or resigned, usually with a tinge of frustration or resentment. Another clue is the content of what's being said. A complaint focuses on a situation that seems wrong or unfair and impossible to change. **To practice recognizing complaints, visit CTsavvy.com/Cquiz.**

Response Step 2: Action—Asking What They Want, Then Asking How They Can Get It

Once you know how to transform your own complaints, you know how to help someone else transform theirs. The only difference is in where you direct your two questions. Instead of asking yourself, "What do I want? What proposal can I make to help get that to happen?" you ask the other person, "What do *you* want? What proposal can *you* make to help get that to happen?"

Remember that the answers need to come from them, not from you. Don't assume you know what they really want. And be careful not to propose your own solutions. It's the other person who needs to make the shift from passive complaining to active problem solving. Any suggestions coming from you are likely to backfire.

A friend of ours, whom we'll call Sam, experienced that type of backfiring recently with a woman who reports to him, Meg. Meg is highly conscientious and precise in her work. This makes her the perfect fit for her job, which requires her to conduct detailed financial analyses. However, in order to prepare those analyses, she needs regular updates from three other people in her department who are not as attentive to detail as she is.

When Meg came to Sam complaining about these coworkers, he did what came naturally: he tried to help.

> *"I just don't know what to do," said Meg. "I'm not getting the data I need. None of this information is in a format I can use. I've explained the guidelines to these people again and again, but nothing ever changes."* (Complaint)
>
> *"Why don't you give them some feedback?" said Sam.* (Proposal)
>
> *"That doesn't work. They don't listen to me," whined Meg.* (Complaint)
>
> *Sam tried again. "Let's take it to a meeting. We'll all get together and discuss what's been happening."* (Proposal)
>
> *"I keep trying and it doesn't get through!" said Meg.* (Complaint)

This cycle of complaints and proposals continued until finally Sam gave up in frustration.

After some coaching from (coauthor) Amy, Sam went back to Meg and tried the conversation again. This time, instead of suggesting solutions, he asked her what she wanted. She said she wanted to get the information she needed from her coworkers. She also wanted greater clarity about each person's responsibilities, to make sure that they all had the same understanding.

The next step was more challenging. When asked what she could do to get what she wanted, Meg started complaining again ("If only people would just do what I've been asking, things would be so much easier"). Sam gently but firmly directed her back to the question of what she could do: "So what can you suggest to help move things forward?" It took several attempts, but eventually he got an answer: "Okay, I suggest we bring everyone together to clarify people's responsibilities. We could schedule a group meeting focused just on this issue." And that's what they did.

Now, as you may have noticed, the idea of holding a meeting is something that Sam had already suggested and that Meg had immediately dismissed. You might be tempted to draw conclusions from this about Meg, thinking that she's resistant to authority and can't take advice, or that she's irrational or inconsistent. But in fact, her change in attitude is exactly what we'd expect from anyone who's been stuck in complaints. In the midst of a passive, helpless pattern of thinking, even the best ideas seem doomed to failure. It's the shift in a person's own mindset, not the introduction of new, better ideas from outside, that makes it possible for them to stop complaining and start taking action.

Helping someone to shift their mindset might not be easy. You might need to be persistent (as Sam was with Meg), repeatedly bringing the person's focus back to what they want and what they can do, as opposed to what they don't like and what makes change difficult. You also might need to ask several rounds of questions. Just as when you're working with your own complaints, the idea is to repeat the strategy as many times as necessary until the solution feels satisfying.

When to Use the Response Strategy, and When Not to Use It
As you build your awareness of complaints, you may start to hear them all around you. Before you jump in and try to help, a few words of caution are in order. Sometimes when a person is complaining, they're not interested in problem solving; they just want someone to empathize with how lousy they're feeling. Even if they do want to reason through the issue eventually, they may want to vent for a little while first.

If the other person hasn't asked for your help, and you're not in a context where helping is part of your role (for instance, a therapeutic or coaching session), ask what kind of response they'd like from you. For instance, you might ask, "What would be most useful for you right now? Would you like me to help you talk through this situation to try to find a way to improve it, or is it better for me to just listen and hear what you're going through?" Respect the answer you get. Don't force a problem-solving conversation on someone who doesn't want to have it.

> **The Upshot:** When you help someone who's complaining to discover what they want and how they can get it, you empower them to start solving their own problems.

Response Step 3: Practice
The best practice for managing others' complaints is managing the complaints in your own life. The exercises beginning on page 163 will get you started. Continue practicing until the transition from complaints to wants and proposals feels natural to you.

Intervention Skill: Turning Around Other People's Complaining Conversations

The negative effects of complaining are multiplied when two or more people are doing it together. Sometimes a couple, work team, or other group gets stuck in a fixed pattern of complaints, to the point where a whining, frustrated tone pervades most of their conversations. The mood can be contagious, so that others who enter the group get drawn into complaining as well. If you're able to intervene skillfully in this type of communication, you can help steer the discussion in a more productive direction.

Intervention Step 1: Awareness

Once you can detect a single individual's complaints, you shouldn't have much trouble recognizing when several people are using them together. See if you can notice not just what other people are saying and how they're saying it, but also how you're starting to feel and how you're inclined to respond. Are you tempted to give one of the trio of unhelpful responses: joining in, arguing, or trying to help? It's your habitual response that you'll need to overcome to put a new strategy into practice.

Intervention Step 2: Action—Giving Two Options: Agree or Propose

The response strategy you learned earlier works well in one-on-one interactions but gets a little complicated when more people are involved. You need to lead each person through the process independently, identifying their individual wants and proposals. As a result, it's likely that different people in the group will come up with different solutions that aren't compatible with one another.

An alternative is to skip asking what each person wants, and ask them to make their proposals directly to each other. Teach the group one simple guideline: when someone makes a proposal, the next person must either (1) agree (explicitly accept the proposal) or (2) make a new proposal. Keep it simple. If the person doesn't accept the original proposal, they don't explain why; they just suggest an alternative. The process continues until there's a suggestion that everybody can agree on. Of course, this strategy can fail if people give extreme or unreasonable proposals that others are certain to reject. It may help to remind the group that their goal is reaching consensus, so they're better off giving proposals that have potential to get agreement from everyone.

No strategy is appropriate in every situation, but for couples or small groups trying to solve relatively straightforward problems, this agree-or-propose technique is often surprisingly effective. Just remember our advice in the section "When to Use the Response Strategy, and When Not to Use It," on page 159. The same rules apply here.

It's best if you can first help the people to recognize the downside of the way they're communicating. Our favorite way to do that, which works with any type of troublesome communication pattern, is to ask, "If you continue talking in this way, do you think things are going to get better or worse?"

Anita posed this question to Theresa and Sarah from our opening story, and the sisters agreed that their conversation about working at the store wasn't getting them anywhere. They were both willing to try something different. However, when Anita explained the agree-or-propose strategy, Sarah shook her head. "There's no point," she said. "We can't do it. I can make a proposal, but Theresa is so invested in the store that she'll never agree." She started to cry. (Remember that complaints are often tied to negative predictions like "It won't work," "Nothing will help," and "I'll never get what I want." If you intervene in the communication, you need to be prepared to encounter the sadness or despair that can be triggered by this type of thinking.)

Anita invited Sarah to test her prediction with facts. "Do you have any information right now that tells you a proposal won't be helpful?" she asked. Sarah thought for a moment and said no. Anita then asked if she'd be willing to try making a proposal. Sarah nodded, looked over at her sister, and said, "I propose we close the store for a week and go on vacation."

Now it was up to Theresa. Anita reminded her of the agree-or-propose guideline: "If you agree with that proposal, say so. If you have your own proposal, make it." Theresa said, "I have a different proposal."

Sarah turned to Anita, rolled her eyes, and said, "I knew it." Anita asked Sarah to hold on until she heard what Theresa had to say. Then Theresa gave her proposal: close the store for 10 days. Sarah's jaw dropped.

When she recovered from the shock, Sarah said, "I don't believe it. You don't really mean it." (Notice how she moved right from a negative prediction into a mind-read.) "No, I mean it," said Theresa. "This would give us a chance to have a big sale to clean out our old inventory. We can put a sign on the door saying 'Closed for Restocking' and advertising the sale, and then spend three days getting the store and the warehouse ready. After that we'll have a full week to get away, and when we come back we can have the sale."

Sarah slowly took in what her sister was saying. "You know, that's a really great idea," she said. "We've been wanting to clean out the warehouse for ages. There's nice stuff in there that customers can't see."

"Yeah," said Theresa, "and if we mark down all the items that haven't been selling, that would clear out the clutter and help us pay for the vacation at the same time."

Sarah smiled. "I think this could actually work," she said.

The plan did work, beautifully. The sisters spent three days cleaning and preparing for the sale, and then took a weeklong hiking trip. When they returned, their sale brought in more than enough money to cover their travel expenses.

Sarah and Theresa were thrilled. In the course of a single coaching session, they'd managed to solve a problem they'd been struggling with for years. Anita was pleased not just that the sisters resolved this issue successfully, but that they now had a strategy they could use to work through future problems instead of complaining about them. Of course, you may not get such dramatic positive results every time you intervene in complaints. This strategy isn't a cure-all. However, it does open the door to creative thinking and problem solving that people simply can't do while they're complaining.

Intervention Step 3: Practice

Once you've made it to this point in the chapter, you've learned everything you can learn just by reading about complaints. Now it's time to practice. If you haven't yet looked ahead to the exercises, go ahead and start them now.

Exercises

Complaints Training Program: Discovering the Underlying Problem

If, like many people, you complain frequently, gaining skill in managing this behavior may make a big difference for you, empowering you to take a more active role in getting what you want. Even if you're one of the rare individuals who never complain, you certainly know other people who do. Learning how to respond or intervene effectively may help improve many of the conversations you have every day.

For general guidelines on how to get the most out of each training program, review "Training Program Guidelines" in Chapter 3, on page 47. Note that this icon—**OO**—marks exercises for which we strongly recommend working with a partner.

Basic Training: Building Awareness and Flexible Thinking

Exercise 1: Your Personal World of Complaints

Goal: Increase your awareness of the ways in which complaining plays a role in your life

Estimated time: 5–15 minutes

In what situations do you encounter complaining in your own life and work? When do you do it yourself? When do you hear others complaining? Make four lists:

1. Topics you complain about
2. Individuals or groups you complain to (this may include yourself, if you complain in your self-talk, or the readers of any blogs or social networking sites where you post complaints)
3. Other individuals or groups that complain to you
4. Situations in which the complaining happens (staff meetings, dinners at home, conversations at the gym, etc.)

See if you spot any patterns. For instance, are you aware of more complaining at home? At work? With friends? Or are many different areas of your life filled with complaints?

Intermediate Training:
Deepening Your Complaint Savvy

Exercise 2: The Experience of Complaining, Fact-Finding, and Proposing ∞

Goal: Notice any emotional shifts that occur when you move from complaining to finding facts and making proposals

Estimated time: 15–20 minutes

In this exercise, we want you to complain on purpose, and then switch to using other types of communication. Pick a subject to gripe about—anything that frustrates you, from taxes and politics to how busy, tired, overworked, underpaid, or unappreciated you are. Then, together with a partner, go through the following steps:

1. **Complaints**
    *   Complain for one minute while your partner listens.
    *   Talk with your partner about how your complaining affected both your emotional state and their emotional state.

2. **Facts**
    *   Give facts about the situation for one minute while your partner listens and provides coaching if they notice you getting off track (for instance, if you're complaining instead of giving facts).
    *   Talk with your partner about the effects on your emotions.

3. **Proposals**
    *   Generate at least five proposals for what you could do in this situation while your partner listens and provides coaching if needed.
    *   Talk with your partner about the effects on your emotions.

4. **Debriefing**
    *   Talk with your partner about any similarities and differences in your experiences of the three types of communication.

At the end, switch roles.

Exercise 3: Four Different Responses to Complaints ∞

Goal: Experience the differences between four types of responses to complaints, from both sides of the conversation

Estimated time: 10–20 minutes

To start, your partner will briefly describe a situation that they find frustrating and then begin complaining about it to you. You'll practice responding in four different ways:

1. **Complaining.** Join in and complain together with them for one minute.
2. **Arguing.** Your partner repeats their complaint, and this time you yes-but or contradict what they're saying. Argue together for one minute.
3. **Making proposals.** When your partner complains, you respond with a proposal. Listen to their response, and then make another proposal. Continue for one minute (stopping early if your partner agrees to one of your proposals).
4. **Asking what they want for a response.** After your partner repeats their complaint, ask them what type of response would be most helpful to them. Whatever they ask for—whether it's advice, help with brainstorming, or just patient listening—do that for one minute.

When you're finished, talk with your partner about those four types of responses. What was it like for you to respond in each of those ways? What was it like for them to be on the receiving end? Which of the responses felt most natural, most comfortable, or most irritating? Then switch roles so you complain and your partner responds.

Exercise 4: Digging Deeper Beneath Complaints ∞

Goal: Identify the underlying wants or needs beneath your complaints

Estimated time: 5–15 minutes

Pick a complaint that you have, on any topic, and keep asking yourself what you want, going deeper each time. Continue until you get to one or more core needs or desires that really matter to you. You can do this exercise either on paper or together with a partner, who can keep prompting you to think more deeply about what you want.

If you have trouble thinking of deeper wants, ask yourself (or have your partner ask) the following questions:

- If I had this, what would the benefit be?
- What need would this fulfill for me?
- Why is this important to me?

> **Exercise 4 Example**
> *Complaint:* My desk is such a mess that I can't find anything.
> *What I want:* To be able to quickly find the papers I'm looking for right now.
> *Deeper want:* To feel confident that I know where all my important papers are.
> *Deeper want:* To feel more in control of the projects I'm working on.
> Etc.

Advanced Training:
Preparing to Apply the Full Complaint Strategies

Exercise 5: Transforming and
Responding to Complaints ∞

Goals:
- Build your skill at shifting from complaining to active problem solving
- Build your skill at coaching another person to shift from complaining to active problem solving

Estimated time: 15–25 minutes

The strategies for transforming your own complaints and for responding to others' complaints are essentially the same. The only difference is whether you're asking yourself what you want and how you can get it, or asking those questions to somebody else. By doing this exercise with a partner, you'll get a chance to practice both variations.

First, work with one of your own complaints, going through the following steps:

1. Complain for one minute about something that's bothering you.
2. Your partner asks, "What do you want in this situation?" Give some thought to the question, and answer honestly.
3. Your partner asks, "What can you do to help get that to happen?" Answer by making a proposal for something specific you could do.
4. Repeat steps 2 and 3 at least two more times. Go a little deeper with each repetition, and continue until you come up with a proposal that feels satisfying.
5. Talk with your partner about your experience. How did shifting your communication affect how you think and feel about your difficult situation? What might you do differently in the future, as a result of going through this process?

When you're finished, switch roles, coaching your partner through one of their complaints. If you get stuck at any point during this exercise, turn back to the section "Troubleshooting the Complaint Strategy," starting on page 153.

Variation: Do this exercise on your own, repeatedly asking yourself what you want and what you can do to help get that to happen.

Want to learn more? Try more exercises at CTsavvy.com/Cexercises, plus the awareness quiz at CTsavvy.com/Cquiz.

8

Blame Games

Each of the communication problems we discuss in this book can wreak havoc on a conversation, but the most challenging of all is the one we've saved for last—the subject of this chapter. To illustrate, we'll share the story of one of our SAVI trainees (we'll call her Laura) as she faced what to all appearances was an impossible, no-win situation. Laura wasn't dealing with a contentious executive team, a stalled contract negotiation, or an impending financial crisis. This was a much more formidable problem: an overtired four-year-old who had suddenly realized that she wasn't going to get what she wanted.

What did this four-year-old (her daughter, Katie) want? What many four-year-olds want, all the time: to Do It All By Herself. On this occasion, what Katie wanted to do all by herself was brush her teeth. But when she walked into the bathroom, she saw that her mother—hoping to speed things along, since Katie kept putting off bedtime—had already squeezed a dollop of toothpaste onto her toothbrush.

This, to Katie, was a crisis of epic proportions. "You're not supposed to put toothpaste on my toothbrush!" she yelled.

Laura took a deep breath and kept her voice very calm as she attempted to reason with her daughter. "It's just toothpaste," she said. "It's not a big deal, honey."

"Yes it IS!" cried Katie, collapsing to the floor.

Laura tried a different tactic: "Let's just wash it off, okay? Then you can start over and do it yourself."

"No!" Katie screamed. "You weren't supposed to do it! You ruined it! I hate you!" She grabbed the toothbrush and used it to whack Laura in the leg.

At this point Laura felt she had no choice. According to their house rules, hitting meant an automatic "time-out." She picked Katie up and carried her, crying and thrashing, back to her bedroom. It was getting harder and harder to keep the edge out of her voice. "Come on," she said. "Why does everything have to be such a drama?"

Laura closed the door on her still-wailing daughter, feeling frustrated, sad, and defeated. She asked herself what had gone wrong in her family. It seemed like Katie was always having a meltdown over something—if it wasn't brushing her teeth, it was pouring milk in her cereal, getting herself dressed, or putting away her toys. Who was to blame? Had Laura failed as a mother? Was Katie a bratty child? Or was this just a difficult stage that all parents and children had to suffer through?

By this point in the book, our answers to Laura's questions should come as no surprise. No, she was not a bad mother, and Katie was not a bad daughter. And while it's only natural for conflicts to arise as a four-year-old struggles to be more independent, those conflicts are not always destined to end in rage and tears. There are ways of communicating that consistently help to defuse frustration or anger, in any relationship. There are also ways of communicating that consistently make things worse, which is what kept happening in Laura and Katie's conversation. To understand what went wrong and what had to change for mother and daughter to reconcile, we need to examine the specific behaviors they were using to talk to each other. In particular, we need to look at one potentially destructive and widely misunderstood behavior: the verbal attack.

Communication Challenge 6: Attacks—Expressing Angry Feelings in Misleading Ways

Verbal attacks are a type of communication that we all use sometimes when we experience anger, frustration, irritation, annoyance, or other similar feelings. Instead of expressing those feelings in a straightforward way ("I'm angry," "I'm irritated," "I'm annoyed"), we vent them indirectly, targeting other people ("She has no right to treat me like this," "Now you've gone and ruined everything," "It's all your fault!"). Every comment Katie made in the opening story is an attack. Her frustration about the toothpaste came out both in hostile words ("You ruined it!") and in the hostile tone of everything she said (screaming and yelling, rather than just talking). A hostile voice tone can make even the most innocuous, neutral words into an attack. (See the following sidebar.)

The Many Faces of Attacks

Verbal attacks take a wide variety of forms:

Accusations and blame. "Thanks to your lack of professionalism, we just lost our largest client!" "If you hadn't been so careless with our money, we could have retired by now."

Accusatory mind-reads. "You think you're better than everyone else in this office." "You never really cared about me."

Labeling, name-calling, put-downs, and profanity. "I've never met anyone so arrogant." "You're too weak to succeed in this business."

Threats and retaliatory remarks. "I'm not going to let you forget this." "You're going to regret the way you've treated me."

Sarcastic jabs. "Oh yeah, that's a *brilliant* idea." "I just bet you were trying to help me."

Expressions of outrage and indignation. "Your presentation was a disgrace!" "You ought to be ashamed of yourself."

Righteous questions (attacks in question form).[1] "Are you really that naive?" "Just who do you think you are?" "Can't you get the simplest thing right?"

Neutral words with a hostile tone or inflection. "Where ARE you?!" "The meeting is starting in FIVE MINUTES!"

You probably don't need us to tell you that attacks tend to escalate, rather than resolve, conflict. That much is obvious. What's less obvious is why they have that effect. The toxic power of attacks stems primarily from how misleading they are.

Our Attacks Mislead Us

There are times when people use attacks deliberately, consciously intending to cause pain. However, in our experience, this is the exception, not the rule.

Much of the time, the person who's attacking has no idea that's what they're doing; they may even believe they're using helpful forms of communication. We all fall into this trap occasionally. While it might be clear to others that we're attacking, we fool ourselves into thinking we're just sharing our feelings, giving facts, asking questions, using humor, or even displaying tactful restraint. We'll discuss each of these possibilities in detail.

Feelings

It's common in couples counseling for one partner to say, "I can never express my feelings, because he gets too upset" or "When I'm honest about how I feel, she yells at me." However, frequently the other person is upset because what's being "honestly" expressed aren't feelings but attacks—comments like "I feel you're being selfish," "I feel as though you're smothering me," or "I feel like you never appreciate how much I do for you." You might hear similar comments in a work context: "I feel you're treating the staff unfairly" or "I feel like you're not committed to this initiative."

Just because someone uses the words "I feel," that doesn't mean they're expressing a feeling. A feeling is an emotional experience, like anger, fear, or happiness. Direct statements of feeling (like "I'm angry," with an angry voice tone that's consistent with the words) are not attacks and usually are not perceived as attacks by other people. Watch out for feeling look-alikes such as *abandoned, betrayed, rejected, ignored, criticized, put down, cheated, used,* or *violated.* Instead of describing your own emotional experience, these words make blameful interpretations of what someone else has done to you ("You abandoned me" or "You betrayed me").

Emotions do get communicated through attacks but not in a direct, clear way. They leak out through the blame in our words, the edge in our voice tone, or both. The feeling underneath "You're being selfish" might be disappointment or anger. The feeling underneath "I feel betrayed" might be anguish or sorrow. Some attacks merge a feeling statement together with an accusation—for instance, "You made me really angry." There's a feeling in there ("angry"), but the main message coming through is blame ("you made me" feel this way).

Facts

Attacks can also masquerade as facts. Something that someone presents as factual may convey no real data, only blame or criticism. A supervisor might tell an employee to "face the reality that you let the whole department down." A parent might tell a teenager to "accept the fact that you're ruining your chance to get into a good college."

Alternatively, factual words may be spoken with a hostile voice tone that transforms them into an attack ("There are TWELVE typos in this report!" "You missed your curfew THREE TIMES this week!"). The facts on their own might potentially be valuable, but when they're delivered with obvious anger, irritation, or contempt, the person on the receiving end is likely to be too upset to get anything useful from them.

Questions

A person who says, "What on earth gave you THAT idea?" or "What were you THINKING?" may believe they're asking a real question. They may expect an answer and be surprised if they get a defensive response instead. However, that sort of question (a righteous question) is not a clear request for a response. Rather than communicating, "Could you give me some information?" it sends the attacking message, "You're wrong!" or "You should have known better!"

Humor

There is sometimes a fine line between a funny joke and a cruel dig or insult, particularly when we speak ironically (using words to express the opposite of what they literally mean). Some irony may get a smile, laugh, or sympathetic groan without causing any bad feelings. For example, a coworker excited by an unexpected gift says, "Wow, you remembered my birthday!" and you reply, "No, it was just an amazing coincidence! These flowers were lying on the road on the way to work today."

At other times, irony comes out through sharp sarcastic comments, which may get a laugh but at somebody else's expense. Your softball teammate trips and drops the ball, and you say, "Impressive play. Keep it up." Or an employee arrives late to a meeting and you say, "Oh, I hope this meeting hasn't disrupted your schedule." Whether these remarks are intended to be hurtful or merely humorous, they function as attacks. In fact, many people experience sarcastic barbs as more painful than other forms of attacks.

Tactful Restraint

Paradoxically, someone who's attacking may think they're doing just the opposite, being patient and biting their tongue. This may be because the attacks coming out of their mouth are less inflammatory than the ones running through their head. A computer support person might snap, "Just let me do it!" instead of "You're so slow and incompetent, you're wasting my time!" Or a teenager might say testily, "No, Mother, as I've already told you three times, there will not be any drinking at this party" instead of yelling, "Leave me alone! Stop being so paranoid!" While these people may feel as though they're showing remarkable restraint, their contempt and annoyance are obvious to anyone who's listening.

Our Attacks Mislead Other People

In addition to misleading the people who use them, attacks also mislead other people who hear them, including whoever is getting attacked. What drives us to attack is something happening internally: a strong feeling like anger or frustration. But the way we're talking focuses all the attention on something external: a situation that's upsetting us, a person who did something we didn't like, or anyone or anything else we're targeting with our hostility.[2] Our own misdirected focus, away from our feelings and onto something else, will tend to mislead those around us.

Think about what happened with Katie and Laura. Katie didn't talk about how frustrated she was; she talked about the toothpaste. Therefore, it's not surprising that when Laura responded, she talked about the toothpaste too. First she tried to convince Katie that the toothpaste wasn't important ("It's not a big deal, honey"). Then she made a proposal to try to fix the problem ("Let's just wash it off").

When Katie's attacks got more personal ("You ruined it! I hate you!"), Laura's responses got more personal too. She counterattacked with a righteous question ("Why does everything have to be such a drama?") and started looking for someone to blame, tempted to target either her daughter (attack), herself (self attack), or the situation (a form of self defense, thinking that it's not her fault since every mother has the same problem). These are all common responses to attacks, and all are highly unlikely to lead to a good outcome (see the following sidebar). Certainly none of them helped to resolve the toothpaste battle.

Ineffective Responses to Attacks

Focusing on the Situation: Avoiding It or Trying to Fix It
- Dismissing the other person's concern ("Don't worry about it." "It's no big deal.")
- Making proposals ("Why don't you . . ." "Have you tried . . . ?")

Focusing on the People: Laying Blame or Diverting Blame
- Counterattacks ("You're so negative!" "You make such a big deal out of everything.")
- Self attack ("It's all my fault." "I always do the wrong thing." "I'm a bad mother/friend/manager/etc.")
- Self defense ("It's not my fault." "I was only trying to help." "I did the best I could in a no-win situation.")

The Upshot: Attacks vent hostile feelings in a way that makes it difficult for those feelings to be understood or get resolved.

When two people are fighting and only one is using attacks, it's easy to lay all the blame for the unpleasantness on that person and see the other as an innocent victim. In fact, we might praise the other person for staying calm and focused on the problem at hand, or else for sticking up for themselves with a strong defense. Typically, however, these responses only add more fuel to the fire. When someone is yelling or raising their voice, staying calm and quiet is more likely to infuriate them than to help them settle down. If that sounds counterintuitive to you, try to remember a time when you felt really angry and someone started reasoning with you or told you to calm down. This response probably left you feeling even angrier, perhaps quieting down on the surface but simmering with resentment inside.

Responding to an attack with self defense can be even more provocative. Attacking and defending go hand in hand, with each one tending to invite the other. Suppose your spouse asks you a neutral question, "Did you pick up my suit at the dry cleaner?" and instead of simply saying, "No," you respond with a litany of excuses: "I really meant to, I've been so busy, the kids needed so much attention, the washing machine broke," and so on. You've just increased the chances that what you'll get in return are attacks: "Thanks to you, I have nothing to wear tomorrow." "You never make time for the things that matter to me."

From there, odds are good that you'll reply with more self defense ("I'm just so overwhelmed these days"), leading to more attacks ("We're all busy! That's no excuse for not keeping your commitments!"). And then you're off and running in a fight that could keep going indefinitely, perpetuated just as much by you as by your spouse. Whenever people get stuck in an attack–self defend communication pattern, the defender holds as much responsibility for the breakdown as the attacker and has at least as much power to repair the breach.

Skills for Managing Attacks

The strategies for managing attacks don't come naturally to most of us and can be extremely challenging to put into practice. However, they are well worth the effort; mastering these skills gives you the potential to transform some of your most difficult conversations into productive dialogues.

Transformation Skill:
Distilling Your Attack into Useful Information

All of us use attacks, at least occasionally. You might not make loud accusations or call people names, but we guarantee that from time to time, some hostility leaks out in your communication. When you start communicating more directly, you help the people around you, particularly those who've been on the receiving end of your attacks. You also help yourself, by increasing the chances that your feelings and concerns will be heard and understood.

Transformation Step 1: Self-Awareness
Frequently, people are not only unaware that they're using attacks; they don't even know that they're angry. Someone may be red in the face, pound-

ing their fists, hollering about their awful boss or neighbor or coworker, but still insist they're not mad. We've had this happen more than once with clients—when a person is ranting about something and we ask what's made them so angry, they say, "I'm not angry! He's just such a jerk!" or "I'm perfectly calm! She's the one who's hysterical!"

Many of us find it hard to admit that we have angry or aggressive feelings. These feelings are widely considered to be negative or destructive, so acknowledging them can bring up guilt and shame, particularly if we got criticized for showing anger when we were young. In a famous scene from the movie *Bambi,* Thumper repeats a lesson he learned from his parents: "If you can't say something nice, don't say nothin' at all." Those of us raised to follow this rule may have grown up holding back, from ourselves as well as from others, any opinion or emotion that isn't considered "nice" or acceptable.

The reality is that feelings themselves don't cause conversations (or work teams, relationships, or families) to fail. It's the way those feelings get expressed that leads to problems. People often confuse anger, a natural, universal human emotion, with verbal attacks. However, verbal attacks are just one method of demonstrating anger—and an indirect, ineffective method at that. To stop yourself from attacking, it's not necessary to eliminate or conceal your angry feelings. All that has to change is the way you express them.

Of course, before you can consciously express an emotion in a new way, you have to be aware that you're feeling it. If you're never aware of your own frustration or irritation, be sure to practice Exercise 2, on page 198. You might also want to have someone else tell you when you start to sound angry or hostile. Proceed with caution, however. Before you ask someone to point out when you use attacks, make absolutely sure you feel ready to hear that information.

Also, be careful about whom you ask. This type of feedback (for instance, "Your voice tone is sounding a little hostile") can be difficult to hear, and you may find yourself reacting with defensiveness or retaliation ("What do you mean, I sound hostile?! I'm not being hostile!"). A supportive coach, mentor, or therapist will typically be less inclined to take your response personally and get upset or hold it against you. They may also find it easier to tell you the unvarnished truth than a friend, spouse, or colleague would. We recommend that you do not ask for feedback on your attacks from people who are dependent on you, like your children or employees.

To help you avoid getting triggered by the feedback, remember that it is giving you information about your behavior, not your personality or motivation. The presence of hostility in your voice tone does not mean that you're a hostile person or that you're intending to be harsh or hurtful. It simply means that strong feelings are coming through, indirectly, in the way you're saying what you're saying.

Transformation Step 2:
Action—Recognize, Strategize, Verbalize

Once you realize you're on the verge of attacking, what can you do instead? If you're experiencing a high level of anger, disappointment, irritation, or another strong feeling, your options are limited. When your emotions are so intense that they're driving you to use verbal attacks, they'll tend to decrease your capacity to think clearly and do the useful things you'd otherwise be able to do: understand other people's points of view, take steps to solve the problem that's leading you into conflict, or even explain what's bothering you in a clear, nonhostile manner.

You can increase your odds of having a productive conversation by giving yourself a chance to calm down first. There is wisdom in the old advice of counting to 10 before you speak. Sometimes that's all you need to do—after you pause and take a few deep breaths, your feelings start to subside and you're better able to communicate clearly, without hostility leaking out. However, in many situations, you'll likely find that it takes additional time and effort to regain your composure. The strategy we're going to teach you is a more focused, deliberate technique for working through intense feelings and preparing to express your concerns in a constructive way. It's a great alternative to try whenever there's an upsetting issue you don't want to drop but don't yet feel prepared to discuss effectively.

This strategy does take time, though, and parts of it must be done in private, either by yourself or together with a person who can act as a coach (see the following sidebar). If you're in the middle of a distressing conversation, you may need to stop the discussion for a little while by saying something like, "I suggest we take a half-hour break to think things through." When stopping the conversation is not an option (for instance, when you're in the middle of a big group meeting), we recommend containing your emotions as best you can and finding time later on to use the strategy.

Choosing a Coach to Help You Transform Your Attacks

It can be very helpful to have assistance from another person as you work through your attacks. Just make sure they meet the following criteria:

- **You trust them.** You're certain that this person won't judge you for what you say and will keep your conversation confidential.
- **They aren't personally involved in your conflict.** It's best to talk to someone who doesn't know, or at least is not close to, the person you're inclined to attack.
- **They are comfortable dealing with strong feelings.** Don't pick a person who gets nervous, fearful, or overwhelmed when other people express anger or hostility.
- **They are clear about their role.** They understand that you don't want them to take sides or agree with you. Their job is simply to listen and to help you calm down and prepare to communicate more effectively.
- **They have freely agreed to take on this role.** Before you begin, ask the person if they feel comfortable helping you in this way, and encourage them to say no if they don't.

When you're ready to start, walk through the three components of the strategy:

1. Recognize (notice your feelings and put them into words)
2. Strategize (set a productive goal for your communication)
3. Verbalize (communicate to the other person in a way that meets your goal)

Part 1. Recognize—Identify Your Feelings

Notice what you're experiencing, and try to identify a feeling word that captures it, such as *annoyed, angry,* or *fearful*. If there is more than one feeling, identify them all. If you have difficulty finding the right words, look through the list in the following sidebar to see which ones seem like the best fit.

Feelings That May Underlie Attacks

When you're tempted to use attacks, this may mean that you're feeling:

agitated	distressed	jealous
alarmed	embarrassed	lonely
angry	enraged	nervous
anguished	envious	overwhelmed
annoyed	exasperated	pained
anxious	fearful	powerless
apprehensive	frightened	resentful
ashamed	frustrated	sad
bitter	furious	scared
bored	grouchy	shocked
confused	grumpy	tense
cranky	guilty	terrified
dejected	helpless	uncomfortable
desperate	hopeless	uneasy
disappointed	humiliated	worried
discouraged	hurt	
dismayed	irritated	

You may experience just one prevailing feeling, or two or more at the same time.

Remember our earlier warning about look-alikes, words that sound like feelings but actually give blameful interpretations (see the section "Feelings" on page 171). If the first word that occurs to you is *abandoned, used, criticized,* or another feeling look-alike, work to translate it into a real feeling word. (For example, the feeling underneath the word *abandoned* may be loneliness, fear, or even rage). If you're working with a coach, ask for their help with this.

Once you've identified one or more feelings, clearly state each of them, with as much authentic emotion in your voice tone as you can muster. For example, you might say, "I'm feeling disappointed" or "I'm really annoyed!" or "I feel furious!" Then rate the strength of each feeling, right in the present moment, on a scale from 1 to 5. (A rating of 1 means "I don't feel this at all right now," and 5 means "I'm feeling this more powerfully now than I ever have before.") By naming and rating your feelings, you not only deepen your self-awareness but also help to calm yourself down. Research shows that simply naming a negative feeling can help reduce its impact.[3] The rating process takes this one step further. Performing mental calculations requires you to engage your rational thought processes, which will tend to decrease your level of emotion.

Part 2. Strategize—Set a Productive Goal for the Communication
Ask yourself what you want to have happen between you and the person you feel tempted to attack. Here are a few examples of productive goals:

- I want to help improve our relationship (as friends/partners/business associates/etc.).
- I want to help resolve a misunderstanding.
- I want us to find a way to get work done more efficiently.
- I want us to find a way of making decisions that we both feel good about.
- I want us to stop repeating the same argument with each other.
- I want us to be able to communicate more effectively together.
- I want to clearly state what I want to be different in the future.
- I want to clearly and directly state why I am choosing to end this relationship.

Goals that focus on punishing the other person or trying to make them change (for instance, getting them to feel guilty or admit they were wrong) are unlikely to lead to a good outcome.

If you can't think of a productive goal—you can't imagine anything good that could come out of talking to the person about what's bothering you, no matter how well you deliver the information—you may decide this is not a conversation worth having. In that case, skip the third part of the strategy (verbalize), and try finding a way to make yourself feel better that does not involve the other person. You might get support from someone else, go for a run, meditate, or distract yourself for a while with another activity you enjoy.

Part 3. Verbalize—Find the Words to Help You Meet Your Goal
Whatever goal you've set, choose the words to help you achieve it. Typically, you'll have the best luck with a combination of feeling statements, fact statements, proposals, or questions. The particular combination you choose will depend on the person you're talking to and the situation you're in.

- **Feeling statements.** Clear, direct expressions of your emotional experience (past or present), with words that are consistent with the voice tone.
- **Fact statements.** Neutrally toned, factual descriptions or pieces of data about other people, things, or events.
- **Proposals.** Suggestions of what to do or how to do it, including proposals for your own actions.
- **Questions.** Neutrally toned requests for information, either narrow (asking for a yes/no, either/or, or specific factual answer) or broad (openly inviting the other person's ideas, opinions, or proposals).

One tip: if you plan to use feeling statements, particularly in a business context, double-check to make sure they're relevant to your goal. Many times, feelings help bring awareness to information that's relevant to the situation at hand but are not, in themselves, important to discuss. For example, feeling frustrated with a colleague can draw your attention to obstacles that are preventing you from working together effectively. While identifying and addressing those obstacles is important to your job, talking about the specific emotions that alerted you to the problems may waste time or even go against company norms.

See Table 8-1, on the following page, for a variety of examples of attack transformations. Whatever message you decide to send, keep practicing until you can state it clearly, without blame or hostility in your words or voice tone. If you're working with a coach, ask for their feedback on whether you're succeeding. If you feel too upset to talk in a nonhostile way, go back and repeat the earlier parts of the strategy (recognize and strategize), and then try again.

Table 8-1. Attacks Transformed into Feelings, Facts, Proposals, and Questions

Remember that whatever you're saying, it's important for your words to match your voice tone.	
Example 1 **Attack:** You always dominate these meetings. You never give serious attention to anyone else's ideas. **Feeling:** I left the meeting today feeling frustrated. **Fact:** My proposal was last on the agenda, and we discussed it for five minutes. **Question:** What can I do to help get more air time for my ideas?	**Example 2** **Attack:** I can't count on you for anything! You totally dropped the ball. **Fact:** I asked you to analyze data from six different regions, and your report addressed three regions. **Question 1:** What happened with the data from the other three regions? **Question 2:** Do you think you can complete the full six-region report by Tuesday?
Example 3 **Attack:** Do you realize how late it is? Did you even think about how worried I would be? You are so irresponsible. **Feeling 1:** When you missed your curfew, I was worried that something bad had happened to you. **Feeling 2:** I'm angry that you didn't call to let me know you'd be late. **Question 1:** What happened? **Question 2:** What do you think needs to change so that this won't happen again?	**Example 4** **Attack:** Your risky investment may have cost us our entire future! **Feeling:** I'm terrified to hear that we might not have enough money for our mortgage payments. **Proposal:** I suggest we make an appointment with a financial advisor to discuss our options. **Question:** Do you have any other ideas of what we could do?

Notice that we're not asking you to mechanically change your voice tone to mask your feelings and try to sound friendly. By engaging your rational thinking, the process of identifying your feelings and setting a productive goal helps to create an internal emotional shift that precedes and supports the shift in what you actually say.

When you're ready to talk directly to the other person, arrange to meet them in a place where you'll both feel comfortable, at a time when you won't feel rushed or get interrupted. Communicate the message that you've practiced, listen to their response, and try to keep the conversation moving in a constructive direction, always keeping your goal in mind. If your first efforts at transforming your attacks don't succeed, you always have the option of repeating the strategy. As soon as you realize you're lapsing back into attack mode, stop the conversation, suggest another time to talk, and try recognizing, strategizing, and verbalizing once more. If you're working with a coach, you may also want to arrange a follow-up conversation with them to review what went well, what didn't go well, and what you could do better in the future.

Three-Part Strategy for Transforming Attacks

Note: For each part of the strategy, we've included coaching tips— either for your coach, if you have one, or for you to use in coaching yourself.

1. **Recognize.** Identify your feelings, state them clearly, and rate their level of intensity.

   (Coach: Listen, with empathy. If necessary, point out feeling look-alikes and gently probe for the true underlying emotional states.)

2. **Strategize.** Identify a goal for what you want to have happen with the person you feel like attacking. Alternatively, make a plan for helping yourself feel better that does not involve the other person.

   (Coach: Check to be sure that the goal is productive, and if you think the person could do better, encourage them to come up with an even more productive goal.)

3. **Verbalize (if appropriate).** Practice clearly stating the feelings, facts, proposals, or questions you would like to communicate to the other person. Continue practicing until you're certain your message is free of hostility, blame, outrage, and other negative overtones. Then identify a good place and time to talk, and work toward achieving your goal.

   (Coach: Check to be sure that the way the person is communicating is not likely to cause additional problems. For example, point out any hostility or blame that is still leaking out. After the conversation, provide consultation on how the discussion went.)

Transformation Step 3: Practice

If you'd like to begin working on transforming your attacks, skip ahead to the exercises starting on page 196. Try the awareness-building exercises before moving on to any strategies; most of us have a hard time recognizing the attacks in our own communication. And when you attempt to change your behavior, be patient with yourself. It may take quite a while to overcome your tendency to discharge negative feelings in the form of attacks, particularly in close relationships that bring out strong emotions.

As you build your awareness of the angry feelings that accompany attacks, you may come to realize that these experiences are very challenging for you to manage. For some people, feeling angry brings up intense guilt, shame, or fear. For others, anger escalates quickly and tends to get out of control. If you recognize either of those two tendencies in yourself, we suggest using this chapter for information only and finding a professional resource (coach, therapist, or mentor) to help you work through your anger without endangering yourself or others.

> **The Upshot:** By following a systematic process, you can use your hostile thoughts and strong feelings as a starting point to plan a meaningful, productive conversation.

Response Skill: What to Do When Someone Attacks You

While transforming your own attacks can be extremely difficult, responding effectively when someone attacks you is an even greater challenge. Not only do you need to manage your own strong emotions (defensiveness, anger, fear, or whatever else you feel when you're verbally attacked); you also need to help the other person to calm down, or at least avoid making them more upset. There's no magic formula guaranteed to work with every attack. However, when used skillfully, the strategy we'll describe here gives you a very good shot at de-escalating hostility and achieving resolution.

Response Step 1: Awareness

The types of attacks that get directed at you will depend on the person who's talking and the situation you're in. At work, you might be insulted by your boss ("Your sales record is pathetic!") or blamed by your employee

("You never gave me any guidance on this assignment"). At home you might hear a righteous question from your spouse ("How could you forget to mail our mortgage payment?!"), snippy retorts from your teenaged child ("ALL RIGHT, I'll clean my room! Stop nagging!"), or accusatory parenting advice from your in-laws ("You're far too lenient with those children.")

Some of these attacks may be subtle and therefore difficult to detect. Frequently a person's words are neutral or friendly, and their irritation comes through only in their voice tone. That happens with many sarcastic comments, like "Yeah, *right*, that's a *great* plan." In our experience, people who don't use much sarcasm themselves have the most trouble recognizing this kind of communication in others.

Even with relatively straightforward attacks, you may feel so reactive that you have a hard time noticing what's happening while it's happening. Suppose your supervisor yells, "You've botched this entire project!" It takes great presence of mind, plus a good bit of detachment, to focus on the communication (thinking to yourself, "He just used a verbal attack") rather than on the other person ("He has no right to talk to me like that!") or on yourself ("I really screwed up" or "It's not my fault"). Attacks are often easiest to identify in retrospect, after you've had time to reflect on the conversation in a calmer state of mind. Gradually, with practice, you'll get better at spotting them spontaneously. **To practice recognizing verbal attacks, visit CTsavvy.com/Aquiz.**

Response Step 2: Action—Resonate, Reflect, Resolve

Recognizing an attack gives you a tremendously useful piece of information, telling you that the person who attacked you is upset. Why is that information so useful? Because it tells you exactly what you need to do next: help that person to calm down. We say this not because it's the nice or "right" thing to do, but because it's a necessary first step before you can accomplish any other productive goal you might have. Remember that when a person's level of feeling is so high that they're using attacks, their ability to think clearly is likely to be limited. What follows is a three-part strategy for de-escalating hostility to the point where you can have a relatively calm, rational problem-solving conversation.

Part 1. Resonate (High Feeling)

When a person is verbally attacking you, there's a good chance they're experiencing a high level of negative feeling. If that's the case, the most effective response is what we call *mirroring*. Mirroring is similar to paraphrasing, but instead of reflecting only the content of what someone has said, it reflects the feeling underneath it as well. For example, if your client yells, "This is not what I asked for!" you could paraphrase by saying, "This isn't what you asked for" or "You're really unhappy with this" in a voice tone that's relatively neutral (not flat or monotone, just not conveying strong emotion). This is usually not an effective response. A mirror might use the same words but with more energy and empathetic feeling behind them: "This isn't what you asked for!" or "You're really unhappy with this!" It's typically best to match the other person's tone of voice, but with slightly less intensity.

As with paraphrasing, you can either repeat the same words the person used or use different words that convey the same underlying message. Just be sure not to add in any new ideas. If your friend says, "I can't believe you didn't visit me in the hospital!" don't embellish: "You're saying I'm selfish for not visiting you in the hospital!" Adding in the idea of being selfish puts words in your friend's mouth, which may make them even more upset.

Occasionally, when someone is very upset, they feel misunderstood unless you repeat their words exactly. For example, suppose your colleague says, "You humiliated me in that meeting!" You say, "I'm hearing I made you look bad!" and she replies, "No! You didn't just make me look bad, you humiliated me!" A response like that is a clear signal to stop rephrasing and stick to faithfully reflecting what you heard, at least until the person calms down a little.

The most important guideline is to keep trying. Don't get discouraged if the other person doesn't immediately regain their composure. Even if you're mirroring skillfully, it might take several attempts before you do it in a way that really resonates with them.

Guidelines for Effective Mirroring

- Match the other person's voice tone but with slightly less emotional intensity
- Use either the same words they used or different words that capture the same underlying message
- Don't add in any new ideas
- Continue until the hostility diminishes

Why is mirroring successful in responding to attacks when nothing else seems to work? Remember that the main message coming through in an attack is the feeling of the person who's speaking. Only by reflecting that feeling can you show that you've really understood what is important to them. And when people feel understood, they tend to be less agitated and upset.

Objections to Mirroring

Whenever we teach mirroring in our trainings, several people always raise concerns. Here we'll address the most common objections we've heard:

- **I can't believe it actually works.** You're not alone. Many people find this strategy to be counterintuitive. We encourage you to test it for yourself by having someone else mirror your strong emotions. (You'll have a chance to do that in the training program.)
- **This sounds like it takes a lot of effort.** It does take a lot of effort, particularly when you're just starting to use the strategy. If you don't expect to have ongoing contact with the person who's attacking you, and you don't have a compelling reason to make your conversation work better, you may decide to save yourself the effort and just walk away. However, if the person, the relationship, or the conversation matters to you, mirroring is usually in your best interest.
- **I don't want to feel angry.** As you mirror someone, you may start to experience the emotion you're mirroring, at least to some degree. Many people are not comfortable feeling anger or other strong emotions. For some, simply raising their voice feels overly aggressive or frightening. Only you can decide whether it's worth it to you to work through your discomfort to gain this new skill. If it is, we recommend getting some help from a counselor or coach.
- **I don't want to agree with the awful things someone is saying about me.** This is an important distinction to make. Mirroring an attack is not the same as agreeing with it. You don't need to say, "I agree" or "You're right" (although doing so can be helpful if you mean it sincerely). It may help to keep in mind that attacks give you information about the person who's speaking, not about you. (See the sidebar on the following page.) If it really bothers you to say back the words of an attack, you could try adding "You're saying" (for instance, "You're saying I let you

down"). Avoid adding "You think" ("You think I let you down"), which invites the response, "I don't just think it, it's true!"

- **I feel like I'm being manipulative.** In a sense, you're being manipulative every time you use any communication strategy. You're consciously choosing to act in a particular way to get the result you want. That doesn't mean you're being insincere, selfish, or malicious. When you consciously use strategies in the service of improving relationships, resolving conflicts, and making better decisions, you'll often make a positive contribution to your work, to your life, and to the lives of those around you.

- **This feels artificial.** If you haven't tried mirroring before, it will probably feel awkward, just like moving around on skis or roller skates feels awkward when you're just starting out. That discomfort should diminish over time, as you gain more experience and proficiency with this way of communicating and see the benefits it brings.

- **I tried this before and it didn't work.** That's certainly possible. No strategy is guaranteed to succeed with every person, in every situation. Another possibility, more common in our experience, is that what you did wasn't actually mirroring—at least not in the way we're describing it here (including matching the person's voice tone and reflecting their message without adding anything new). Mirroring anger is a high-level skill that few people can do successfully without intensive practice or training. Even if you managed to do it for a little while, you might not have kept it up long enough for it to be effective.

Taking Attacks Less Personally

You may recall that in Chapter 4, on mind-reads, we talked briefly about the negative impact of taking things personally. When you take someone's comments personally, you focus all your attention on what you think they're saying about you, as opposed to anything else they might be thinking or experiencing. In the case of verbal attacks, this response may seem unavoidable, particularly when the person is directly criticizing something about you (your personality, appearance, work ethic, etc.). We'll give you one very good reason not to take an attack personally: it's not actually about you. The primary information expressed in any attack is about the person who's delivering it.

Suppose your business partner says, "You've been utterly irresponsible, rushing ahead with that proposal." Strange as it may sound, this statement doesn't tell you anything about your proposal, your personality, the way you go about your work, or anything else about you. The only information it gives you is about your partner, telling you there's something going on for them emotionally (perhaps anger, fear, anxiety, frustration, or disappointment).

Even that information is vague and indirect. It's not clear exactly what the emotion is or where it's coming from. Their reaction may be related to their personal preferences (they prefer to deliberate for weeks about major decisions and feel anxious that you made a decision more quickly); their expectations (they thought you would consult with them before making certain commitments, and you didn't); or their opinions (they think another course of action would work better than the one you've chosen).

Learning to take attacks less personally makes it easier to stay grounded and avoid getting defensive ("Hey, I'm just looking out for the best interests of the company") or launching a counterattack ("If it were up to you, we'd never move forward with anything!"). Plus, when you stop focusing on yourself, you can direct your energy toward more useful goals—like helping the other person to feel heard, calm down, and possibly resolve the underlying concern that led them to attack you.

Part 2. Reflect (Medium Feeling)

Once your mirroring has been successful and the other person has settled down a bit, you can shift to the second part of the strategy. How can you tell they're feeling calmer? A good indication is that their tone of voice becomes less hostile or edgy. You might also notice that you start to get a clearer sense of what their concern is. Instead of just venting blame and outrage ("How could you do this?!" "You've ruined everything!"), they make more coherent, substantive statements about what's bothering them ("The numbers on that proposal were incorrect," "Martin called me and pointed out five discrepancies").[4]

At this point, you can show that you've heard and understood the person's message by giving a paraphrase ("You're saying the numbers were wrong, and Martin found five different errors"). As their voice tone becomes more neutral, yours does as well; the focus is now on the content of what they're saying rather than on their feelings. However, it's still important to avoid adding in new ideas of your own. Stick to using the same words they used or different words that have the same meaning.

If you switch too soon from mirroring to paraphrasing, or if you fail to paraphrase accurately, you'll get a clear signal: the person will get more upset. (For example, your colleague says, "Your analysis was so off-base it's embarrassing." You reflect, "The analysis was way off-base," and they yell, "You never listen! That's your problem! It was so off-base it's embarrassing!") That's your cue to return to mirroring ("It wasn't just off-base; it was embarrassingly off-base!"). Continue to mirror them until they calm down a little further, and then try paraphrasing again.

One trap many people fall into is waiting to paraphrase until the other person has talked about several different things. At that point, there are so many ideas on the table that the person trying to paraphrase has to pick and choose which ones to reflect. Since we all sometimes fail to hear what we don't want to hear, it's easy for the parts of the message that are most important to the other person to get lost, leading them to feel misunderstood. If this happens to you, try asking the person to tell you one idea at a time, so you can make sure you understand everything they're saying. Then, after each idea they tell you, immediately paraphrase what they've just said.

Part 3. Resolve (Low Feeling)

In the final part of the response strategy, you work together with the other person to resolve the underlying concerns beneath their attacks. This type of discussion is possible only if the person is calm enough to be capable of rational thinking. If you suspect that they are, try asking a neutral, broad (open) question. For instance, with the situation we just described, where your colleague didn't like your analysis, you might ask, "What specifically was off-base in my analysis?" or "What were you hoping to see in the analysis that wasn't there?"

The reply you get will tell you what to do next. If the person responds with attacks ("Everything was wrong!" "I already told you what I was looking for!"), go back to mirroring. If they're not attacking but still aren't answering your question, go back to paraphrasing. If, on the other hand, they answer your question calmly and directly ("What was wrong was . . ."

or "What I wanted to see was . . ."), you can begin the process of problem solving together. This might mean gathering facts, sharing facts of your own, asking for proposals, giving your own proposals, or building on each other's suggestions. If the problem you're trying to solve is personal—for example, if you're trying to repair damage to a romantic relationship—you might also ask about the other person's feelings and, if that works well, share your own.

Three-Part Strategy for Responding to Attacks	
What they're expressing	**How you respond**
High feeling	Resonate (mirror their emotions as well as their ideas)
Medium feeling	Reflect (paraphrase their ideas)
Low feeling	Resolve (engage in problem solving)

The three-part attack response strategy has helped many of our students and clients to resolve challenging conflicts. Laura, from our opening story, was familiar with this method, having practiced it the previous month in an intensive training with (coauthor) Ben. After she carried her daughter, Katie, to her room and had a few minutes to calm down, she was able to recognize that Katie had been using attacks, that her own responses had not been helpful, and that the new strategy she'd learned might get better results. She decided it was worth a try and walked down to Katie's room.

Katie's door was half-open. Laura peeked in and knocked.

"Go away!" Katie yelled. "I don't want to talk to you!"

Laura mirrored back empathetically, "You don't want to talk to me!"

"No, I don't!" said Katie. "You're mean! It's not fair!"

Laura mirrored again: "You're saying I'm mean! This isn't fair!"

"Yeah." Katie nodded. Her voice was softer now. "It's not fair I have a time-out."

Laura paraphrased, with empathy, "It's not fair that you have a time-out."

Katie nodded again. "You weren't supposed to do the toothpaste."

"I messed up," said Laura. "I was supposed to let you do the toothpaste, and I didn't."

"Uh huh," said Katie.

"I really made a mistake didn't I?"

"Yeah, you did." At that point Katie actually smiled a little. She looked up at her mother.

Laura asked, "What do you think about giving us one more try with brushing your teeth?"

Katie hesitated. "I can do it all by myself?"

"You can do it all by yourself."

"Well," said Katie. "I guess . . . Yeah . . . I'll do it." And Katie's teeth finally got brushed.

The Upshot: When someone verbally attacks you, you can often de-escalate the conflict by helping them to feel heard and understood—through skillful mirroring and paraphrasing— before moving on to constructive problem solving.

Response Step 3: Practice

Of all the strategies you learn in this book, responding to attacks is likely to feel the most difficult and unnatural. Allow yourself plenty of opportunities for practice (see the training exercises starting on page 196) before you attempt to use this skill in real-life conversations.

Intervention Skill: Coaching Other People through Attacks

When two people have a pattern of verbally attacking each other and you're in a position to intervene (meaning you have all the necessary skills, authority, and motivation), there are two primary ways you can make a useful contribution. The first—intervening right at the moment when the attacks are happening—is the work of advanced negotiation or therapy, and beyond the scope of this book. The second option, which we'll focus on here, is to give one-on-one coaching. Depending on your role and your relationships with each individual, you may end up coaching both people or just one or the other.

If you've already started working with a coach to transform your own attacks, you know how useful it can be to get this type of help. In the sections that follow, we'll give you guidelines for deciding if and when it makes sense for you to take on a coaching role, as well as what types of coaching tend to be most effective.

Intervention Step 1: Awareness

Once you're able to notice your own verbal attacks, as well as those that people direct toward you, you shouldn't have too much trouble detecting them in other conversations. Whenever you hear an attack aimed at someone else, either to their face or behind their back, take a moment to notice your reaction. Does your energy level increase, decrease, or stay the same? Do you start to feel uncomfortable, anxious, fearful, frustrated, or angry? If you have a strong negative response to attacks, it's important to be aware of that. Before you attempt to coach another person, you need to be comfortable with your own strong emotions.

In addition to strong feelings, a number of other factors can influence your ability to be an effective coach. When you're deciding whether to take on a coaching role in a particular situation, run through the checklist in the following sidebar.

To Coach or Not to Coach

Before you offer to coach someone who's been using attacks, be certain that you meet all of the following criteria:

____ **I have authority to act as a coach.** The other person has explicitly asked me to help them communicate better, or I'm in a role (professional coach, mentor, therapist, etc.) that gives me authority to do that.

____ **I've successfully worked through my own attacks.** I have experience transforming my attacks into more effective communication.

____ **I feel comfortable dealing with strong feelings.** I don't get nervous, fearful, or overwhelmed when other people express anger or hostility.

____ **I can focus on the communication rather than the issue.**
I understand that my role is to help the other person communicate
more skillfully, not to figure out or resolve the issue they're communicating about.

____ **I can stay neutral and nonjudgmental.** I'm not personally
involved in this conflict, and I don't feel tempted to take sides.

If you do not meet all of these criteria, you risk doing more harm
than good by taking on a coaching role.

Intervention Step 2:
Action—Guiding an Attack Transformation

After reading the earlier sections of this chapter, you've already learned
the strategy for coaching someone through attacks; you just learned it
from a different perspective, as the person being coached. We won't reit-
erate the full strategy, which is laid out on pages 177–183. Instead, we'll
give you some tips for troubleshooting each of the three parts: recognize,
strategize, and verbalize.

Part 1. Recognize—Identify Feelings

Some people have a very hard time putting their feelings into words. Be
patient. There are a few common difficulties you might run into:

- **The person simply can't think of a word that fits.** Have them read
  the list of feeling words in the sidebar on page 179 and try to pick one.
  If they can't find a word that fits exactly, ask them to pick the one that
  seems closest to what they're feeling.
- **The word they choose doesn't seem strong enough.** For instance,
  the person says they're just disappointed, but their face is red
  and their voice tone is extremely hostile. Gently ask if they can
  identify any additional feelings. (For instance, "Is there any other
  emotion in there, in addition to disappointment?" "How do you feel
  toward [the other person] for doing something that disappointed
  you?")
- **The word they choose is a feeling look-alike such as** *betrayed, criti-*
  cized, **or** *used.* Coach the person to identify the underlying emotion

they're experiencing. You might refer them back to the list of feeling words on page 179.

- **Their statement of feeling sounds flat, inauthentic, or uncertain.** Encourage them to let themselves feel their emotion fully before they state it out loud, so that it comes through in their voice tone. (For example, the expression of strong anger would be a forceful, "I'm angry!")
- **They have difficulty rating their level of feeling from 1 to 5.** Have them try limiting themselves to three choices: 1 (not feeling the emotion at all), 5 (feeling it at maximum intensity), and 2–4 (somewhere in the middle).

Part 2. Strategize—Set a Productive Goal for the Communication
Your role in strategizing is relatively simple. If the person identifies a goal, check to make sure it's productive, not focused on punishing the other person or making them change (something like "I want to find a better way of talking to each other," rather than "I want him to understand how insulting he's been"). If they can't think of any productive goals, see if you can come up with some that they might have overlooked. After they've stated a productive goal, encourage them to continue to explore, searching for an even more productive goal (for instance, transitioning from "I want to find a balance of responsibilities in this department that will work for me" to "I want to find a balance of responsibilities in this department that will work for all of us").

Part 3. Verbalize—Find the Words to Help Meet Their Goal
As the person practices their combination of feeling statements, fact statements, proposals, or questions, give feedback on how they're coming across. Have them continue practicing until their message comes through clearly, with no blame in their words or voice tone. If they find this impossible to do because they're still so upset, encourage them to repeat the earlier parts of the strategy (recognize and strategize) and then try again. (If you reach a point where both of you have tried your best and they still can't manage to transform their attacking behavior into direct, clear statements, you might refer them to a therapist, counselor, or anger management specialist.) Your final task as coach is to consult with the person after they've had their conversation. Discuss what went well, what didn't go well, and what they could do better in the future.

> **The Upshot:** When a person needs help to transform their attacks into more productive communication, skillful coaching can significantly boost their chance of success.

Intervention Step 3: Practice

Helping someone work through their attacks is not a task to take on lightly. It requires a great deal of patience and skill, as well as the ability to stay grounded and focused in the face of strong emotions. Be sure to get lots of practice—first with transforming your own attacks, and then with the coaching skills—before you try to use this strategy spontaneously. Start now by continuing on to the training program.

Exercises

Attacks Training Program: Using Feelings as Information, Not Ammunition

To our knowledge, we have yet to encounter anyone who never uses attacks. The attacks may be subtle, and they may primarily be internal—coming out more in what you think about other people than in what you say to them—but they're happening. Whether or not you decide to practice the response or intervention strategies, we recommend trying at least a few of the exercises that focus on your own attacks. You may be surprised to discover the ways in which your anger or irritation tends to leak out, as well as the new possibilities that open up when you transform your attacks into more useful communication.

For general guidelines on how to get the most out of each training program, review "Training Program Guidelines" in Chapter 3, on page 47. Note that this icon—OO—marks exercises for which we strongly recommend working with a partner.

Basic Training:
Building Awareness and Flexible Thinking

Exercise 1: Feeling Statements and Their Look-Alikes

Goal: Test and enhance your ability to distinguish between direct expressions of feeling and other, similar-sounding statements
Estimated time: 5–10 minutes

Identify whether the following comments are feeling statements (clear, direct expressions of emotional experience) or other types of communication. Mark each one either *F* for feeling or *O* for other. (Note: It is often impossible to know what type of communication is being used without hearing the voice tone. Assume that for each of these, the voice tone is consistent with the words, without being threatening, hostile, or whiny.) Answers are at the end of this chapter, on page 203.

1. I'm mad.
2. I'm mad at you.
3. I'm mad about how selfish you've been acting for the past few weeks.
4. I'm feeling disrespected by you.
5. I'm feeling irritable.
6. I'm so angry that I'm having a hard time even talking to you.
7. When I heard I wasn't getting promoted, I was enraged.
8. You make me so angry!
9. I'm feeling nervous about this job.
10. I feel underappreciated in this job.
11. I feel like I don't belong in this job.
12. After hearing your presentation, I feel like you're trying to pass off other people's work as your own.
13. I feel like this relationship is never going to work.
14. I feel hopeless about our relationship.
15. I feel like my feelings don't really matter to you.

Exercise 2: Putting Words to Your Feelings ∞

Goals:
*   Gain skill at detecting and naming your negative feelings
*   Learn to shift focus from your thoughts about someone else to a direct experience of your own emotional state

Estimated time: 10–20 minutes

This exercise is particularly helpful if you have a hard time putting words to your feelings. Together with a partner, walk through the following steps:

1. Think of a person in your life whom you strongly dislike, or who does things that really bother you.
2. Come up with an adjective that captures what you don't like about this person (pushy, lazy, annoying, etc.).
3. Think of a specific thing the person has said or done recently that seems consistent with that adjective (something they did that seemed pushy, lazy, etc.). Recall the details of the situation as vividly as you can, and describe them to your partner.
4. As you remember that incident, identify what emotion you're feeling, and say it out loud (for instance, "I'm annoyed," "I'm frustrated," or "I feel angry"). If you have difficulty thinking of a feeling word, look through the list of examples in the sidebar and see if any of those seem to fit. Your partner might also be able to make some suggestions.
5. Rate your feeling on a scale from 1 ("I don't feel this at all right now") to 5 ("I'm feeling this more powerfully now than I ever have before").
6. Talk with your partner about anything that surprised you or that you learned from this exercise. What was it like to shift focus from your negative thoughts about someone else to an awareness of your own feelings? How might this awareness of your feelings influence your future interactions with this person?

Common Negative Feelings

Words to describe common negative feelings include:

agitated	distressed	jealous
alarmed	embarrassed	lonely
angry	enraged	nervous
anguished	envious	overwhelmed
annoyed	exasperated	pained
anxious	fearful	powerless
apprehensive	frightened	resentful
ashamed	frustrated	sad
bitter	furious	scared
bored	grouchy	shocked
confused	grumpy	tense
cranky	guilty	terrified
dejected	helpless	uncomfortable
desperate	hopeless	uneasy
disappointed	humiliated	worried
discouraged	hurt	
dismayed	irritated	

When you're finished, switch roles with your partner. Repeat this exercise as often as you like, thinking of different people and different situations each time.

Variation: Do this exercise on your own, writing your responses down on paper.

Intermediate Training:
Deepening Your Verbal Attack Savvy

Exercise 3: Building Your Mirroring Muscles ∞

Goal: Develop skill at accurately mirroring others' feelings

Estimated time: 15–30 minutes

Work together with a partner to practice the skill of mirroring. Go through the following steps:

1. Think of a verbal attack you'd like to practice responding to. Tell it to your partner, and coach them until they can deliver the attack convincingly, with feeling.
2. Your partner directs the attack at you.
3. Respond by mirroring. (Remember that a mirror is like a paraphrase, but instead of just reflecting content, it reflects the person's feeling tone as well.)
4. Your partner responds naturally. (That means they talk more calmly only if they genuinely feel calmer as a result of your mirroring. If they feel more upset, they let that show.)
5. Talk with your partner about whether your mirroring felt accurate and helpful, and, if not, what might improve it.
6. Repeat steps 2 through 5 until both you and your partner are satisfied with your mirroring.
7. Talk together about anything that surprised you or that you learned from this exercise.

When you're finished, switch roles, so you deliver a verbal attack and your partner mirrors you. Continue practicing for as long as you like, switching after each successful mirror. Once you feel skilled with the basic version of this exercise, challenge yourself with Variation A.

Tips for Effective Mirroring
- Match the other person's voice tone but with slightly less emotional intensity
- Use either the same words they used or different words that capture the same underlying message
- Don't add in any new ideas

Variation A: Instead of aiming for accuracy, go for variety, seeing how many different ways you can mirror. Experiment with using the same words your partner used, and then with using various combinations of your own words. In addition to trying to match your partner's voice tone, see what happens when your tone is much less intense or much more intense. Discuss which types of mirroring work best, and why.

Variation B: Try this exercise in a trio. While one person attacks and another mirrors, the third person provides feedback and coaching.

Exercise 4: Four Different Responses to Attacks ∞

Goals:
- Experience the differences between four types of responses to attacks, from both sides of the conversation
- Improve your ability to recognize four types of responses to attacks

Estimated time: 20–30 minutes

To start, think of a situation in which someone might verbally attack you, and describe it to your partner. Then do a role-play together. Your partner takes on the role of the person using attacks, and you practice responding in four different ways:

1. **Counterattacks.** Every time you get attacked, strike back with criticism or blame of your own. Continue attacking each other for one minute.

2. **Self defense.** Respond to your partner's attacks by getting defensive, explaining why you shouldn't be blamed or why the situation isn't your fault. Continue for one minute.

3. **Proposals.** This time, when you get attacked, respond with a proposal for improving the situation. Listen to your partner's response, and then make another proposal. Continue for one minute (stopping early if they agree to one of your proposals).

4. **Mirroring.** Respond to your partner's attacks with empathetic mirroring. Continue for one minute (stopping early if they calm down fully). If they don't calm down at all, stop and ask whether they're feeling understood. If they're not, ask them how you could improve your mirroring, and try again.

When you're finished, talk with your partner about the four types of responses. What was it like for you to respond in each of those ways? What was it like for them to be on the receiving end? Which of the responses felt most natural, most comfortable, or most irritating?

Then switch roles, so you launch attacks and your partner responds. If you have a hard time with mirroring, get more practice with Exercise 3, then come back and try this exercise again.

Advanced Training:
Preparing to Apply the Full Attack Strategies

Exercise 5: Responding to Others' Attacks ∞

Goal: Develop skill with the complete strategy for responding to attacks, from de-escalating strong feelings to problem solving
Estimated time: 20–40 minutes

Think of a situation in which another person has verbally attacked you, and describe it to your partner in detail. Then coach them until they can role-play this person convincingly. Go through the following parts of the attack response strategy:

1.   **High feeling (they attack, you mirror)**
     Partner: Verbally attacks you, not easing up until your responses make them feel genuinely calmer.
     You: Mirror their message.

2.   **Medium feeling (they describe their concern, you paraphrase)**
     Partner: After calming down a little, talks more specifically about what is bothering them.
     You: Paraphrase their message.

3.   **Test question (you ask, they respond)**
     You: When you suspect your partner is ready to do rational problem solving, test this by asking a neutral question. If they answer calmly and directly, continue on to the next step. If they don't, return to paraphrasing or mirroring.
     Partner: If you feel ready to answer the question calmly and directly, do so. If you don't, give whatever other response comes naturally.

4.   **Low feeling (you both engage in problem solving together)**
     Both: Talk together about the problem underneath the attacks, and attempt to reach a mutually satisfying solution.

When you're finished, talk with each other about how this exercise went. What do you think worked well, and what didn't work well? What could you do in the future to make your mirroring, paraphrasing, questioning, and problem solving more effective? Then switch roles, so you deliver attacks and your partner responds.

Repeat this exercise as many times as you can, over several days or weeks. Be patient. It may take a while for you to feel fully comfortable with the strategy.

Answers to Exercise 1

F = Feeling statement, O = Other type of communication

1. F
2. F
3. O (The main message that comes through is not an expression of feeling but an accusation that the other person has been selfish.)
4. O ("Disrespected" is a blameful judgment, not a feeling.)
5. F
6. F
7. F
8. O (This statement doesn't just express a feeling; it blames the other person for causing it.)
9. F
10. O ("Underappreciated" is a blameful judgment.)
11. O (This is the speaker's opinion, not their feeling.)
12. O ("You're trying to pass off other people's work as your own" is not a feeling but an accusation.)
13. O ("This relationship is never going to work" is a negative prediction.)
14. F
15. O ("My feelings don't really matter to you" is an accusatory mind-read.)

Want to learn more? Try more exercises at CTsavvy.com/Aexercises, plus the awareness quiz at CTsavvy.com/Aquiz.

9

SAVI®: An All-Purpose Tool to Improve Any Conversation

In the preceding chapters, you've learned about six different troublesome forms of communication, from yes-buts to attacks, together with six sets of strategies for turning them around. You now have the keys to resolving the six most common causes of conversation breakdowns.

In this final chapter, we're going to go one step further, showing you that the six different topics we've covered aren't really so different. Yes-buts, mind-reads, negative predictions, leading questions, complaints, and attacks all belong to a larger class of communication behaviors that cause trouble in predictable ways, for the same underlying reasons. Likewise, all the behaviors that we recommend as strategies share something in common that makes them effective.

You may be familiar with the first line of Leo Tolstoy's novel *Anna Karenina*: "Happy families are all alike; every unhappy family is unhappy in its own way." The same can't be said of our conversations. Not only are successful conversations very much alike; unsuccessful conversations are alike as well. Both the good and the bad follow consistent patterns. To help you discover that for yourself, the next section walks you through an experiment that tests whether your own conversations fall into the patterns we're talking about.

SAVI® is a registered trademark of Anita Simon and Yvonne Agazarian.

Experiment: Is There a Pattern to Your Good and Bad Conversations?

Throughout this book, we've been focusing on how people talk rather than what they're talking about. You've learned to look at communication in terms of specific verbal behaviors (particular combinations of words and voice tones), such as complaints, mind-reads, paraphrases, broad questions, and so on. While the range of topics you could discuss is infinite—from the price of milk to the meaning of life—the range of behaviors you use in those discussions is actually quite small. In fact, anything you could possibly say, in any conversation, can be categorized within the nine-square grid shown in Figure 9-1 on the following page.

Use this grid to try our experiment. First, read through the names of the behaviors. Many of them are common terms, such as facts, proposal, and agreement. Some you will have encountered in Chapters 3 through 8, where we introduced a few less familiar behaviors, such as righteous questions and mirroring. Other terms may be completely new to you. Check the sidebar on pages 207–208 for definitions of several behaviors you might not recognize.

Now you're going to relate these behaviors to your personal experience. You'll need a grid you can write on, so either make a copy of Figure 9-1 or simply draw a three-by-three grid on a piece of paper, numbering the squares from 1 to 9. You can also try this experiment online at CTsavvy .com/bw. Start by bringing to mind the worst conversation you've ever been in. Try to recall a situation in which the more people talked, the worse things got—morale was low, very little was accomplished, and you couldn't wait for it all to be over. This may have been a board meeting, a family discussion, a negotiation with clients, an argument with friends, or any other unproductive interaction.

Think back to some of the specific things that were said. Then refer to Figure 9-1, and identify seven behaviors that you think played a big part in making the conversation go badly. For each of those behaviors, put a W (for "worst") in the corresponding square. (For instance, if you chose *joking around*, you'd put a W in square 2; if you chose *proposal*, you'd put a W in square 6; etc.) Take a few moments to do this now. Don't think too hard. Go with your first impression.

Figure 9-1. Grid to Classify Any Verbal Behavior

1	2	3
Attack/Blame	Mind-Reading	Yes-But
Righteous Question	Negative or Positive	Discount
Sarcasm	Prediction	Leading Question
Self Attack/Defend	Gossip	Oughtitude
Complaint	Joking Around	Interrupt
	Thinking Out Loud	
	Social Ritual	
4	**5**	**6**
Personal Information Current	Facts & Figures	Opinion
Personal Information Past	General Information	Proposal
Personal Opinion/ Explanation	Narrow Question	Command
Personal Question	Broad Question	Social Reinforcement
7	**8**	**9**
Inner Feeling	Answer Question	Agreement
Feeling Question	Clarify Own Answer (with data)	Positives
Answer Feeling Question	Paraphrase	Build on Other's Ideas or Experience
Mirror Inner Experience	Summarize	Work Joke
Affectionate Joke	Corrective Feedback	
Self Assertion		

This grid was adapted from the SAVI® Grid with permission from Anita Simon and Yvonne Agazarian, 2011. © Anita Simon and Yvonne Agazarian, 2011. SAVI® is a registered trademark of Anita Simon and Yvonne Agazarian.

Next, think about the best conversation you've ever been in—a situation in which morale was high, you accomplished your goals with ease, excitement, and good humor, and you left feeling good about everyone involved. Identify seven behaviors that you think played a big part in making that conversation go well and place a *B* (for "best") in the corresponding square. Again, just go with your first impression.

When you've finished, look at your final result. Some of the squares will have *W*s in them, some will have *B*s, some may have both *W*s and *B*s, and some may have neither *W*s nor *B*s. What conclusions can you draw from what you see? Are there any clear patterns? Are your *W*s randomly distributed throughout the grid, or do they seem to cluster in certain areas?

What about the *Bs*? Based on what you're seeing, can you make any guesses about how the different behaviors are organized within the grid? Stop and give some thought to this question before reading any further.

Unfamiliar Terms in the Grid

- **Joking around.** Joking about a serious topic, or telling tangential stories or jokes that take the discussion away from the issue at hand. (Examples: "Have you heard the one about the salesman who wore two hats?" "If you think this situation is tough, you should have seen the crazy problem I ran into this weekend with my dog Chester . . .")

- **Thinking out loud.** Incoherent ramblings, incomplete thoughts, or partial phrases. (Example: "Well, what I think is . . . it's just like, you know . . . but of course, I can't really say . . .")

- **Social ritual.** Predictable, socially determined expressions that are rattled off with little or no emotion. (Examples: "Hi, how's it going." "Excuse me.")

- **Oughtitude.** Statements implying that the speaker has a direct line to the absolute truth, which everybody ought to know. Oughtitudes are frequently shaming and are often stated with a voice tone that is haughty or superior (though not hostile). (Examples: "Everybody should know that." "That just isn't done.")

- **Social reinforcement.** Neutral space-fillers that neither oppose nor explicitly agree with what another person is saying. (Examples: "Uh huh," "You don't say," "I see.")

- **Affectionate joke.** Warm, interpersonal humor that expresses intimacy and good feelings between people. (Example: "It would be a lot more fun to argue with you if you'd stop being right all the time!")

- **Self assertion.** Clear, nonhostile, neutrally toned, descriptive "I" statements of what the speaker will or will not do. These are often used to set limits or draw boundaries. (Examples: "I will not help you cheat on this exam." "If you don't meet this deadline, I'll reassign the project to somebody else.")

- **Corrective feedback.** Neutral, nonhostile statements that give data (not opinions) correcting a previous statement. (Example: Person 1 says, "The store closes at six o'clock tonight." Person 2 says, "Actually, due to the holidays, the store will stay open until nine o'clock.")
- **Work joke.** In-group jokes, puns, and plays on words that are relevant to the work being done or the goal of the group. (Example: "There's just one problem: now that we're making decisions so efficiently, how are we going to fill all three hours of our staff meetings?")

Of course, we can't see your pattern of Ws and Bs, but we can make a good guess about how it turned out. Wherever people have tried this experiment—in different types of organizations, different cities and states, and even different countries—they've come out with the same basic result: more Ws on the top row and more Bs on the bottom row. Such consistent results clearly reveal some sort of underlying pattern in the grid.

Did you come up with a theory about what that pattern might be? The answer may seem obvious: all the bad, oppositional, and nasty communication behaviors are at the top, while all the good, friendly, and cooperative behaviors are at the bottom. You might be surprised to learn that in fact, the organization of the grid has nothing to do with what's good or bad, or with any other kind of value judgment. There is one simple yet crucial factor that differentiates the behaviors in the top row from those on the bottom, a factor that underlies all the communication challenges and strategies we've described in this book. It can be summed up in a single word: *noise.* The behaviors that consistently cause communication problems are noise producers, and the behaviors that help resolve those problems are noise reducers. What does it mean for communication to be noisy? Keep reading, and we'll explain.

The Universal Conversation Killer: Noise

Imagine walking along a city street while talking to a friend on your cell phone. You're discussing something important, and you're both engrossed in the conversation. Suddenly, there's static on the line, so you can hear only bits and pieces of what your friend is saying. Then a truck drives by, honking loudly, followed by a police car and ambulance with sirens blaring. What happens to your conversation, and to your frame of mind? The more noise there is, the harder it is for someone to get their message through to you, and for you to get your message through to them. This can be extremely frustrating.

Static, horns, and sirens are all examples of external, physical noise. These sorts of barriers to communication may be maddening, but at least they're obvious. When people are competing with loud sounds in their environment, there's no mystery about why they're having trouble understanding one another. Much more difficult to perceive are factors *within* a conversation that make it hard for information to get through.

Noise within the communication itself can cause just as much misunderstanding and frustration as external, physical noise, but all too often it goes unnoticed. We'll describe this type of noise briefly here, and show how it relates to the specific communication behaviors that can make or break a conversation. (Note: The conception of noise we're using was originally developed by Yvonne Agazarian, building on the work of Claude Shannon and Warren Weaver).[1]

Noise within conversations takes three distinct forms:

1.   **Ambiguity.** An ambiguous message is one that's unclear or that could be interpreted in more than one way, making it hard for listeners to figure out what the speaker means and how they should respond. For example, suppose your business partner asks, "Don't you think Kevin is doing a great job?" (a leading question), and you don't think Kevin is doing particularly well. What do you say? It's not clear whether your partner wants your honest opinion or just wants you to say yes.

     You face a similar problem when friends make vague remarks like "What an unusual pair of shoes" or "That's an interesting perspective" in a flat voice tone that gives no clue as to what they're really thinking. These comments are so ambiguous that it's impossible to know whether you're being complimented or insulted.

2.   **Contradiction.** In contradiction, two opposing messages are coming through at the same time. Often the tone of voice contradicts the words, as in sarcasm ("I can't *wait* to spend three hours in another committee meeting"). Yes-buts represent a different type of contradic-

tion, saying yes and no simultaneously ("Yeah, it would be great to get away, but I'm too busy right now"). It's always difficult to take in two conflicting pieces of information at once.

3. **Redundancy.** In a redundant communication, the message is so repetitious that listeners tend to tune out. Think of any class or talk you've attended where the presenter went on and on, saying the same thing in five different ways. That's the most obvious form of redundancy: repetition of *what's* being said. Repetition of *how* something is said can also be a problem. Hearing the same communication behavior over and over can be as off-putting as hearing the same idea over and over. Although people generally aren't used to noticing this sort of redundancy, it has a significant impact on many conversations. You saw one instance of that in Chapter 7, where we discussed the complaint-proposal-complaint-proposal pattern, in which one person repeatedly complains and the other person keeps making unsuccessful attempts to help.

Another common example is a redundant string of narrow questions. Imagine being stuck on the receiving end in the following exchange:

"Have you started your new exercise program?" (Yes.)
"Do you do it every day?" (Pretty much.)
"Did you miss any days last week?" (I don't really remember.)
"Do you ever skip more than two days in a row?" (Well, doesn't everyone?)

After answering a few of these questions in a row, you'd probably start to feel irritated, though you might not understand why. The discussion starts to feel like an interrogation, not because of the topic you're discussing but because of the redundant pattern of questioning.

These three forms of noise—ambiguity, contradiction, and redundancy—work against the very purpose of communication. The whole point of communicating is to get information from one place or person to another, and noise makes that significantly more difficult. As a result, noise tends to increase stress. When information isn't getting through, people generally start feeling frustrated and annoyed. The converse is also true: stress tends to increase noise, because when people are frustrated, they're more likely to use noisy behaviors. The result is a vicious cycle—noise in the conversation generates frustration, which in turn generates more noise, and so on.

> Three forms of noise in communication:
>
> - Ambiguity
> - Contradiction
> - Redundancy
>
> Each of these makes it more difficult for information to get through, which tends to increase stress and frustration.

The concept of noise ties in directly to the nine-square grid in Figure 9-1 (page 206). That grid is part of a comprehensive framework that categorizes all verbal behaviors[2] in terms of how they affect the flow of information, including whether they increase or decrease the level of noise. This framework, developed in 1965 by Anita Simon and Yvonne Agazarian, forms the foundation for all the communication skills we teach. It's called SAVI® (pronounced *savvy*), which stands for the System for Analyzing Verbal Interaction.[3]

In the remainder of this chapter, we'll introduce you to some fundamental elements of SAVI theory and practice. We won't go into a lot of detail, but we'll give you enough background so you can see how this system unites everything you've learned about the six most common communication challenges (including the strategies to resolve them), and how it holds the key to tackling many other communication challenges you might encounter.

Information Traffic Jams

Take a look at the full version of the SAVI grid in Figure 9-2 on the following page. (To access a full-color downloadable grid, visit CTsavvy.com/grid.) Notice how the rows are labeled. They're based on the model of a traffic light, with each row having a different color: red, yellow, and green. Whenever you're unsure about how to get your message across effectively, or how to respond to a difficult message coming at you, these colors provide

Figure 9-2. The Complete SAVI® Grid

System for Analyzing Verbal Interaction

| | PERSON | | TOPIC |
	Personal	Factual	Orienting
RED Light	**1 FIGHTING** Attack/Blame Righteous Question Sarcasm Self Attack/Defend Complaint	**2 OBSCURING** Mind-Reading Negative or Positive Prediction Gossip Joking Around Thinking Out Loud Social Ritual	**3 COMPETING** Yes-But Discount Leading Question Oughtitude Interrupt
YELLOW Light	**4 INDIVIDUALIZING** Personal Information Current Personal Information Past Personal Opinion/ Explanation Personal Question	**5 FINDING FACTS** Facts & Figures General Information Narrow Question Broad Question	**6 INFLUENCING** Opinion Proposal Command Social Reinforcement
GREEN Light	**7 RESONATING** Inner Feeling Feeling Question Answer Feeling Question Mirror Inner Experience Affectionate Joke Self Assertion	**8 RESPONDING** Answer Question Clarify Own Answer (with data) Paraphrase Summarize Corrective Feedback	**9 INTEGRATING** Agreement Positives Build on Other's Ideas or Experience Work Joke

Silence, Laughter, Noise

an invaluable guide. (You may also notice that the columns of the grid are labeled as well. We'll talk about those later on.)

Red Light: Blocking the Flow

The behaviors in the top row of the SAVI grid have the same effect on information as a red light has on traffic. They don't stop everything from getting through, but they do tend to block the flow. Why? Because they're so noisy. Conversations containing a lot of red-light behaviors are filled with ambiguity, contradiction, redundancy, or some combination of the three.

All that noise makes it hard to get information across. This, in turn, makes it hard to accomplish whatever it is that we're trying to do, whether it's negotiating a budget deal, planning a course of medical treatment, making a hiring decision, resolving a marital conflict, deciding where to move or go on vacation, or any of the countless other things we try to achieve through talking. That helps to explain why the results of the best/worst experiment keep turning out the same; no matter what people talk about in their "worst" conversations, the behaviors causing the trouble come mainly from the top (red-light) row. It also explains why, as you may have noticed, all the communication challenges we've covered in this book are red-light behaviors.

While the consequences of using red-light behaviors are often negative, we want to emphasize that the behaviors themselves aren't bad. Yes-buts aren't bad. Complaints aren't bad. Even attacks aren't bad. The people who use these behaviors aren't bad, either. In fact, we all use many of these behaviors every day. Red-light communication actually carries very important information, often including information about the emotional state of the person who's talking (for instance, the fact that they're angry or frustrated or worried about something). The problem is that this information comes embedded in a murky haze of ambiguity, contradiction, and redundancy, which makes it difficult for other people to get the message and do something useful about it.

Red-Light Communication

- Contains the most noise (ambiguity, contradiction, and redundancy)
- Makes it difficult for information to get through
- Carries important embedded information that tends to get lost or misunderstood
- Includes all the communication challenges discussed in this book

The three red-light squares on the SAVI grid carry different types of embedded information.

In square 1 (fighting), what's embedded is mainly personal, with strong feelings and other deeply meaningful information coming out in noisy ways. For instance, in Chapter 8, we saw Katie venting her frustration indirectly at her mother, through verbal attacks. Likewise, the sisters in Chapter 7 didn't directly state what

1 FIGHTING
Attack/Blame
Righteous Question
Sarcasm
Self Attack/Defend
Complaint

they both intensely wanted (time off from working at their store to take a vacation). Instead, that desire got buried in complaints about how bad their situation was ("We don't do anything fun anymore," "I'm fed up with being in the store all the time").

Square 2 (obscuring) behaviors talk about other people, activities, or events—not directly but through gossip, assumptions, tangential jokes, and other highly ambiguous remarks. Any actual data about the topic at hand is embedded in so much noise that the reality of the situation gets obscured.

2 OBSCURING
Mind-Reading
Negative or Positive Prediction
Gossip
Joking Around
Thinking Out Loud
Social Ritual

Remember from Chapter 4 that Ben's untested mind-reads of his friend Alan ("Clearly Alan was still upset," "He had no interest in talking to me") blocked him from discovering the reality that his friend had actually forgiven him, or from even considering that possibility. Similarly, when the school negotiators in Chapter 5 got caught up in negative predictions ("If we try to present the facts, he'll just laugh and make sarcastic jabs," "It's the students who will lose out in the end"), they failed to see the options they had for improving their chances of success.

In square 3 (competing), the embedded information is a point of view that differs from what's previously been said. Rather than being stated in a clear, direct way, this different perspective introduces competition by opposing, contradicting, interrupting, preempting, or putting down previously expressed viewpoints. For

3 COMPETING
Yes-But
Discount
Leading Question
Oughtitude
Interrupt

example, in Chapter 3, you saw how Rob and Amanda Parker kept expressing their concerns in the form of yes-buts—"I don't expect you to be over it, but that was almost a year ago," "Sure, it was almost a year ago, but we don't even talk about it anymore"—with the result that neither of them really heard and understood the other person's point of view. For Ricardo Garza, from Chapter 6, presenting ideas in the form of leading questions ("Isn't that right?" "Wouldn't you agree?") contributed to the near collapse of his sales team.

Once a conversation starts moving into square 1, 2, or 3, it can quickly get stuck in red light. Remember the vicious cycle in which noise increases frustration, which then further increases noise? Whenever you use complaints, mind-reads, yes-buts, or any other noisy, red-light behaviors, you make it more likely that other people in the conversation will get frustrated and join you up in red light.

Green Light: Greasing the Wheels

Now let's look at the other end of the communication spectrum: the behaviors at the bottom of the SAVI grid. Just as a green light is a welcome sign at a traffic intersection, green-light behaviors are usually good news for a conversation. These behaviors contain a minimum of noise and therefore make it easier for information to get through. In addition, each of these behaviors gives evidence that information has already gotten through. For instance, when someone states a mind-read of you and you accurately paraphrase it, you show that you understand what they've said. When someone asks a question and you answer it, you show that you understand their question. Green-light behaviors grease the wheels of communication, encouraging a free and open flow of information and ideas.

When a conversation is in trouble, green-light behaviors are often the safest bet for turning things around. You may have noticed that many of the strategies you learned in this book involve green-light behaviors like mirroring, paraphrasing, and building. By meeting red-light behaviors with a green-light response, we help ensure that the embedded information they carry doesn't get lost but instead gets actively processed.

The behaviors in square 7 (resonating), on the following page, help to process feelings and other deeply personal information. For example, through mirroring, Laura (from Chapter 8) showed that she understood the emotions behind her daughter Katie's attack and also helped to soothe those emotions. When feelings aren't so high, we can use square 8 (responding) behaviors to demonstrate understanding and provide clarification. A good example is the leading question response strategy. By paraphrasing the embedded opinion, the embedded question, or both, you show that you understand the message while at the same time helping to clarify that mes-

7 RESONATING	8 RESPONDING	9 INTEGRATING
Inner Feeling	Answer Question	Agreement
Feeling Question	Clarify Own Answer (with data)	Positives
Answer Feeling Question		Build on Other's
Mirror Inner Experience	Paraphrase	Ideas or Experience
Affectionate Joke	Summarize	Work Joke
Self Assertion	Corrective Feedback	

sage. (For instance, to paraphrase the leading question "Isn't that too expensive?" you might say, "You want to know if I think this is too expensive.")

The third green-light square, square 9 (integrating), contains behaviors that integrate previously stated ideas or experiences by joining, validating, or building on them. Recall the powerful shifts that happened when the Parkers (from Chapter 3) stopped yes-butting each other and started building instead; the very issues that had been driving them apart (grief over infertility and desire for a closer romantic connection) became areas of common ground that brought them closer together.

In addition to using green-light behaviors yourself, you can invite others to move into green light by asking a question. Any direct answer to a question is a green-light behavior, giving proof that information is flowing and making it easier for that flow to continue. It's no accident that questions play a large role in many communication strategies, including the ones we've discussed in this book. In yes-but conversations, broad questions can help promote creative thinking and problem solving. In conversations dominated by mind-reads or negative predictions, questions can help replace assumptions with data. And when someone is complaining, asking the right types of questions can help them shift from helpless passivity to constructive action. Just keep in mind that for any question to be effective, it needs to get answered. It's the potential to shift a conversation into green light—by soliciting an answer to create a two-way exchange of information—that makes questions so powerful.

Green-Light Communication
- Contains minimal noise
- Gives evidence that information has gotten through

- Makes it more likely that new information will get through as well
- Is often the best bet for moving difficult conversations in a more constructive direction
- Is included in all of the communication strategies discussed in this book, either directly (going into green light yourself) or indirectly (asking a question to open the way for a green-light response)

Yellow Light: Food for Thought or Fuel for the Fire

Up to this point, we haven't said anything about the central row of the grid. Look back at your pattern of *W*s and *B*s from the best/worst conversation experiment. You probably have more *W*s on the top and more *B*s on the bottom, but what's going on in the middle? Results vary somewhat from person to person. Most frequently, there's a mixture of a few *W*s and a few *B*s, meaning that yellow-light behaviors are showing up in both successful and unsuccessful conversations.

The behaviors in the yellow-light row—facts, opinions, proposals, questions, and so on—are quite different from those in the other two rows. They don't make it harder for information to get through (like red-light behaviors), but they also don't show that information has already gotten through (like green-light behaviors). They simply bring more information into the discussion.

Sometimes the information is personal, relating to ourselves, our preferences, and our relationships (square 4, individualizing: "I really like the blue version of the logo"). Sometimes it's related to facts in the external world (square 5, finding facts: "The designer gave us three different logo options to choose from"). And sometimes it sets a new direction for the conversation (square 6, influencing: "Let's see which option other people prefer").

4 INDIVIDUALIZING	5 FINDING FACTS	6 INFLUENCING
Personal Information Current	Facts & Figures	Opinion
Personal Information Past	General Information	Proposal
Personal Opinion/ Explanation	Narrow Question	Command
Personal Question	Broad Question	Social Reinforcement

We refer to yellow-light behaviors as *contingent* because their effects on communication are contingent on the pattern of other behaviors that have been used in the conversation (the *communication climate*). Depending on the communication climate that's been established, the same yellow-light contribution can be used either as a resource to help get work done or as ammunition to perpetuate a fight.

Say you're in a meeting and you make a proposal: "Let's look into hiring a new administrative support person." If the meeting so far has included a lot of green-light behaviors (questions are getting answered and ideas are getting explored through builds and agreements), the odds are good that your proposal will be worked through in a productive way. People might build on your suggestion ("Having more administrative support could free us up to start new creative projects"), or they might ask broad, exploratory questions ("What tasks would this person take over?" "What would be the financial pros and cons?"). However, if the climate is predominantly red-light (people are yes-butting, discounting, attacking, and interrupting each other), your proposal will likely be ignored, criticized, or shot down ("That would be great, but we can't afford it," "We'd never get approval to make a new hire," etc.).

There's also a third possibility. Sometimes a conversation takes place almost entirely in yellow light. That means a lot of information is coming in, but it isn't being used. You might hear one opinion, then another, then another, or a long string of different proposals. (In our example, your suggestion might be followed by several others: "Why don't we cut back on a few projects?" "How about automating some of our systems?" etc.) Nobody shows any sign of agreement or disagreement, or builds on anybody else's ideas. It's hard to tell if anyone's even heard what other people have said.

When people complain about tedious, boring meetings that don't go anywhere, an all-yellow communication pattern is often to blame. Particularly common are long strings of opinions: "This is the best time to buy," "The best time to buy will be after the holidays," "Maybe we should rethink this issue," and so on. Groups that never make it from yellow light to green light can wind up having essentially the same meeting five, ten, or twenty times. SAVI cocreator Yvonne Agazarian has labeled this sort of pattern "as-if work," because it sounds as if people are working, but nothing ever gets accomplished.[4]

Yellow-Light Communication

- Brings unsolicited information into a conversation
- Neither helps nor blocks the flow of information
- May be used as a resource in a constructive dialogue or as ammunition in a fight
- Is insufficient, on its own, to get anything significant accomplished

The Power of Three

You may have noticed in Figure 9-2, on page 212, that each of the SAVI rows includes three separate squares. There's a good reason for this. In addition to the three rows, the SAVI grid also includes three vertical divisions (columns), with each column focusing on a different type of information. Column 1 behaviors focus on personal information, such as feelings (square 7) and information about oneself (square 4). Column 2 behaviors focus on factual information about the outside world, whether it's real data like facts and figures (square 5) or imagined data like mind-reads and negative predictions (square 2). Column 3 behaviors orient the direction of a conversation, either by introducing a new viewpoint (square 6), supporting or building on a previously introduced viewpoint (square 9), or competing with a previously introduced viewpoint (square 3).

The nine SAVI squares are formed by the intersection of the three rows and the three columns. Once you know what square a particular behavior is in, you know quite a bit about how it is likely to influence a conversation, including both how it affects information flow (its row) and the type of information it's bringing in (its column). For example, when you see that attack is in square 1, you know that it's mainly focused on personal information (column 1). You also know the behavior is noisy (since it's in the red-light row), so it will be difficult for that personal information to get through to the listener effectively. The same characteristics (personal focus and a high level of noise) apply to all other square 1 behaviors, from *self attack* ("I'm such a bad mother") to *complaints* ("Nothing ever gets done around here unless I do it").

A Master Strategy for Communication Breakdowns: Diagnosis and Repair

Resolving a communication breakdown is much like fixing a broken-down car: you need to first diagnose the underlying problem, and then find an effective way to repair it. In the previous chapters, you've learned about six specific problems that arise in conversations, together with corresponding strategies to help repair them. The SAVI grid enables us to go one step further, revealing an overall diagnosis for communication troubles and an overall strategy for repair.

- **Master diagnosis.** In almost any conversation where the more people talk, the worse things get, the pattern of communication is predominantly in red light, yellow light, or some combination of the two.
- **Master strategy.** You can make a positive change by shifting the difficult conversation to a green- and yellow-light pattern. To do so, you'll probably—at some point—need to move into green-light communication yourself, pose questions that invite others into green light, or both.

These general guidelines not only unite all the skills we've covered in this book; they also provide a foundation for understanding other communication skills you may learn. Test this out for yourself whenever you read books or articles on effective communication. In the large majority of cases, you'll find that the problems they identify are in yellow and red light, and the solutions they recommend are in yellow and green.

Any time you find yourself stuck in a frustrating or upsetting conversation, you can use the master strategy to help navigate your way out of trouble. Start by making an intentional mental shift: instead of thinking just about *what* you want to say, focus on *how* you want to say it—what communication behaviors you want to use. Make the choice to use a green-light behavior, a yellow-light question, or a combination of the two.

If you recognize one of the red-light behaviors from this book, either in what you've said or in what someone else has said, you can try the strategy we've discussed for handling that particular communication challenge. (For instance, if you realize that you've been yes-butting or someone has yes-butted you, you can try the yes-but transformation or response technique.) If not, simply try whatever combination of green-light and yellow-light behaviors you think might work best. Be prepared to make more than one attempt. If your first attempt fails and you get a red-light response, try a different behavior, and then another, until you get to where you want to be: in a green-yellow conversation, where information is flowing and everyone's ideas are getting heard and understood.

Backup Plan

You may occasionally run into situations where the master diagnosis doesn't seem to work: everyone is communicating in yellow and green light, but the conversation is still going nowhere. This typically means that the problem lies not in how information is flowing (as indicated by the SAVI rows), but in the types of information being shared (as indicated by the SAVI columns). The types of information people are discussing may be poorly suited to the goals they're trying to achieve. For instance, coworkers trying to make a financial decision may get stuck talking about their personal preferences (column 1), instead of working through facts and proposals (columns 2 and 3). Or spouses trying to repair their relationship may primarily discuss facts (column 2), without sharing their feelings (column 1). You can resolve this sort of problem by shifting into a different column, or combination of columns, while still remaining in yellow and green light.

It Takes a Pattern (to Wreck or Save a Conversation)

Did you notice that both the master diagnosis and the master strategy refer to *patterns* of communication, not just individual behaviors? Whether you're trying to figure out what went wrong with a conversation or what needs to change to make things better, it's the patterns that you need to keep your eye on. Remember that in and of themselves, red-light behaviors aren't bad and green-light behaviors aren't good. One lone yes-but, leading question, complaint, or attack is rarely a problem; it's what comes next that matters. For example, while an attack followed by self defense is often the start of a fight, the same attack followed by an empathetic mirror may lead to a meaningful exchange that draws people together and gives them a renewed sense of purpose.

What this means is that when you're trying to understand why your conversation is going badly, it's not enough to notice what the other person is saying. You also need to consider what you're doing to contribute to the breakdown. If you find yourself getting increasingly frustrated while talking with a friend, spouse, or colleague, the problem is not just that they're attacking, yes-butting, or complaining; it's that you're responding to those behaviors with more red-light (or at least non-green-light) communication. Instead of working to understand their perspective or build on what they're saying, you may be defending yourself, arguing with them, telling them what to do, or expressing your ideas in some other unconstructive way.

The good news is that by changing your own behavior, you automatically start to change the communication pattern. By mindfully and consistently shifting yourself into green and yellow light, you can help to shift the whole discussion into green and yellow light, giving both of you a better chance of reaching your goals.

Watch What You Say, but Only When It Matters

Sometimes when we teach people about the different types of behaviors, they worry that they ought to be monitoring everything they say, mentally categorizing every sentence in their conversations as red, yellow, or green light. We want to be clear that even if this were possible (which it isn't), it's not what we'd recommend. It's certainly not what we strive for in our own communication. Think back to the car analogy. If your car is running fine and getting you where you want to go, there's no need to keep checking under the hood. The same is true of conversations. It's only when you start to see signs of trouble, such as anxiety, irritation, or misunderstanding, that you have a compelling reason to search for underlying problems and work toward finding solutions.

It's Not Easy Being Green (Light)

Using the master strategy—shifting your communication from a red/yellow to a green/yellow pattern—is no easy task. In Chapter 2, we discussed one reason for this: it's difficult to change any deeply ingrained pattern of behavior. You need to inhibit your habitual response and consciously choose to try something new, which may feel awkward and uncomfortable until you've had a fair amount of practice.

There's also another reason why this change is difficult: being in green demands more from you than being in red. Remember that using green-light behavior involves processing information. That takes mental work. To paraphrase someone accurately, you need to hear and understand what they're saying while restraining your own impulse to be heard first. To build on someone's idea, you need to take in that idea and integrate it with your own point of view while at the same time resisting the impulse to bring up opposing ideas.

Along with all the mental work, there's often some emotional work you need to do as well. Simply going through the motions of green-light behavior isn't enough. If you don't transform your hostility or irritation into genuine interest in the other person's perspective, you can say all the right words for a build or mirror or paraphrase but still come across as critical or blameful. When you're feeling frustrated, angry, anxious, or even just tired and bored, summoning the energy and curiosity you need to stay in green light can be quite a struggle.

In contrast, red-light behavior is literally a no-brainer. To interrupt a conversation or say, "That won't work," "Yes, but we can't afford it," "It's all your fault," or "Don't blame me," you don't need to be paying close attention to the other person's message. You hardly need to hear a word they're saying. You can stay totally checked out, running on autopilot, and let your impulses take over.

Given how much work it takes to move out of red light and into green, why should we bother? When people choose to make that effort, it's generally because they know it will get them better results—often much better results. Just because it's easy to use red-light behavior, that doesn't mean it's easy to live with the consequences: failed meetings, damaged relationships, hurt feelings, and all the time and energy that get wasted on needless conflict and misunderstandings. When the outcome of a conversation matters to you, the benefits of communicating with awareness and skill usually more than compensate for the effort you put in.

We're Not Only the Authors . . .

In one of the most frequently parodied advertising slogans of the 1980s, Sy Sperling announced, "I'm not only the Hair Club president, I'm also a client." As this book draws to a close, we—Ben, Amy, and Anita—would like to make a similar disclosure of our own. We don't just teach the strategies you've been reading about; we use them ourselves, in every area of our lives.

Our SAVI training doesn't make us immune from using red-light behaviors or getting triggered when someone else uses them with us. When the pressure is high or our buttons get pushed, we're as vulnerable as anyone else to falling back into habitual patterns of noisy communication. What we get from working with SAVI is a heightened awareness (so we're more likely to notice what's happening) and a set of skills (to help us get out of trouble and back on track). Usually, we can resolve our conflicts in minutes rather than hours, days, or weeks.

It's fair to say that if the three of us didn't have these skills, we wouldn't have been able to write this book together. Coauthoring a book is a stressful undertaking. We feel fortunate that we had the tools we needed to manage our differences. When we got caught in a conflict between Amy and Anita's negative predictions ("We're going to miss our deadline") and Ben's positive predictions ("We'll finish in plenty of time"), we sought out data and made contingency plans (like negotiating an extension, just in case). When any one of us started complaining ("I don't know what to do . . . Things just aren't coming together . . . This chapter is so hard to organize"), someone else would step in to help them figure out what they wanted and how they could get it. And on countless occasions when we had conflicting opinions, we worked through our yes-buts to discover what we liked about each other's ideas.

As a result, we ended up with a final product that we all agree is a much better book than any of us could have written alone. And because we actively improved our working relationships as we went along, we finish this process as closer friends and colleagues than we were when we began.

The issues that you deal with in your life and work will differ from ours. Instead of writing a book, you may be trying to solve a budget problem, design a new product, improve your students' test scores, plan for retirement on a fixed income, settle a disagreement about how to discipline your kids, plan long-term care for a patient or family member, or adjust to a new job, new relationship, new baby, or other major changes. But whatever challenges you face, the way you talk about those challenges will either be part of the problem or be part of the solution. We hope that reading this book is a first step toward making your own communication a powerful force for positive transformation.

Afterword:
What's Next?

If you've been working through the training programs in this book, you know how difficult it can be to transform your own communication. Changing communication patterns throughout a group or organization is an even greater challenge. Whether you're seeking to deepen your own skills or to make a broader difference in your work team, department, or organization, there are many resources available to help you take the next steps toward positive change.

Next Steps for Your Team or Organization

Is your team or organization experiencing any of the following:

- Frustrating, contentious, or unproductive meetings?
- Excessive turnover rates?
- Lack of buy-in or follow-through?
- Chronic failure to meet deadlines?
- E-mails or phone calls left unanswered?
- Distrust and spreading rumors about the organization's policies or intentions?
- Unresolved conflict between individuals, small cliques, or entire departments?

If you answered yes to any of these, your group is an excellent candidate for training based in SAVI®, the communication framework that underlies all the skills and concepts you've learned in this book. When applied within a team or organization, SAVI provides a common language that helps to bridge differences, boost morale, foster productive collaboration, and resolve conflicts in creative, mutually satisfying ways. Focused, targeted training can help any group, small or large, to transform unproductive behaviors into new, effective patterns of communicating.

You can explore a wide range of options for group skill development on the Conversation Transformation website, a clearinghouse for SAVI-related trainings of all types. The most common components of these programs include:

- **Free team assessment.** Following electronic testing and/or live interviews, you receive a free assessment of your team's current level of communication skill, together with specific recommendations for improvement. Visit CTsavvy.com/assessment.
- **Live trainings.** Through a series of in-person trainings—tailored to the particular needs of your industry, organization, and team members— your group begins to systematically replace dysfunctional behaviors with powerful new communication techniques. You may choose to focus these trainings on specific challenges your team is facing—such as cross-cultural misunderstandings, sensitive internal conflicts, or major company-wide changes such as mergers or downsizings—or stick to a broader focus on increased understanding and skill in communication. Visit CTsavvy.com/onsite.
- **Online learning.** As part of the training process, all team members receive full access to the online SAVI Learning System. This enables each individual to intensively practice and refine their skills and identify areas for further improvement. Visit CTsavvy.com/LearnIt.
- **Interactive teleseminars.** Between live training sessions, your team meets with trainers via web-based conference calls to refine previously learned skills and troubleshoot real-life work challenges. Visit CTsavvy.com/tele.
- **One-on-one coaching.** Should you or any of your colleagues want more focused, personalized attention, you may choose to enroll in one-on-one coaching. Visit CTsavvy.com/coaching.

Next Steps for You Personally

There are many options for continuing your own personal learning beyond this book:

- **Webinars from any location.** Live and prerecorded webinars enable you to continue your learning. Visit CTsavvy.com/webinars.
- **Open trainings.** A variety of one- and two-day trainings are available to help you prepare to apply SAVI as a consultant, coach, or trainer, or to simply take your skill to the next level. Visit CTsavvy.com/open.
- **Online learning.** Enrolling in the online SAVI Learning System gives you unlimited 24-hour access to challenging activities designed to deepen your knowledge and refine your skills. Visit CTsavvy.com/LearnIt.
- **Coaching.** Whether you're seeking to boost your general level of skill or resolve a specific high-stakes communication challenge, receiving one-on-one coaching is one of the most efficient, effective ways to move toward your goals. Visit CTsavvy.com/coaching.
- **Certification training.** To learn about becoming a certified SAVI trainer, visit CTsavvy.com/cert.

How to Get Started

There are three easy ways to learn more about possible training options:

1. Visit CTsavvy.com and click on Training.
2. Call 800-600-1522.
3. E-mail info@ConversationTransformation.com.

Yes, I want to transform my team!

I would like to learn more about SAVI®-based training opportunities.

Our key challenges are:

☐ Training the next generation of leaders

☐ Improving cross-cultural communication

☐ Breaking down the barriers between silos

☐ Handling conflict within the team or across teams

☐ Making meetings more effective

☐ Navigating major changes (e.g., mergers, relocations, layoffs, etc.)

☐ Improving communication with customers, clients, suppliers, etc.

☐ Enhancing productivity and effectiveness

☐ Improving morale/reducing turnover rates

☐ Other: _____

How to contact me:

Name: _____

Company name: _____

Address: _____

City, state, zip code: _____

E-mail address: _____

Daytime phone number: _____

Fax number: _____

Team size: _____

Type of business or organization: _____

The best way to reach me is:

☐ Phone   ☐ Email   ☐ Fax

Four easy ways to connect with SAVI® trainers:
1. Fill out this form online at CTsavvy.com/contactme
2. Fill out this form and submit it by fax to 888-863-4499
3. Call 800-600-1522
4. E-mail info@ConversationTransformation.com

Acknowledgments

This book wouldn't have been possible without the generous help, support, and intellectual contributions of many individuals.

First we thank Yvonne Agazarian, a woman of remarkable knowledge, insight, and vision. Yvonne is codeveloper with Anita of SAVI® (the System for Analzying Verbal Interaction), which forms the basis for everything we teach in this book. We're also deeply grateful to SAVI experts Claudia Byram and Fran Carter, who graciously sacrificed much of their limited free time to give extensive, invaluable feedback. And we thank Susan Gantt for helping us to clarify the boundaries between SAVI and Systems-Centered Training (SCT®).*

On the publishing side, we thank our agent Claudia Gere for masterfully guiding us through every step of the publication process, from proposal creation to final manuscript preparation. We've benefited greatly from her skill, expertise, patience, and insight. For connecting us with Claudia, we're grateful to Alesia Latson, one of the most inspiring people we've ever had the pleasure of working with.

We couldn't have asked for a better experience with our publisher. Everyone we've worked with at McGraw-Hill has been knowledgeable, responsive, and dedicated to producing the best book possible. Our acquisitions editor, Leila Porteous, has been truly exceptional, gracious, and conscientious from beginning to end. We also thank editing manager Jane Palmieri, developmental editor Joe Berkowitz, and publicist Pamela Peterson.

---

*SAVI® is a registered trademark of Anita Simon and Yvonne Agazarian. SCT® is a registered trademark of Dr. Yvonne M. Agazarian and the Systems-Centered Training and Research Institute, Inc.

For public relations, Tara Goodwin Frier has already been a wonderful resource, and we look forward to continuing to benefit from her expertise—and that of the rest of the Goodwin Group team—in the months to come.

For web-based content, we're indebted to Jeff Korn, our website designer, and Joel Gluck, the creative programming master behind our online learning system and other computerized book resources. We've relied heavily on their technical savvy and overall good judgment.

One of the greatest gifts people have given us is sharing real stories from their lives and work. Some we've used in the book, and others have had a more indirect influence on our thinking and writing. (We hope to incorporate some of the wonderful stories we couldn't include here into future books or articles.)

Individuals we've mentioned by name include Claudia Byram, Fran Carter, Mark Johnson, Clauda Marchessault, and Beulah Trey. Others who've contributed, directly or indirectly, include Shea Adelson, Maria Åkerlund, Karen Ball, Darren Burgess, Dayna Burnett, Ginny Christensen, Rowena Davis, Wayne Dorris, Amy Elizabeth Fox, Joel Gluck, Sharon Grady, Carl Harvey, Barbara Haskell, Jessica Kern, Michelle Lynskey, Mike Maher, Jane Maloney, Daniel Nordlander, Felix Rust, Carol Salloway, Steve Weinstein, Nancie Zane, Angelika Zollfrank, and Alida Zweidler-Mckay.

For Chapter 2, we're grateful for the substantial contributions of Ed Josephs, as well as the input of others with specialized knowledge in neuropsychology: Janet Crawford, Juliet Koprowska, Russell Poldrack, and Michael Robbins.

In developing the training programs for Chapters 3 through 8, we relied on insightful feedback from volunteer beta-testers, including Regina Au, Alison Bentley, Ali Farquhar, Claudia Gere, Sharon Grady, Curdina Hill, Cynthia Johnson, Merry Jones, Alesia Latson, Alexei Levine, Margo Levine, Lorri Lofvers, Libby Mahaffy, John Malloy, Diane Margolis, Anne Orens, Ellen Robinson, Michael Rutter, Ibrahim Skandarani, Gale Taylor, Maya Townsend, Eric Volkin, Nancy Wells, and Anna Xia. Special thanks to Diana Hammer, who not only gave great, thorough feedback, but also helped collect and synthesize others' comments.

Additional help reviewing or researching portions of text came from Ashley Adams, Alicia Cahill-Watts, Christine Junge, Jessica Kern, Irene McHenry, Felix Rust, Russell Sackowitz, Sonja Scali, James Sellman, Maya

Townsend, Eric Volkin, Amy Wyeth, and Cynthia Yeager. The book is stronger as a result of their efforts.

On an individual level, Ben thanks Mary-Louise White for her help and support through the long development and realization of this book. Both Ben and Amy thank Ariana Goterch and Catie Colliton, who expertly manage the countless administrative tasks that make the rest of their work possible. In addition to going far above and beyond the call of duty, they both have made our office a much more lively, fun, and pleasant place to be. Amy also thanks her husband Michael Rutter for being her greatest source of sanity, fulfillment, and joy, throughout the book-writing process and always. Anita thanks her sister Ruth for her countless useful suggestions and for making a nurturing home for her while she was building a home for SAVI. She also wants to acknowledge two individuals who inspired her to focus on verbal behavior as the critical data for studying and improving human interactions: Ned Allen Flanders for his work on improving teacher behavior and Robert Freed Bales for his work in methods of quantifying behavioral data.

Finally, we thank all of our students and clients, past and present. Thank you for giving us a reason to do what we do, and for all that you've taught us throughout the years.

Notes

Chapter 1

1. Hardeep Singh, Aanand Dinkar Naik, Raghuram Rao, and Laura Ann Petersen, "Reducing Diagnostic Errors through Effective Communication: Harnessing the Power of Information Technology," *Journal of General Internal Medicine* 23, no. 4 (2008): 489–494; and Kathleen M. Sutcliffe, Elizabeth Lewton, and Marilynn M. Rosenthal, "Communication Failures: An Insidious Contributor to Medical Mishaps," *Academic Medicine* 79, no. 2 (2004): 186–194.
2. We developed this dialogue for a training session we led at a major Boston hospital. It does not reflect one specific case but rather is an amalgam of several similar clinical conversations.
3. You may notice that throughout the book, we use the words *they, their,* and *them* as singular, gender-neutral pronouns. While some grammarians view this usage as unacceptable, we've found it preferable to the awkwardness of *he/she, he or she,* and other alternative phrasings.

Chapter 2

1. For in-depth accounts of the history of neuroplasticity research, see Norman Doidge, *The Brain That Changes Itself: Stories of Personal Triumph from the Frontiers of Brain Science* (New York: Viking, 2007; Penguin Books, 2008); and Sharon Begley, *Train Your Mind, Change Your Brain: How a New Science Reveals Our Extraordinary Potential to Transform Ourselves* (New York: Ballantine Books, 2007; Ballantine Books Trade Paperback, 2008). (Citations refer to the paperback editions.)
2. In line with most popular discussions of neuroplasticity, we are focusing our attention on changes that occur within the brain. However, plasticity is

a property of the entire nervous system. For much of this chapter, "brain" serves as a shorthand for "nervous system."

3. In the words of neuroscientist Alvaro Pascual-Leone and colleagues, "Plasticity is not an occasional state of the nervous system; instead, it is the normal ongoing state of the nervous system throughout the life span." Alvaro Pascual-Leone, Amir Amedi, Felipe Fregni, and Lotfi B. Merabet, "The Plastic Human Brain Cortex," *Annual Review of Neuroscience* 28, no. 1 (2005): 379.

   The seminal paper demonstrating that neurogenesis continues to occur late in life is Peter S. Eriksson, Ekaterina Perfilieva, Thomas Björk-Eriksson, Ann-Marie Alborn, Claes Nordborg, Daniel A. Peterson, and Fred H. Gage, "Neurogenesis in the Adult Human Hippocampus," *Nature Medicine* 4, no. 11 (1998): 1313–1317.

4. For a useful review of research on how different sorts of mental activity influence the brain, see Begley, *Train Your Mind, Change Your Brain*, 131–160.

5. Alvaro Pascual-Leone, Nguyet Dang, Leonardo G. Cohen, Joaquim P. Brasil-Neto, Angel Cammarota, and Mark Hallett, "Modulation of Muscle Responses Evoked by Transcranial Magnetic Stimulation during the Acquisition of New Fine Motor Skills," *Journal of Neurophysiology* 74, no. 3 (1995): 1037–1045.

6. Eleanor A. Maguire, Katherine Woollett, and Hugo J. Spiers, "London Taxi Drivers and Bus Drivers: A Structural MRI and Neuropsychological Analysis," *Hippocampus* 16, no. 12 (2006): 1091–1101.

7. For explanations of three key principles of brain change—"neurons that fire together wire together" (commonly known as Hebb's Law, after neuropsychologist Donald Hebb), "neurons that fire apart wire apart," and "use it or lose it"—see Doidge, *The Brain That Changes Itself*, 45–92. For a more technical discussion of the distinction between reinforcing established pathways and creating new pathways, see Pascual-Leone et al, "The Plastic Human Brain Cortex," 379–382.

8. Doidge, *The Brain That Changes Itself*, 209.

9. Doidge, *The Brain That Changes Itself*, 242.

10. For a compelling, though technical, discussion of how a stable character can emerge from repeated patterns of responses, see Jim Grigsby and David Stevens, *Neurodynamics of Personality* (New York: The Guilford Press, 2000), 305–326.

11. Doidge, *The Brain That Changes Itself*, 242.

12. See discussions of the work of Edward Taub in Begley, *Train Your Mind, Change Your Brain*, 120--126; and Doidge, *The Brain That Changes Itself*, 132–163. See also Jeffrey A. Kleim and Theresa A. Jones, "Principles of Experience-Dependent Neural Plasticity: Implications for Rehabilitation After Brain Damage," *Journal of Speech, Language & Hearing Research* 51, no. 1 (2008): S225–239.

13. The primary book on this topic geared toward OCD patients is Jeffrey M. Schwartz and Beverly Beyette, *Brain Lock: Free Yourself from Obsessive-Compulsive Behavior* (New York: HarperCollins, 1996; New York: Harper Perennial, 1997). Dr. Schwartz's work with OCD is also described at length in Doidge, *The Brain That Changes Itself*; Begley, *Train Your Mind, Change Your Brain*; and Jeffrey M. Schwartz and Sharon Begley, *The Mind and the Brain: Neuroplasticity and the Power of Mental Force* (New York: Harper-Collins, 2002; Harper Perennial, 2003). All citations refer to the paperback editions.

14. V. S. Ramachandran and Eric L. Altschuler, "The Use of Visual Feedback, in Particular Mirror Visual Feedback, in Restoring Brain Function," *Brain* 132, no. 7 (2009): 1693–1710.

15. The treatment is not a miracle cure; symptoms may take weeks or months to subside and may never fully disappear. But with persistence and effort, people can dramatically decrease their obsessions and compulsions while reducing or eliminating their need for medication. Schwartz and Beyette, *Brain Lock*, 74, 194–195, 208.

16. Jeffrey M. Schwartz, Paula W. Stoessel, Lewis R. Baxter, Jr., Karron M. Martin, and Michael E. Phelps, "Systematic Changes in Cerebral Glucose Metabolic Rate After Successful Behavior Modification Treatment of Obsessive-Compulsive Disorder," *Archives of General Psychiatry* 53, no. 2 (1996): 109–113. These findings are also documented in Schwartz and Beyette, *Brain Lock*, 57–59, and in Schwartz and Begley, *The Mind and the Brain*, 88–90.

17. Dr. Josephs is cofounder of the Canadian Foundation for Trauma Research and Education (CFTRE). For more information, see www.cftre.com.

18. Ed Josephs, telephone interview with coauthor Amy Yeager, February 16, 2011.

19. Grigsby and Stevens, *Neurodynamics of Personality*, 372.

20. Ed Josephs, telephone interview, February 16, 2011.

21. M. M. Merzenich and R. C. deCharms, "Neural Representations, Experience, and Change," *The Mind-Brain Continuum: Sensory Processes*, ed. Rudolfo Llinás and Patricia S. Churchland (Cambridge, MA: MIT Press, 1996), 62–64, 71. See also Begley, *Train Your Mind, Change Your Brain*, 156–60, and Schwartz and Begley, *The Mind and the Brain*, 327–342.

22. Kleim and Jones, "Principles of Experience-Dependent Neural Plasticity: Implications for Rehabilitation After Brain Damage," S231–232; and Katja Stefan, Matthias Wycislo, and Joseph Classen, "Modulation of Associative Human Motor Cortical Plasticity by Attention," *Journal of Neurophysiology* 92, no. 1 (2004): 66–72.

23. Schwartz borrows the concept of the "Impartial Spectator" from philosopher Adam Smith. See Schwartz and Beyette, *Brain Lock*, 10–12.

24. In Schwartz's four-step OCD treatment program, these are Step 1 ("Relabeling") and Step 2 ("Reattributing"). See Schwartz and Beyette, *Brain Lock*, 5–69.

25. Schwartz and Beyette, *Brain Lock*, 187.
26. Schwartz and Begley, *The Mind and the Brain*, 76–78.
27. Jon Kabat-Zinn, *Wherever You Go, There You Are* (New York: Hyperion, 1994), 4.
28. Ezra Bayda, *Being Zen: Bringing Meditation to Life* (Boston: Shambhala Publications, 2003), 18.
29. Bayda, *Being Zen*, 19.
30. See Britta K. Hölzel, James Carmody, Mark Vangel, Christina Congleton, Sita M. Yerramsetti, Tim Gard, and Sara W. Lazar, "Mindfulness Practice Leads to Increases in Regional Brain Gray Matter Density," *Psychiatry Research: Neuroimaging* 191, no. 1 (2011): 36–43; and Lisa A. Kilpatrick, Brandall Y. Suyenobu, Suzanne R. Smith, Joshua A. Bueller, Trudy Goodman, J. David Creswell, Kirsten Tillisch, Emeran A. Mayer, and Bruce D. Naliboff, "Impact of Mindfulness-Based Stress Reduction Training on Intrinsic Brain Connectivity," *Neuroimage* 56, no. 1 (2011): 290–298.
31. This is the third step of Schwartz's treatment program ("Refocus"), described in Schwartz and Beyette, *Brain Lock*, 70–95.
32. Dopamine, a neurotransmitter (chemical messenger) associated with pleasure and reward, plays a crucial role in neuroplastic change. See Thérèse M. Jay, "Dopamine: A Potential Substrate for Synaptic Plasticity and Memory Mechanisms," *Progress in Neurobiology* 69, no. 6 (2003): 375–390; and Doidge, *The Brain That Changes Itself*, 71, 106–107, 170.
33. See Schwartz and Beyette, *Brain Lock*, 71; and Doidge, *The Brain That Changes Itself*, 170.
34. For examples of how these rewards function in one computerized brain-training program, see Doidge, *The Brain That Changes Itself*, 70–71.
35. Kleim and Jones, "Principles of Experience-Dependent Neural Plasticity: Implications for Rehabilitation After Brain Damage," S230.
36. See Doidge, *The Brain That Changes Itself*, 149, 156, where Doidge explains Edward Taub's use of "massed practice" in stroke rehabilitation.
37. Schwartz and Beyette, *Brain Lock*, 71, 79–80.
38. Doidge discusses this feature of Edward Taub's work in *The Brain That Changes Itself*, 147, 149, 155.
39. Schwartz and Beyette, *Brain Lock*, 72, 79.
40. Ed Josephs, telephone interview, February 16, 2011.

Chapter 3

1. In other cultural contexts, yes-butting may not be common at all. We once trained a corporate group in which half the employees were based in the United States and the other half were based in India. When we led an exercise on yes-buts, both teams found it challenging, but for entirely different reasons. The U.S. employees had a strong tendency to use yes-buts, and it was a struggle for them to break that habit. The Indian employees, on the

other hand, found yes-buts so unnatural that they had a hard time coming up with any. They explained to us that their cultural norm was to agree with an idea for several hours, or even days, before mentioning any potential problems. This was a big "aha" moment for the U.S. employees, who had often become frustrated when members of the Indian team would say, "Yes, we can do that," and only later mention all the roadblocks that stood in their way.

2. We define broad questions as open-ended requests for other people's thoughts, conclusions, opinions, or proposals. We'll give a much more detailed explanation of different types of questions in Chapter 6, "Question Traps."

3. For more information on leading questions, see Chapter 6.

Chapter 4

1. Keep this in mind as we move on to the skills section. Our strategies were developed with Western cultural norms in mind and might not always be appropriate in other cultural contexts.

2. We draw the idea of taking things personally from Yvonne Agazarian's Theory of Living Human Systems. For more information, see Yvonne M. Agazarian, *Systems-Centered Therapy for Groups* (London: The Guilford Press, 1997), 28, 70–71.

3. Undoing mind-reads is a Systems-Centered® technique developed by Yvonne Agazarian and used to help groups and systems establish a reality-testing climate. (See Agazarian, *Systems-Centered Therapy for Groups*, 31, 76–78, 81, 154.) The strategy described here is an adaptation of that technique.

Chapter 5

1. Various elements of our strategies for managing negative predictions are adapted or taken directly from Yvonne Agazarian's Theory of Living Human Systems. (See Yvonne M. Agazarian, *Systems-Centered Therapy for Groups* [London: The Guilford Press, 1997], 31, 68–69, 76–77, 154–157.)

2. P. A. Lewis, H. D. Critchley, A. P. Smith, and R. J. Dolan, "Brain Mechanisms for Mood Congruent Memory Facilitation," *Neuroimage* 25, no. 4 (2005): 1214.

3. These odds apply to plane flights in traditional first-world countries, such as the United States, Canada, and Japan. See Arnold Barnett, "Cross-National Differences in Aviation Safety Records," *Transportation Science* 44, no. 3 (2010): 322.

4. Passing rates are posted online by the American Institute of CPAs (www .aicpa.org) in their section on becoming a CPA. Passing rates for the first half of 2011 averaged around 44 percent.

5. Agazarian's Theory of Living Human Systems describes such discomfort as anxiety from being "at the edge of the unknown." This feeling is extremely common, since "everyone has apprehension when we do not know what is going to happen next." However, it's possible to change the quality of that apprehension by "mobiliz[ing] one's curiosity." (Yvonne M. Agazarian, "Systems-Centered Therapy [SCT] Applied to Short-Term Group and Individual Psychotherapy," in *Systems-Centered Therapy: Clinical Practice with Individuals, Families and Groups,* ed. Susan P. Gantt and Yvonne M. Agazarian [London: Karnac Books Ltd, 2011], 75.)

Chapter 6

1. Daniel Goleman, Richard E. Boyatzis, and Annie McKee, *Primal Leadership* (Boston: Harvard Business School Press, 2002), 93. The term *CEO disease* originally appeared in an article in *Businessweek*: John A. Byrne, William C. Symonds, and Julia Flynn Siler, "CEO Disease," *Businessweek,* April 1, 1991: 52–59.
2. In defining just four categories of questions, we're omitting mention of a couple of finer distinctions. Most of the narrow and broad questions we discuss in this chapter are focused on the external world. Those are the types of questions you'll encounter most frequently, at least in professional contexts. Other types include personal questions, which ask people for relatively superficial information about themselves, and feeling questions, which focus on emotions and other deeply meaningful, personal issues. Both personal and feeling questions can be either narrow or broad—for instance, "Are you hungry?" (narrow personal question), "What would you like to eat?" (broad personal question), "Are you angry?" (narrow feeling question), "How did you feel when you heard the news?" (broad feeling question).

Chapter 7

1. Suppose someone had already walked away with Joan's coat. That would in no way diminish the value of her shift from complaining to taking action. By making a plan and carrying it out, Joan could at least reassure herself that she'd done all she could to get it back. She might feel sad or angry that the coat was gone, but she'd avoid the unnecessary anxiety of worrying about what might be happening while she did nothing.

Chapter 8

1. For a refresher on the different types of questions, turn back to the sidebar "Four Types of Questions" in Chapter 6, on page 124.

2. The target of the attack may be the original cause of the frustration or may have landed in the line of fire purely by accident. We've all had the experience of coming home after a really tough day and snapping at our spouse, child, dog, or roommate, or whoever else had the bad fortune to cross our path.

3. Matthew D. Lieberman, Naomi I. Eisenberger, Molly J. Crockett, Sabrina M. Tom, Jennifer H. Pfeifer, and Baldwin M. Way, "Putting Feelings into Words: Affect Labeling Disrupts Amygdala Activity in Response to Affective Stimuli," *Psychological Science* 18, no. 5 (2007), 421–428.

4. If the person starts out at this lower level of emotion, you may want to try part 2 of the strategy right from the beginning.

Chapter 9

1. The concept of noise comes from information theory (the technical study of how quantities of information are measured, stored, and transmitted), as articulated in Claude E. Shannon and Warren Weaver, *The Mathematical Theory of Communication* (Urbana, IL: The University of Illinois Press, 1949). This idea was picked up and further developed by Yvonne Agazarian in her Theory of Living Human Systems and is the basis for the discussion of noise that we give in this chapter. For more information, see Yvonne M. Agazarian and Susan P. Gantt, *Autobiography of a Theory: Developing the Theory of Living Human Systems and Its Systems-Centered Practice* (London: Jessica Kingsley Publishers Ltd, 2000).

2. When we talk about verbal behaviors, we're referring to a combination of words and voice tone, not body language or other visual cues. Much of the time, body language is reflected in the voice tone. (For instance, if a person is rolling their eyes, their tone of voice tends to be sarcastic). We think of voice tone as the body part of the verbal message.

3. Simon and Agazarian met as graduate students in the psycho-educational processes program at Temple University. They discovered that they shared a common interest in the idea that verbal behaviors were profoundly and crucially different from the content those behaviors contained. For more on the beginnings of SAVI®, see the following publications: Agazarian and Gantt, *Autobiography of a Theory*; Yvonne M. Agazarian, "A theory of verbal behavior and information transfer," *Classroom Interaction Newsletter* 4, no. 2 (1969): 22–33; and Anita Simon and Yvonne M. Agazarian, "SAVI—the System for Analyzing Verbal Interaction," in *The Process of Group Psychotherapy: Systems for Analyzing Change,* ed. Ariadne P. Beck and Carol M. Lewis (Washington, D.C.: American Psychological Association, 2000), 357–380.

4. See Simon and Agazarian, "SAVI—the System for Analyzing Verbal Interaction," 358, and Yvonne M. Agazarian, *Systems-Centered Therapy for Groups* (London: The Guilford Press, 1997).

SAVI® is a registered trademark of Anita Simon and Yvonne Agazarian.

Index